CW00924887

The Fandom of David Bowie

Toija Cinque · Sean Redmond

The Fandom of David Bowie

Everyone Says "Hi"

Toija Cinque
Faculty of Arts and Education
Deakin University
Melbourne, VIC, Australia

Sean Redmond
Faculty of Arts and Education
Deakin University
Melbourne, VIC, Australia

ISBN 978-3-030-15879-8   ISBN 978-3-030-15880-4   (eBook)
https://doi.org/10.1007/978-3-030-15880-4

© The Editor(s) (if applicable) and The Author(s), under exclusive license to Springer Nature Switzerland AG 2019
This work is subject to copyright. All rights are solely and exclusively licensed by the Publisher, whether the whole or part of the material is concerned, specifically the rights of translation, reprinting, reuse of illustrations, recitation, broadcasting, reproduction on microfilms or in any other physical way, and transmission or information storage and retrieval, electronic adaptation, computer software, or by similar or dissimilar methodology now known or hereafter developed.
The use of general descriptive names, registered names, trademarks, service marks, etc. in this publication does not imply, even in the absence of a specific statement, that such names are exempt from the relevant protective laws and regulations and therefore free for general use.
The publisher, the authors and the editors are safe to assume that the advice and information in this book are believed to be true and accurate at the date of publication. Neither the publisher nor the authors or the editors give a warranty, expressed or implied, with respect to the material contained herein or for any errors or omissions that may have been made. The publisher remains neutral with regard to jurisdictional claims in published maps and institutional affiliations.

Cover image: dpa picture alliance/Alamy Stock Photo
Cover design by eStudioCalamar

This Palgrave Macmillan imprint is published by the registered company Springer Nature Switzerland AG
The registered company address is: Gewerbestrasse 11, 6330 Cham, Switzerland

For my big sisters, Helen and Fiona, for introducing me to the wonder of David Bowie. Those Bowie albums that went 'missing' from your bedroom: I still have them …
Sean Redmond

For my dear friends across time, places and in fandom, Dimity (Stower) Barlow and Peter Green. And my brother, Stephen—thank you for not throwing all my David Bowie books away when I moved out of home!
Toija Cinque

ACKNOWLEDGEMENTS

We would like to acknowledge Deakin University and the School of Communication and Creative Arts for the support of our research. In particular, we are indebted to Geoff Boucher for championing our field-work and for providing us with research grants to complete the work.

We want to extend a special thanks to all the David Bowie fans—our fellow space cadets—who patiently and enthusiastically completed our survey, attended our Focus groups and answered our questions. It has been our privilege to experience how amazing you are. This book is for you.

Chapter 4 'Lazarus Rises: The Migrant Fandom of David Bowie' first appeared in the *Journal of the International Association for the Study of Popular Music*, vol 6, no., 1. 2016: 7–24.

Contents

LIST OF FIGURES

LIST OF TABLES

CHAPTER 1

Introduction: 'We're Just the Space Cadets, and He's the Commander'

OVERVIEW

Everyone Says "Hi": The Fandom of David Bowie explores the way that fans reflect upon their identification with, and connection to, this seminal figure of contemporary art and culture. Built from the stories and memories that self-defined Bowie fans shared with us, the book is a journeyed account of individual life stories and collective fan practices, revealing the way Bowie existed as a figure of renewal and redemption, lining these collated recollections with hopeful, desiring and enchanted reflections. *Everyone Says "Hi": The Fandom of David Bowie* also critically assesses this fandom, showing how Bowie navigated individual traumas and loneliness, his outsider status resonating with those on the margins of society, marginalised often because of their gender, sexuality, race and ethnicity.

In this book we seek to find Bowie in the streams of fandom that swell around him, including harvesting nostalgic fragments, recollections (via personal interviews), memorabilia, diaries, letter writing, collective and communal gatherings, and artistic impersonation. Within the context of contemporary changes to the media landscape, the book will also assess the nature of the present digital conversations taking place about David Bowie and the fan interactions that emerge on social media. Finally, and perhaps rather uniquely, the book assesses Bowie's own fandom and the fandom of the authors, who draw upon auto-ethnography to make personal sense of what he means to them. By the end of the book we will have

© The Author(s) 2019
T. Cinque and S. Redmond, *The Fandom of David Bowie*,
https://doi.org/10.1007/978-3-030-15880-4_1

seen the remarkable influence that David Bowie has exerted over those who gladly call themselves his space cadets.

MIXING METHODS, THEORIES AND STORIES

The idea for this book started by way of a chance conversation before a dreary work meeting, where we discovered we were both Bowie fans and agreed on how little there was written about him at the time, particularly from a fan's perspective. In a very direct way, this conversation and the route it took mirror the mixed methodological and theoretical approach we have since taken here. First, we began our conversation with our very own fan stories, in effect adopting the storying the self approach to memorial work. This approach draws on a,

> Model of the self as 'storied' and of culture as both moulded and moulding through the personal stories of individuals… It extends the idea of 'culture' and media beyond the organizational structures of, say, the culture industries, broadcasting or the published media, into the everyday modes in which we express and construct our lives in personal terms, telling our own stories. (Finnegan 1997: 69)

The emphasis on 'writing the personal' (Probyn 2011) has also been central to the epistemological and political interventions of popular culture theorists and those interested in 'hearing' the stories of the marginalised and politically disenfranchised. Connected to this approach is the recognition that researchers also have stories to share and in a way that democratises the empirical process—no one story is more important than the other—and through shared storytelling, experiential equivalences and thematic 'clusters' emerge. Through storying the self, we find out about how people directly experience their own, often marginalised, subject positions, and within this context, we found out how important David Bowie is to the modern narratives of selfhood our respondents shared with us.

Second, our different academic backgrounds meant that we approached the question of fandom through different critical entrance points, recognising and embracing these differences to foster an innovative mixed methods approach. However, this fusion approach to the research design is not simply to do with having both qualitative and quantitative data at our disposal but through the mechanisms that data are collected, organised and interpreted. Through this 'triangulation' or 'multiple operationalism', we follow

Denzin (1978) who identified four types of interlocking data gathering and interpretation:

a. data triangulation or the use of a variety of sources in a study;
b. investigator triangulation or the use of several different researchers;
c. theory triangulation or the use of multiple perspectives and theories to interpret the results of our study; and
d. methodological triangulation or use of multiple methods to study Bowie fandom.

The project design of *Everyone Says "Hi": The Fandom of David Bowie* involved five central data gathering methods. First, self-defined Bowie fans were asked to respond to an online questionnaire. These fans were recruited from within our peer network, through wider fan networks, and by a call to participate, circulated across media, screen and cultural studies listservs. Entitled, *Turn to Face the Strange: The Fandom of David Bowie*, the online questionnaire was composed of 16 questions and offered in both English and Japanese languages (see Appendix A). Answers to the questions produced both qualitative and quantitative data (see Appendix B). The questions were designed to elicit both factual and descriptive responses and to allow and enable participants to emotively story their memories, recollections and interests. For example, 'Question 15. Do you have a cherished piece of David Bowie memorabilia?' was designed to not only have respondents recall these favourite items but to allow us to gauge the level of affective attachment they had through the way they remembered them—the word choices, the scene setting and the personalisation. The question would also allow us to count 'items' if we so desired to see if repeated forms of memorabilia were cherished.

Second, focus groups were held in seven international locations during 2016: Melbourne (February), Tokyo (June), London (June), Amsterdam (June), New York (July), Berlin (September) and Lisbon (September). Each focus group comprised of between 5 and 30 people and lasted for approximately 60 minutes. Participants were invited to respond to questions about David Bowie's star image, music and art, and the role it plays (has played) in their lives. Participants were also asked to bring a special piece of memorabilia that they were invited to speak to, but not compelled to discuss. For the London, New York and Tokyo focus groups, participants were drawn from those who had previously completed the online survey and who had indicated a willingness to do so, furnishing us with 'deeper' or 'extended' data. For the Amsterdam and Lisbon focus groups, these took place in 2016 as part of academic conferences: the former the *3rd International Celebrity Studies Conference: Authenticating Celebrity* (28–30 June) at the University of Amsterdam, and the latter the *David Bowie Inter-art|text|media* CEAUL/ULICES–University of Lisbon Centre for English Studies *Conference* (22–24 September) in Portugal. The participants for the Berlin focus group were lifelong friends of Sean. To ensure anonymity and alleviate denotive meaning that might arise from any names assigned to the participants, albeit that they be false, all the quotations drawn upon in this book are referred to by random alphabetical letters and/or numbers.

Our reasoning for the organisation of these focus groups was as follows: London, New York and Tokyo are key locations in Bowie's own mythology, and the intention was that these locations would draw out pilgrimage-type conversations. Amsterdam and Lisbon were chosen because they were a part of conferences with an interested sample population, and because we wanted to draw into our study the role of the Aca-Fan. Berlin was chosen for two reasons: it would allow Sean to undertake his own pilgrimage, being a key Bowie location, and it would allow him to gather with his friends to assess together their own life stories.

We also felt that the focus group method (and the questionnaire, for that matter) would allow us to draw upon narrative and storytelling, which Laurel Richardson (1990: 183) observed, 'is the best way to understand the human experience because it is the way humans understand their own lives'. As Bochner (2012) contends,

> Scholars taking "the narrative turn" pointed inquiry toward "acts of meaning" (Bruner, 1990), focusing on the functions of stories and storytelling in creating and managing identity; the expressive forms for making sense of lived experience and communicating it to others; the entanglements that permeate how interpersonal life is lived and how it is told to others; the reflexive dimensions of the relationship between storytellers and story listeners; and the canonical narratives that circulate through society, offering scripted ways of acting.

Third, we employed auto-ethnography, 'a form or method of research that involves self-observation and reflexive investigation in the context of ethnographic field work and writing' (p. 43). Carolyn Ellis (2004) defines autoethnography as 'research, writing, story, and method that connect the autobiographical and personal to the cultural, social, and political' (p. xix). It was this latter connection which allowed us to move from the personal to the cultural that particularly interested us.

The point of convergence in our cultural analysis is on fan interactions as being broad and accounting for the myriad of ways that the wider social struggles (in which a number might feel themselves to have a stake) are brought to the surface. Richard Schickel gestures that there are two interlocking fantasies embedded in the life of a star. On the one hand is the 'dream of autonomy' whereby the star lives a life uncompromised by obligation (Schickel 2000: 255). On the other hand is the familiar 'dream of intimate, almost familiar connection' (Schickel 2000: 255). An important narrative here is around the affective role that stars play so we turned then to the in-depth analysis by Gregg and Seigworth (2010) in which Clough (2010: 206) conjectures that the challenge of affect theory, against every other form of inquiry, is to show how 'bodily matter' bears 'information'. The sheer delight of fans witnessed at a Bowie concert might attest to this claim. The allure was to unravel the existing and mutual relationship between 'our star [man]' together with his associated textual objects including '*neo*-communicative contexts', and the receptive individual or fan. Indeed, the intricate dialectic of culture conjoins and remerges texts and bodies as components in a code that suggests a wide range of messages.

Remaining constantly evocative, however, is the notion of 'star' because they dramatise the search for identity temporarily suspending everyday reality and introducing new possibilities into human imagination (Stevenson 2006). Moreover, stars have cultural resonance (Vincendeau 2000: viii). With an upward trajectory, the star reaches evocative iconic status upon their fame becoming prevalent through the modulation of their cultural meaning, significance and values that correspond with and reflect key changes in society (Holt 2004). Eagar and Lindridge (2014: 304) considered arguments like punctuation marks in time to describe David Bowie's iconicity as 'an emergent process as his symbolic meanings [have evolved] over various time periods from counter-culture musician and as a symbol of sexual ambiguity (1970s), to mainstream musician and aging rock star (1980s and 1990s), and finally into the merging of Bowie and Ziggy as a unified cultural icon (2000s)'. Woodward's (2017: 505) apropos discussion adds further to the deeper contemplations swirling around Bowie:

> The Ziggy Stardust jumpsuit that Bowie wore in 1972 when he performed on the popular BBC television show *Top of the Pops* became not only iconic

but also part of the Bowie myth. In [Roland] Barthes's writing text is plural as well as singular and different meanings are interwoven (1977). Bowie embodies the interrelationship between image, music and text and his significance has become immediately recognizable whatever form it takes, the jumpsuit, carnivalesque make up, or cool Fedora, the white shirt and the suit. The figure of Bowie has been appropriated in different cultural fields and crosses the boundaries between genres. For example, the myth of Bowie transgresses not only heteronormativity and hegemonic binary logics of sex and sexuality, but also different cultural domains. Different cultural components combine to produce the cultural figure and Bowie's mythological status but myths are reproduced, reformed and reconstituted with impact upon other cultural terrains.

This capacity for his meanings to transubstantiate across time, place and cultural contexts denotes that David Bowie is no longer tethered to a particular time or setting and is absorbed as significant into the weft of society (see Boorstin 1964). This can of course be layered with complexity when the star seeks to shed light on a particular sociocultural issue such as that raised in Bowie's music video 'Let's Dance' (*Let's Dance*, 1983) for example. But, the 'Let's Dance' song was interpreted as personally powerful for Indigenous affairs editor for *The Guardian* Australia, Stan Grant (2016, n.p.) who recalls that for them: 'It was 1983 and I was at university when I first saw the film clip. Here was a music superstar featuring my own people, putting Indigenous faces on a world stage … it contained a message that resonated with us: "when all is against you, what else can you do? Put on your red shoes and dance the blues!"' (also see Chapter 2 for a more critical reading of the *Let's Dance* music video). Here is a parallel to the timeless existential work of Albert Camus' *The Myth of Sisyphus* (1955), a work that takes storytelling as method to impart to readers the profound philosophical ideal that no matter how unbearable one's life might give the impression of being, it is still worth it for them to stick around to see what happens next. 'The Next Day' if you will, to be playing off Bowie's 2013 track and album title of the same name. At the level of the individual fan, emotional growth and subsequent active agency may be developed. For Daniel Cavicchi (1998: 59), fandom is emotionally experienced and '*a process of being*' whereby the star performer acts not as a particular possession or even an activity but as 'a continuing presence to which they [the fan] may turn again and again'. Not in a regressive, going backward sense but instead, moving forward.

Our fourth approach in *Everyone Says "Hi": The Fandom of David Bowie* is marked by a set of intersecting theoretical positions: first, it draws heavily on cultural studies when defining human subjectivity and individual identity; second, it draws upon subcultural theory and the media-specific work done on pop music, stardom and fandom; third, it draws on psychological aspects of the self, including a concern with trauma and desire; finally, it draws upon phenomenology and affect theory to get to the emotions and affects that the authors think cannot be simply read off language and representation. The book draws these sometimes-competing positions through a process of entanglement and de-entanglement, looking to see and hear in fans' responses the complete human sensorium.

From one important perspective, the book draws from the subtlety of Sara Ahmed's notion of 'stranger fetishism' (2000) to better capture the ways that the consumption of a cultural icon (such that David Bowie is) can work to make the strange familiar or one in which the stranger's relationship is based on closeness, proximity, perhaps even incorporation (p. 4). Otherness and strangeness here are, not tied to simple us/them binaries, but is rather an alien alterity that shifts sides and folds into itself. For Bowie fans, the desire for the Other, for the strange, may radiate out from a Western cultural centre that is lacking, and which stems from a need that is about owning both the exotic Other, and devouring or ingesting them so that their energy becomes (y)ours. Of course, Bowie's Japonism and his huge Asian fan base complicate the Western/Eastern dichotomy. It is through an analysis of David Bowie fandom that the book is able to explore broader spatial and cultural intersections of place, race and identity.

Ratiocinating from a slightly different angle, in David Bowie a number of our participants often saw something of themselves and individual sensibilities being mirrored; he a like-minded entity for certain shared human subjectivities. As participant MC stated during our focus group in Lisbon: 'People have never been OK with me, my clothes, hairstyle, my focus on objects and Bowie was a route to understand different things'. Where this fan's perceived weirdness made them feel at times adrift from those around them, David Bowie was comfortably nestled in the recesses of their heart affording them emotional fortitude.

Finally for this book, in addition to our other methodological and theoretical approaches, we undertook an analysis of online Bowie fan sites and Facebook pages, alongside the analysis of data furnished through Twitter. Twitter hashtag research specifically involves searching Twitter for tagged tweets, collecting these tweets and using a range of analytic methods to interpret and display the data. Such research assesses how people are using the platform to communicate and interact with its content. A systematic Twitter search process used the most commonly occurring David Bowie-related hashtags, previously determined through repeated scans of Twitter, as follows: #Bowie, #David Bowie #Blackstar. Because data can be difficult to collect retrospectively from Twitter, a six-month period between 2015 and 2016 was initially chosen to begin gathering data for the 2016 release of the *Blackstar* album as part of the preparatory research for this book. As it turned out, it was also the time that David Bowie died. Following the quantitative analysis, tweets about Bowie identified as being written by fans/or images posted by fans at the time of David Bowie's death were further analysed by their linguistic or image content which formed a narrative coding. We explore how digital content shared publicly on this popular social platform can generate meaningful data for scholarly analysis in the context of David Bowie online fan cultures. The focus is because the digital sphere holds a place in the primary function of remembrance and documentation. Increasingly important aspects of stardom and celebrity in contemporary societies find an interplay between fans and stars engaged in the digital mediasphere.

Bowie Data

The Questionnaire

The questionnaire aimed for a participation rate of at least 100 people to enable the research to have statistical power and for extrapolation purposes. We had a meaningful response: 292 completed the questionnaire, which was advertised across Bowie fan sites and newsletters as well as academic list-servs such as MECCSA, the Fan Studies Network and the Cultural Studies Association. The questionnaire notifications went out in January 2016.

The survey data were processed using SPSS and NVivo. We found that 58.3% of our respondents identified as female, 40.3% identified as male, with 1.4% not specifying their gender (see Table 1.1). In terms of sexual orientation, 70.3% identified as straight, 14.5% identified as bisexual, and 11.3% identified as gay (see Table 1.2). Two facts potentially emerge from these results: Bowie has a larger female fan base and those identifying as non-straight are higher in proportion to sexual orientation statistics generally, although one's sexual orientation is found not to be static and shifts with age (see David Spiegelhalter 2015). That Bowie would have a

Table 1.1
Self-declared gender of participants responding to the *Turn to Face the Strange: The Fandom of David Bowie* online survey

Gender	Frequency	%
Female	165	58.3
Male	114	40.3
Not specified	4	1.4

Table created by the authors

Table 1.2
Self-declared sexuality of participants responding to *Turn to Face the Strange: The Fandom of David Bowie* online survey

Sexuality	Frequency	%
Straight	199	70.3
Bi	41	14.5
Gay	32	11.3
Other	11	3.9

Table created by the authors

Table 1.3
Self-declared race/ethnicity of participants responding to the *Turn to Face the Strange: The Fandom of David Bowie* online survey

Race/ethnicity	Frequency	%
White	61	21.0
Caucasian	59	20.3
White British	25	8.6
Unassigned	11	3.8
British	4	1.4
Chinese	4	1.4
White Caucasian	3	1.0
European	3	1.0
Other	121	41.6

Table created by the authors

high gay/bi/queer fan base is not surprising, of course, and as we will see through the data gathered, Bowie's own sexual orientation and play with gender binaries opened him up to non-normative fan readings.

Respondents were drawn from right around the world but with the majority coming from Europe, North America and Australasia. As outlined in Table 1.3, our data finds that in terms of racial diversity just over 50% of our respondents identified as White, Caucasian or white British, and over 40% identified as non-white.

The racial and ethnic diversity of the participants was something that we felt demonstrated Bowie's international appeal, confirming again how his star image offered positive and progressive entry points for those on the supposed margins or periphery of dominant white culture.

The Focus Groups

As noted above, the participants for the New York, London and Tokyo focus groups were drawn from the questionnaire pool. For the Amsterdam and Lisbon focus groups, conference delegates were asked to sign up to the session and were then emailed with the broad details of how they would be run. For the Melbourne focus group, participants were recruited through listserv communication, flyers and Bowie friendship networks. All these focus groups were organised around a loose set of questions (see Appendix C), and as we note above, delegates were asked to bring a piece of Bowie memorabilia with them or to share knowledge of a cherished Bowie memento, if they had one. The workshop rooms, which took place in universities and/or libraries, were 'dressed' before the respondents arrived: Bowie photographs were visible, PowerPoint slides of his many star images were shown on rotation, and Bowie music was played. Our intention here was to humanise the encounter, to create an affective space for sharing. The Berlin focus group was differently constituted and run: it took place in a hotel room around a coffee table, where Sean and his friends shared personal memories of their growing up together, and how they viewed David Bowie.

DATA ANALYSIS

As we note above, the analysis of the data involved both triangulation and the utilisation of different theoretical writing to make sense of the responses that we received. The analysis of the data was led by the 'voices' of the respondents, something we were committed to ensuring. We wanted Bowie fans to speak and feel and for these affective registers to be the melodic chorus that harmonises the findings of this book. Nonetheless, we looked for patterns and repetitions across the data and sought to complement these voices through comparative and narrative means. Where qualitative data clearly showed relational clustering, we used that, developing a layering approach to the findings. Nonetheless, the quotations that were drawn upon had to be selective: as can be seen from Appendix C, we had a wealth of material to draw upon. The voices of the fans led us ultimately to structure the book in the way that we have, something that we will now briefly discuss.

CHANGING CHAPTERS

The Fandom of David Bowie: Everyone Says "Hi" has nine interlocking, entangled chapters. Each Chapter stands in their own anthemic right, but dialogue with the next, and so forth. Each chapter is built out of themes and stories, each contributing to the bigger narrative—what types of fandom does David Bowie call forth and crystallise. Some chapters explore a wide canvass, such as the question of identity in Chapter 2, while others focus closely on a salient theme, such as migration in Chapter 3—both these chapters are locked together in an affective membrane.

The nine chapters provide a cross-cutting, rhizomic journey, albeit one that begins with an entangled overview of how fans identify with him and with what fandom is. The book then turns to undertake a critical analysis of Bowie fandom, drawing upon such key concepts as participatory culture, subcultural group formation, selfhood and sexuality, otherness, desire, the parasocial, the carnival, immersion and mimicry, liminality and transgression, and emotion and affect.

CHAPTER 2: THE FANDOM OF DAVID BOWIE

In this chapter, the central deposits of fandom are defined and then outlined in relation to how fans affectively identify with David Bowie. Drawing on scholars such as Henry Jenkins and Matt Hills, the chapter sees Bowie fandom as a positive and creative set of formations, practices and processes, and Bowie fans as powerful indicators of the potentiality and possibility of fandom. This chapter sets up the core themes and findings of the research, alongside an integrated definition of what fandom constitutes, which is then be taken up in the rest of the book.

CHAPTER 3: STORIES OF DIFFERENCE AND OF AWAKENINGS

This chapter explores the way our respondents wrote and spoke about how David Bowie impacted upon their identity and sense of self, and the empowerment he often gave them through his representations and performances. Here, we find stories of difference emerging, either framed through culturally empowering narratives of gender and sexual transformation, or around discourses of outsiderdom and alienation, which our respondents suggested Bowie provided escape from and a 'home' to arrive in. We also find narratives of awakening and sublimation where Bowie—his body—gave people experiences that were heightened and charged, electrifying and liquefying their being-in-the-world.

Chapter 4: Lazarus Rises: The Migrant Fandom of David Bowie

In this chapter, we focus upon the ways that 'migrants' in Melbourne have used David Bowie to story and make sense of their arrival to Australia, often as refugees or as people looking for a better life. We argue that Bowie's alternative and outsider status resonates keenly with people who find themselves 'strangers' in a new land. Lyrically, musically and in terms of star representation, Bowie becomes the figure through which migrants navigate themselves through new cultural and social environments. This part of the research is focused upon the 1970s Italian and Greek migrant community in Melbourne, Australia, with links and conversations to other groups in the other four cities under exploration.

Chapter 5: Bowie Contagion

In this chapter, we explore two interlocking themes: first, the way memories are called upon to manage and imagine fans relationship to, and identification with, David Bowie. Second, the chapter examines the way that David Bowie memorabilia contextualises and provides anchor points for fan identifications, becoming a 'home' or 'contagion' of treasured objects that are embodied and self-narrated. As Hoelscher and Alderman suggest, 'people now look to this refashioned memory, especially in its collective forms, to give themselves a coherent identity, a national narrative, a place in the world' (2004: 348–349). We will look at two forms of memory, personal and collective, private and communal, although as our work suggests, memory shifts, folds into itself, so that it is very often personal and shared, private and collective, as soon as it is 'told'.

Chapter 6: Being There/Being Him

This chapter's focus is on how David Bowie embodies the symbolic complexities of artistic and cultural forms in critically important aural and visual ways. His creative works have adroitly positioned specific narrative frames whereby his fans find room to contemplate and assemble their identity positions through imagination. In this chapter, the book explores the nature of David Bowie's performances with a specific purpose to examine closely instances in which fans themselves metaphorically and physically 'perform' (as) David Bowie either in professional and social contexts or in domestic and personal ways and the authors seek to meet these performances in real-life and 'live' encounters. In this chapter the authors find that because there is no 'definitive David Bowie', multiple interpretations are therefore rendered possible as a result. David Bowie presents fans with a range of reflexive resources that become useful for a multitude of ways of sustaining a coherent sense of self-identity. Here, the chapter probes some of the important ways that fans adopt, transcode and extend various Bowie star images or personae. There is a resulting flow 'within/without' whereby Bowie seems to be felt from *within* the body by resonating with/in his fans, and *without* as fan perform in tributes, wear costumes, dress up, form ideological affinities and engaging in overarching joyful celebration.

CHAPTER 7: ACA-FANS ON TRACING BOWIE STARDOM FOR BEING AND BECOMING

This chapter applies notions of aca-fandom built in and around star and celebrity figures (Hills 2002, 2012; Jenkins 2012) to draw on the stories of participants attending and presenting at academic conferences focused on David Bowie or celebrity. We search here for how Bowie's work has been interacted with, shared, translated and interpreted particularly by aca-fans. The use of auto-ethnographic methods to allow our fellow aca-fans to 'story' their own reactions to David Bowie enables us to delve into the types of emotional responses or tendencies that are stirred by Bowie fandom in/for a professional life. Here, we perpend the ways aca-fans' interlinked feelings and memories are traced back and forward, emotionally entwined in remembrances of Bowie and intimately shared for what their fandom might have contributed to their professional practice via being and becoming.

CHAPTER 8: BOWIE NETS AND ONLINE INTERACTIONS

This chapter explores the ways that fans have been provided with an interpretative framework for their inner-contemplation and creativity through

Bowie fandom online, raising questions of the value of stars and their art for individual 'becoming' or positive self-actualisation. Precisely because the star performer can establish an intimate connection with a willing individual, a fan can be affected positively (and sometimes negatively) as they navigate their way through key life moments. A relationship is able to form between the celebrity/star performer and a listening body who might self-identify as 'fan' as they closely connect virtually to an experience of a particular medium, a particular materiality and a particular cultural phenomenon that matters. This chapter uses a non-intrusive methodology to specifically question the role and use of the Internet and social media by David Bowie and his fans for their shared experiences online and the multi-layered nature of creative practices or shared stories that emerge therein. In this chapter, we locate these intertextual links and cultural echoes for the expansive dialogic matrix in which they function and are used by his fans online.

Chapter 9: Ghostly Pilgrimages

'Time may change me'; tracing time takes not a realist's view of temporality, but exists in a circularity of continually folding back upon itself. Here, we find spaces to reinterpret our memories, feelings and experiences and all the intervals in between. In this chapter, we give thought to how David Bowie is an artist who always is/always was, futuristic and nostalgic, always present in memorial motifs and haunted places through time and the temporal. With reference to Jacques Derrida's neologism, 'hauntology', we focus on fans' tracing of times and places for the conversational rhythms, for the physical journeys through memorial spaces and of cities associated with David Bowie. Here, we find pilgrimage to live events and locations as recalled by the fans, offers deep exploration of their motivating circumstances and desires.

Chapter 10: Conclusion: Everyone Says 'Goodbye'

In this conclusion, we gather the threads of the book together to reflect upon the articulations of Bowie fandom and to summarise what it tells us about the present conditions of social life. We suggest that storying fandom leads us not to micro-conclusions about everyday life alone, but to the myriad of ways that individuals traverse the messy politics of the global world. We will conclude the book with fans' stories and our own. Sean reflects on not finding Bowie's Château du Signal (situated next to the Sauvabelin forest above Lausanne) and the processes of remembering associated with mediated nostalgia together with a weightier search for temporal mooring in this great city. Against the relentless melting of time, we called upon the fans to reflect on how they heard about David Bowie's passing in 2016 and what his death might mean for them going forward.

Vale David Bowie.

REFERENCES

Ahmed, Sara. *Strange Encounters: Embodied Others in Post-coloniality.* London: Routledge, 2000.

Albert, Camus. *The Myth of Sisyphus and Other Essays.* Translated by O'Brian. New York, NY: Knopf/Doubleday. Original work published in 1955, reprinted 2012.

Bochner, Arthur. "On First-Person Narrative Scholarship Autoethnography as Acts of Meaning." *Narrative Inquiry* 22 (1) (2012): 155–164.

Boorstin, Daniel J. *The Image: A Guide to Pseudo-Events in America.* New York: Harper & Row, 1964.

Cavicchi, Daniel. *Tramps Like Us: Music & Meaning Among Springsteen Fans.* New York: Oxford University Press, 1998.

Clough, Patricia T. "The Affective Turn: Political Economy, Biomedia and Bodies." In *The Affect Theory Reader*, ed. Melissa Gregg and Gregory J. Seigworth, 206–228. Durham, NC: Duke University Press, 2010.

Denzin, Norman K. *The Research Act: A Theoretical Introduction to Sociological Methods.* New York: Praeger, 1978.

Eagar, Toni, and Andrew Lindridge. "Becoming Iconic: David Bowie from Man to Icon." In *NA-Advances in Consumer Research*, ed. June Cotte and Stacy Wood, Vol. 42, 302–306. Duluth, MN: Association for Consumer Research, 2014.

Ellis, C. *The Ethnographic I: A Methodological Novel About Autoethnography.* Walnut Creek: AltaMira Press, 2004.

Finnegan, Ruth. "Storying the Self: Personal Narratives and Identity." In *Consumption and Everyday Life*, ed. Hugh Mackay, 65–112. London: Sage, 1997.

Grant, Stan. "How David Bowie's Let's Dance Shone a Light on Australia's Indigenous Struggle." *The Guardian*, 12 January 2016. https://www.theguardian.com/music/2016/jan/12/how-david-bowies-lets-dance-shone-a-light-on-australias-indigenous-issues. Accessed 5 July 2018.

Gregg, Melissa, and Gregory J. Seigworth, eds. *The Affect Theory Reader.* Durham: Duke University Press, 2010.

Hills, Matt. *Fan Cultures.* London: Routledge, 2002.

Hills, Matt. "'Proper Distance' in the Ethical Positioning of Scholar-Fandoms: Between Academics' and Fans' Moral Economies?" In *Fan Culture: The-*

ory/Practice, ed. K. Larson and L. Zubernis, 14–37. Newcastle: Cambridge Scholars Publishing, 2012.

Hoelscher, Steven, and Derek H. Alderman. "Memory and Place: Geographies of a Critical Relationship." *Social & Cultural Geography* 5 (3) (2004): 347–355.

Holt, Douglas B. "How Brands Become Icons." *The Principles of Cultural Branding*. Boston: Harvard Business School Press, 2004.

Jenkins, Henry. *Textual Poachers: Television Fans and Participatory Culture*. London: Routledge, 2012.

Probyn, Elizabeth. "Glass Selves: Emotions, Subjectivity, and the Research Process." In *The Oxford Handbook of the Self*, ed. Stuart Gallagher, 1–10. Oxford: Oxford University Press. 2011.

Richardson, Laurel. "Narrative and Sociology." *Journal of Contemporary Ethnography* 19 (1990): 116–135.

Schickel, Richard. *Intimate Strangers: The Culture of Celebrity in America*. Chicago: Ivan R. Dee, 2000.

Spiegelhalter, David. *Sex by Numbers: What Statistics Can Tell Us About Sexual Behaviour*. Harvard: Profile Books, 2015.

Stevenson, Nick. *David Bowie, Fame, Sound and Vision*. Cambridge: Polity, 2006.

Vincendeau, Ginette. *Stars and Stardom in French Cinema*. New York: Bloomsbury, 2000.

Woodward, Kath. "Lived Actualities of Cultural Experience and Social Worlds: Representing David Bowie." *Continuum* 31 (4) (4 July 2017): 499–508.

CHAPTER 2

The Fandom of David Bowie

INTRODUCTION: THE BOWIESPHERE

This book is driven by a series of intersecting questions around how the fandom of David Bowie manifests. Drawing on the empirical work we have outlined in our Introduction, it seeks to both emotionalise and contextualise the way fans make sense of his star image. We start with these questions, which we then take up fully in the chapters that follow.

1. How has David Bowie been used or consumed by his fans in everyday life? What fan practices emerge? What life stories are retold? What pilgrimages have been made?
2. How does Bowie's fan base actively make new meanings out of his artistic and commercial work? What sort of remediation and adaptation do fans engage with, and to what affect/effect?
3. What types of identity positions does David Bowie embody and call forth? What sort of identities does Bowie fans imagine for themselves? Are these identities progressive, subversive, liberating?
4. Has Bowie's star image been consumed and commodified by the entertainment industries? Does Bowie become simulacra and commodity fetish, branded and corporatised?
5. Finally, what does his death mean to his fans? What sort of personal and cultural memorial work is employed to deal with, make sense of Bowie's passing?

© The Author(s) 2019
T. Cinque and S. Redmond, *The Fandom of David Bowie*,
https://doi.org/10.1007/978-3-030-15880-4_2

These questions we knit and weave together, to allow us to make critical sense of what we would like to call—borrowing a term from a fan page on Tumblr—the BowieSphere or the various orbits and constellations his star image travels to and entangles with. As the owner of the fan page suggests, 'Bowie created a small alternative universe and some of us feel at home in there' (https://bowiesphere.tumblr.com/).

What now follows in this chapter is the setting up of the core themes and findings of the research, alongside an integrated definition of what fandom constitutes, which will then be taken up in the rest of the book.

Fanning David in Everyday Life

David Bowie has a large and loyal fan base. These fans are part of networks and associations that involve running and attending events, conventions, band nights and social activities. At the everyday level, Bowie fans speak of the way he was central to a whole set of ritualistic and event-based milestones in their lives, including 'coming out', cross-dressing, sexual awakening and the extension of personal freedoms. For example, in response to Question 6 of our study, 'Please recall and describe what your first memory of encountering David Bowie is?', one of our respondents (A1) writes:

> When I was 14, my parents divorced, my mother became a hippie and moved me and my brother to a crappy little redneck town in Tennessee where I had to finish 9th grade. I had long hair, and the boys all wanted to demolish me. Lonely, isolated, I stayed inside as much as possible. I'd won the first Kiss album from a radio station in Florida. A hillbilly girl in Tennessee offered to trade a "weird" album for it: Ziggy Stardust. The album was like a message to me from across the world: You are not alone. It saved my life.

Here, we can immediately see the life story entanglements that Bowie's fans recall. A1 places hearing Bowie in terms of a series of life crisis and the loneliness and alienation that followed. Bowie is seen to rescue them from this sense of outsiderdom, giving them an image and a sound to identify with and to take sustenance from. This is a facet of Bowie's star image: he is often seen to challenge gender norms, particularly embodied notions of the straight and masculine, opening up new spaces of belonging as he does so. As Peri Bradley and James Page argue,

Bowie's rebellion through the creation of his androgynous persona Ziggy Stardust can be seen to offer other artists a new way to explore their own performances, and the audience a new way to explore their own identity, therefore bringing about a gradual but unstoppable transformation in the criteria for gender performance. Bowie effectively demonstrated to the world the liberation offered by rejecting stringent gender roles and labels thereby ensuring that it did not 'repeat itself to infinity' and also offering a voice and form of expression to marginalised groups. (2017: 586)

Fandom can be seen to be 'dis-alienating' since it can provide a communal and collective space for the marginalised to gather together to resist and reject the conformity they face in everyday life, something we discuss in depth in Chapter 3. If we take heavy metal fans at a live gig, we see that:

Fans rage, swear, chant with middle fingers and metal horns, and other billingsgate. They body thrash, mosh, body surf, and delight in parade stripping rituals. As in Bakhtin's carnival, amid sweaty bodies pushing, grabbing, swaying, rubbing, and touching, the crowd is made 'concrete and sensual.' Among the 'pressing throng, the physical contact of bodies, … [t]he individual feels that he is an indissoluble part of the collectivity, a member of the people's mass body' (Bakhtin [1936] 1984:255). This subtler yet powerful carnival experience may be among the most transgressive aspects of heavy metal carnival, for it grates against a society that places primacy on autonomy, self-interest, and individualism. (Hanlon 2006: 40)

Similarly, in our study we found, as A2 and A3 put it:

A2: I have seen him many times in many countries. the excitement and anticipation build up until the moment he comes on stage. The experience is magical, you're transported up out of your body and into a better place. Maybe this is what is meant by rhapsody. For me it is an all-consuming experience and I am so sad that I will never have that again.

A3: … David singing Heroes at the wall in the Glass Spider tour, the crowd building up behind the wall as he sang to those in the west - that covered me in goose bumps and still does…

(Question 11: Have you ever seen David Bowie live in concert or on stage?)

Fandom can afford an individual with a sense of empowerment and, in relation to pop stardom, hearing the music of the one you are devoted to can be responsible for indescribable, unlocatable sensations. For example,

Simon Frith has argued that music is of fundamental importance because it,

> Seems to make possible a new kind of self-recognition, to free us from every-day routines, from the social expectations with which we are encumbered... Music constructs our sense of identity through the experiences it offers of the body, time, and sociability, experiences which enable us to place ourselves in imaginative cultural narratives. (Frith 1996: 275)

Such forms of imaginative transcendence have also been termed encounters of 'enchantment' (Bennett 2001: 5–6) whereby heightened musical connections can be seen to occur in the presence of the performer, or in their absence, as in the case of recorded music, entailing:

> A mood of fullness, plenitude, or liveliness, a sense of having had one's nerves or circulation or concentration powers tuned up or recharged—a shot in the arm, a fleeting return to childlike excitement about life... One also notes that the word enchant is linked to the French verb to sing: chanter. To "en-chant": to surround with song or incantation; hence, to cast a spell with sounds, to make fall under the sway of a magical refrain, to carry away on a sonorous stream.

As our respondents often highlight, fandom can provide a vehicle for powerfully sensorial encounters. In response to Question 8, 'What does David Bowie mean to you?',

> A4: He has been my only constant since I was little. I have adored his voice, his face, his music, his style, intelligence, humour, films, interviews, choice of books.... he has always been a rich tapestry to fill my life with joy, with solace, with the new and the familiar. I feel joyous and comforted when I hear him. I don't have a "God" - but if I did - David Bowie would be it.

These sensorial encounters are often expressed or experienced through fan pilgrimages where a location, space and environment connected to the star is visited and dwelled in. These visits are meant to connect the fan to the location, to the lived biography of the star, granting them access to the 'roads they have travelled', but also, more complexly, to their interiority since these spaces are where seminal work was produced, star memories made, and life traumas played out. For example, fans visit Graceland because Elvis, '... is the guide along the way, a helper on the pilgrim's path, a vehicle and medium through which the pilgrim may come into contact with and encounter a higher truth and reality' (Reader 1993: 224). As Phil Cousineau (1998: 185–186) recalls:

> James van Harper, who visited Graceland on Valentine's Day in 1998 with his wife, says he has been inspired all his life by the singer and suggests that his pilgrimage to the shrine was a chance to get close to the "relics" of the King of Rock "n" Roll. "My pilgrimage taught me that no matter what heights we reach, we all have struggles. Being there at Graceland somehow allows me to carry my burden with a little more grace".

Our respondents undertook pilgrimages in similar ways:

> A5: I really love a restaurant on Heddon Street and remember when the plaque was going up for Ziggy falling to earth. I couldn't believe that I had been there so many times! I would try to imagine peering through time and space to see this young man creating an image that would become so iconic. I know how it feels to walk through busy London streets dolled up to the nines and the looks that you get… I should think it was much crazier for him at that time.

> A6: Berlin. It has an aching heart and Bowie's cathartic album trilogy written while he was there expressed this. I had to feel it for myself. There it was. A city constantly rebuilding itself trying to escape and embrace the past simultaneously. I felt the minor key signatures in the air. London. An exciting place with so much history. I was there for his Meltdown show. It was a place to meet many friends I had only known before as virtual people on Bowienet. Los Angeles. I live here now and a five minute drive from his star on Hollywood Blvd. Close to the studios he recorded at, I have been in the house he stayed at in the 70's. Los Angeles, particularly Hollywood is a much better place now than it was during the 70s, but if you close your eyes and listen, you can still hear shreds of why he wrote what he did when he was here.

(Question 13: Have you ever visited a site or place that is given significance within David Bowie's career?)

Both A5 and A6 are engaged in multiple processes of identification and memorial work: they imagine they have an empathetic relationship with Bowie by being in these spaces, imagining what it was like for him traversing gender norms, creating what would become iconic images and anthemic sounds. As they recall these memories, two types of past tense are reared into simultaneous view—their looking backwards on their own pilgrimages, and pilgrimage as the literal seeing into Bowie's own past, his own lived experiences. A6 divides up their response into the cities they lived in, connecting these urban recollections to the proximity with the production of Bowie's art, as if by living in these spaces they are connected to Bowie's creativity. Space and time consistently flood the recollections and remembrances shared with us.

Bowie Representations and Fan Identities

In terms of representation, David Bowie very often encapsulates a vexing form of otherness. He:

> Is human and flawed (visibly so with a damaged eye) as well as extraordinary in appearance, demeanour and projected self- belief. The ethereal aspect central to Bowie's star persona and epitomized in many of his characterizations – Major Tom, Ziggy Stardust, Aladdin Sane and so on – overtly embraces the 'otherness' of the outsider. (Hunt 2015: 178)

Similarly, as noted briefly above, Bowie's androgyny, cross-dressing and play with sexuality, through such characters as Ziggy Stardust, openly challenged dominant notions of masculinity and heterosexuality. Bowie can be seen as a figure who offered counter-meanings to dominant forms of binary gender classifications that were produced in media culture during his career. Bowie's open and contested play with gender and sexuality created positive, empowering identity spaces for those who felt socially marginalised. In Nick Stevenson's empirical study of David Bowie fandom, we find, for example, one fan, Guy, commenting:

> People tend to go back to it [Bowie's music] when they're having problems, they deal with it by secluding themselves through Bowie and turning to him for, like a guide, inspiration… or just to cope… (Stevenson 2009: 84)

Similarly, in our research we find that fans regularly refer to the way Bowie's perceived difference, imagined through a number of identity positions, enabled them to find themselves:

A7: As a queer kid growing up in a small town, there was also this sense that he gave me a vocabulary for my own sexuality, just through his "I don't even care; this is all part of being human" presentation of his bisexuality. And I love that he let himself be weird, without having to be weird all the time. This is the guy who could be Major Tom, Ziggy Stardust, Gareth the goblin king, and give a remarkably understated performance of Nicholai Tesla.

(Question 8: What does David Bowie mean to you?)

A8: … At the time though, as a sensitive teenage I wasn't really cool, struggling with ideas – was I gay – which at the time it was really, really hard, it was something I really didn't want to be, it was a big 'no no' to be gay, as it was not cool to be gay. I like feminine things. Now I would be seen as transgender and I would have been on that sort of path. But, what I saw in Bowie was the kind of person that had that kind of tension and femininity and I wouldn't use the word 'queer', but there was something different about him but he was cool and people treated him as a cool guy. So, it was like Boy George or Marilyn or people who look very, very feminine but someone who seemed to be struggling within this cage of conventional masculinity.

(Lisbon Focus group: open discussion about Bowie and desire)

Bowie fandom is often shown to be transformative and liberating: gay people in particular were able to see themselves powerfully embodied in Bowie's various star images, opening up the possibility for self-expression and self-actualisation. This is true of queer fan and star relationships more generally. For example, in Richard Dyer's reading of Judy Garland she emerges as a crisis figure who had 'a special relationship to suffering' (1986: 143), a 'gay sensibility' (154) that gay men particularly identified with. When Judy Garlands sings, there is an 'intensity and irony' (ibid.) to the performance that reverberates from the body of the screen into the bodies of gay men, a connection so profound that it feels exactly like the marginalisation they face in the world. As A9 beautifully responds:

Let's Dance in 1983 during a youth camp. Shouting out "tremble like a flower" Made me feel free and that was the starting point to explore my Desire for boys. My outing was framed with Bowie.

(Question 6. Please recall and describe what your first memory of encountering David Bowie is?)

However, Bowie also flirted with a potent form of white masculinity, one which carried a version of hyper-whiteness forward that held the connotations of (post)colonial power and racial superiority. Bowie's idealised whiteness was most notably found in the figure of the Thin White Duke, a character he created in the late 1970s, with iconography that drew upon Nietzschean imagery, and in the music video to *Let's Dance* (1982). In this music video, shot in Sydney and the Blue Mountains, Bowie draws upon 'primitive' aboriginal myths and rituals from the exalted position of his status a hyper-white rock star, offering the two aboriginal dancers a sermon (on a mount) on how to be truly free. The video suggests this 'freedom' is a return to (their) 'nature', as we witness the dancers return to the 'bush', leaving their Western clothes behind them. Bowie's white masculinity is exalted and placed in a position of surveilling power and influence. As one of our respondents (A10) writes:

> Watching the video clip for *Let's Dance* in 1985 and feeling overwhelmed with fascination / confusion. It felt raw and shocking to see a white pop star in the same physical space as First Nation Australians.
>
> (Question 6: Please recall and describe what your first memory of encountering David Bowie is?)

During his Berlin period, Bowie has, of course, been connected to fascist imagery and accusations that he was drawn to right-wing thinking and philosophy. Few fans comment on this or touch upon some of the accusations of sexual violence that was reported on in the popular media. There are a series of absences or gaps, then, in terms of the way fans remember and eulogise him. In one sense, this is not unexpected: the phenomena of the anti-star belong to people who openly challenge and critique celebrity culture. Anti-fans can form in two different ways. First, through derision and distaste they can take issue against a particular star for the way they embody fame or because they compete with other stars they have forged close affiliations with. Second, anti-fans can take critical issue with the whole apparatus of celebrity culture, forming groups that openly attack what stars stand for. As can be seen, from our respondents, there is both a drawing to the shimmering vectors of stardom and an enchanted worshipping of David Bowie.

Nonetheless, we do find elements of what can be termed parafandom/parastardom, where Bowie fans champion the way he exists on the margins of cultural acceptability and visibility. While parastardom draws from mainstream stardom, leaches off its representations and identification streams, it functions in opposition to dominant star images and their ideological and sensorial qualities. The parastar is often a transgressive and liminal figure, appears in cult texts and is defined by their excess, both within the texts they appear in and in public life. They are excessively embodied, and their bodies are exaggerated carriers of emotion and affect. The parastar offers the parafan a set of unruly pleasures, within 'a counter-aesthetic turned sub-cultural sensibility devoted to all manner of cultural detritus' (Sconce 1995: 372). They operate as border crossings for the alienated, the marginal and the dispossessed. Our respondents find these para-attractions and desires in their responses describing Bowie as 'alien', 'otherworldly', and as someone who challenged the conventions of music and performance.

However, one can determine a darker side to these fascinations, one that coalesces around perversion, something we go onto discuss in Chapters 3 and 5, where our respondents imagine both desiring Bowie as a father figure and of dreaming of him within eroticised and non-binary sexual encounters. These fantasies are also unearthed in the creative work of fandom.

CREATIVE FANDOM

It can be argued that fandom constitutes an alternative and oppositional set of practices to the profit-orientated mechanisms of neoliberal capitalism: a *gift economy*. In the fan-gift economy, it is the exchange of gifts between fans that drives interactions, builds and fosters social networks and which disrupts the capital and commodity flow of dominant forms of media production. As Karen Hellekson argues,

> Fan communities as they are currently comprised, require exchanges of gifts: you do not pay to read fan fiction or watch a fan-made music vid. They are offered for free [...] yet within a web of context that specifies an appropriate method of 'payment'. (2009: 114)

One of the core 'gifts' of fan communities is creativity, creative artwork, that reinscribes the text in question and extends the star's artistic universe in so doing. Such fan artwork is unique and personal—it suffers less from cultural mediation and mass reproduction, re-signing it with an 'aura', a sense-based quality. For example, Simon Jacobs (2014) handmade and drawn graphic novel, *Saturn*, explores through a semi-autobiographical lens, 16 short story imaginings with David Bowie, each story a 'story of the self' set within a semi-fictional universe. For example, in the story *David Bowie in a Baconian Nightmare*:

> He Can no longer tell his screaming face from the background

Many of our respondents indicated that they took part in the fan-gift economy and that Bowie was a conduit for their own creativity:

> *A11*: I have a Space Oddity shirt I use only in special occasions and as a teenager I had a lot of newspaper and magazines clipping. I have the catalog of the big exhibit about him, gift from a friend to help me in the grief I'm feeling with his death. And I have the indirect memorabilia. I always have at least one pair of red shoes. So, when I have a depression or anxiety crisis and the world is too much, I use it to remember to "put on your red shoes and dance the blues"

> (Question 15: Do you have a cherished piece of David Bowie memorabilia?)

A12, who took part in the London focus group, makes Bowie dolls, each one encapsulating a different Bowie star image. These dolls, made of cloth and stitching, were made as homages to Bowie and to become a part of the trade and traffic in the gift economy. They are also part of the way Bowie is seen to be commodified and how fans see part of his career as built on selling his brand.

Brand David Bowie

Bowie's music and many of his star images are found licensed and reproduced in various commercial contexts. Bowie appeared in adverts for such products as Takara sake (1980), the soft drink Pepsi (1987), Vittel bottled water (2003) and fashion labels Tommy Hilfiger (2003) and Louis Vuitton (2013). His songs have been regularly used in adverts including *Fame* for the Cadillac Escalade (2015) and *Changes* for BMW Diesel series (2015). The track *Heroes* has been used across numerous cultural contexts and adverts, from Westpac banking commercials in Australia (2018) to being played as athletes from Great Britain entered the Olympic Stadium during the 2012 Summer Olympics opening ceremony, as well as after medal ceremonies during these Games.

David Bowie's iconic lightning bolt image of Aladdin Sane has been re-appropriated by various cultural industries, including urban design, sanctioned street art, advertisements, repackaging Bowie's androgyny in more 'palatable', commercial forms. Numerous artists have adopted or transcoded aspects of Bowie's star images, including Brett Anderson of Suede, Brian Molko of Placebo and Lady GaGa. Gary Kemp of Spandau Ballet has described Bowie's influence on his career in terms of the music and performances providing him with a sense of cool and of difference and of creative influences that shaped the band's own music (2013).

One can read Bowie's career through the lens of proto-capitalist production and as an artist who disrupted the way he could be sold and marketed as a product. As Andy Bennett writes:

> In a very real sense, early in his career Bowie embraced the music business concept of identity production, acquiring a highly reflexive understanding of himself as an object to be fashioned and marketed and skilfully adapting this into a tantalising mode of DIY (do-it-yourself) iconicity. (2017: 574)

David Bowie's understanding of his value in the marketplace was best illustrated in 1997 when he came up with a cash-generating scheme involving selling 'Bowie bonds', which awarded investors a share in his future royalties for 10 years. The bonds, which were bought by US insurance giant Prudential Financial for $55m (£38m), committed David Bowie to repay his new creditors out of future income and gave a fixed annual return of 7.9% (Espiner 2016). Twenty-five albums released between 1969 and 1990—which included *The Man Who Sold the World*, *The Fall and Rise* of *Ziggy Stardust* and *Heroes*—were involved in the deal.

This commercialisation of Bowie is something picked up by our respondents. In response to being asked to choose an image of David Bowie, from 50 or so images provided, and to explain that choice, at the Lisbon focus group:

> *B1*: The interesting thing, the thing I wanted to say is that 80s Bowie, often thought of as the mainstream Bowie, the sell-out Bowie when he said "the biggest mistake I ever made was saying that I am bi-sexual": at the time one of the things that I saw in Bowie was the strain and tension behind this, from this blonde guy in a suit, very mainstream appearing as a

very straight business-man, and I think there is a real queerness about that straight Bowie ... reminiscent of the social times of AIDS fear, Reaganism [US], Thatcherism [UK], economic rationalism and he was representing that fear that tension, trying to repress that queerness inside himself and not really hiding it – I liked that. Here was someone that looked straight, passes as straight but was not really straight and he was really conveying the tension but he was getting away with it.

Our respondent here deftly ties together the issue of corporate Bowie with wider tensions in culture in the 1980s, seeing the repression in/of his bisexuality as actually revealing the way normative masculinity functions. The respondent quoted, however, is what might be termed an aca-fan, taking part in our Lisbon conference focus group, and therefore versed in making such cultural readings (see Introduction). An aca-fan is both a scholar of fandom and a fan of the star text being researched, moving in and across these spaces of critical and personal engagement, something we pick up later in this book (see Chapter 7). Matt Hills (2011) argues for:

Acafandom which strives for "proper distance" (Silverstone 2007) from all its constituencies. My rendering of "proper distance" implies critical and multi-dimensional reflexivity. I think scholar-fandom remains important to the extent that it is able to engage critically with the contemporary limits of what can be said in academic and fan communities. The notion of moral economy is thus useful - or rather, the interference pattern created by intersecting, multiple moral economies.

These moral economies are written large across our questionnaire and focus group responses, but here open up the question of Bowie fandom to other intersecting types of fans—from professional musicians to writers and artists, to bankers and service workers. In this sea of exchanges, fans swim together in the same self-reflecting surfaces and in the same depths of famed water and yet one has to be mindful of power inequalities as they manifest in culture more broadly.

SHARING AND COLLECTING BOWIE

Active star fandom involves two, sometimes interrelating, forms: one that is individualised and individually sanctioned and one that takes place in fan communities, defined as 'the shared social contexts within which fan reading and creative practices occur' (Jenkins 2006). Those star fans who individualise their active participation also often share and partake in communities, involving themselves in both a 'private' form of intimacy with the star they identify with, and a 'public' one, where the sharing of knowledge, readings, desires and the creation of homages and transcoding of existing star texts takes place. According to Henry Jenkins (2010), fandom is a key facet of participatory culture, where:

> [f]andom refers to the social structures and cultural practices created by the most passionately engaged consumers of mass media properties; participatory culture refers more broadly to any kind of cultural production which starts at the grassroots level and which is open to broad participation.

The participatory culture that builds around star fandom can be argued to be regenerative, affecting the production and reception of the figure, as fans creatively resign their meaning, produce and transmit new ways of understanding the star and engage in new forms of collective interaction with other like-minded fans. As Charles Soukup suggests in relation to online fandom communities:

> On the Chris Carter Web sites, fans analysed the themes and symbols of The X-Files episode by episode. In these situations, the fan appears to be actively constructing meaning and refusing to "accept" the dominant interpretation of the media text. Rather than (relatively) passively reading the text as "intended" by the producers or interpreted by mainstream critics, these fans offer unique, alternative, and sometimes quite elaborate readings of the text. By actively reinterpreting the text, the fan is creative and empowered. Perhaps in the most dramatic example, a fansite dedicated to the musician Moby had a page of remixed songs (originally recorded by Moby) posted by fans. In a number of similar examples, fans rewrote or wrote new versions of songs by artists like David Bowie and Bob Dylan. (2006: 327)

Our respondents were highly active in forms of participatory culture around their Bowie fandom, as B2 and B3 share:

> B2: He and his music have been there for me during times of joy and times of horrificness. I have made many dear friends and travelled to places I had never thought to do so because of him. My tastes in music, art, film and life are because of him. One dear friend who is now gone from this physical world referred to him once as "Daddy". It stuck. And it makes perfect sense. Our family of societal outsiders has looked to him as a role model, a confidante, our encouragement, our father …

(Question 8: What does David Bowie mean to you?)

> *B3*: My first experience of seeing Bowie live was at the album launch of 'Reality'
> in 2003. I won tickets through the fan section of his website and the whole
> experience was just so special. From meeting fellow fans who I'd only ever
> spoken to online (who are still friends almost 13 years on) to seeing him
> performing in such intimate surroundings, the whole thing was magical.

(Question 11: Have you ever seen David Bowie live in concert or on stage?)

B2 connects their fan relationship to Bowie through an affective triangulation: their individual fandom, their joint fandom with a close friend
now dead and their collective fandom framed in terms of outsider identifications. Bowie becomes a father figure (also see Chapter 3), but one
framed in childlike language and affinities: he is Daddy. Of course, we are
also seeing the role of the digital media in creating new 'micro' sites of
engagement and attachment. And these digital micro-communities can be
liberating and resistant to dominant culture. As Lothian, Busse and Reid
comment in relation to Slash fandom:

> Our experience in slash fan communities on LiveJournal.com (LJ) suggests
> that participation in electronic social networks can induct us into new and
> unusual narratives of identity and sexuality, calling into question familiar iden-
> tifications and assumptions. Slash fandom's discursive sphere has been termed
> queer female space by some who inhabit and study it; we want to explore the
> function of this space in the lives of the people who occupy it, how it is
> structured, and what it can do. (Lothian et al. 2007: 103)

B3's response recounts a unique experience where they won tickets to see
the launch of the album *Reality*, meeting with fellow Bowie fans who
then became lifelong friends. This 'special' moment of course connects the
winning of the golden ticket to both the fan-gift economy, won on Bowie's
own fan website, and the commercial tentacles of the music industry, since
this is a promotional event for the album.

The various focus groups that we facilitated can be seen to have engen-
dered their own participatory culture, or rather, they become in almost all
instances an intimate and open fan gathering where the sharing of memories, stories, events, meetings and traumas brought people together. This
communing was of course built around Bowie: he was the totemic gift that

fostered the conversation, bounded the 'strangers' in the various rooms we held the focus groups in. All of the focus groups took place after his death, and this produced both a celebratory discourse but also one of melancholy and loss. As B4 writes so powerfully:

> Uncountable shows from 1974 - 2003. Since I am writing this one week after his death, one show is foremost in my mind. I was at the Area 2 show in the middle of the woods in Massachusetts with my best friend who was so very sick. I didn't know how long he was going to live, but he was with me that day. When Bowie sang "Everyone Says Hi" we both had tears streaming down our faces. He lived another year-and-a-half, which was wonderful. Bowie gave me that moment with a man I loved so much that I cried listening to him sing about taking the big trip, about dying.
>
> (Question 11: Have you ever seen David Bowie live in concert or on stage?)

One of the focus groups, held in Berlin was differently constituted: as we note in the Introduction, it was composed of one of the author's (Sean) lifelong friends, who had come to Berlin for the sole purpose of catching up. At this focus group, tears were shed not for Bowie's passing but for the passing of time and the thickness of friendship and the way Bowie was one of the coordinates of their growing up together. For two of the participants, including Sean, this involved remembering and recalling how tough it had been for them—the brute reality of Thatcher's economic policy hitting their families particularly hard. Bowie, it was remembered, was an escape from such harsh realities.

Through its core practices and processes, star fandom is an emotive apparatus that engages with common modes of feelings and at its most heightened, delirious forms of affect. Stars situate themselves within broad economies of intimacy that seem particularly strong and heartfelt. All the subsets of emotion—from love, anger, surprise to sadness and grief—are made manifest through the way stars circulate in the lives of fans. We cry with and for them. They dance in our dreams. They occupy the spaces of event spectacle calling forth our emotions to receive and exalt them. Stars register as figuring in key biographical events and memorial exchanges where fans story and remember them through the event moments they help shaped. The emotion of celebrity matches or catches the emotional encounters fans go through, providing the meta-context for love, romance, heartache and desire. Fans live emotional lives in, and through the emotions of the stars, they connect and entwine with.

Fantasy is crucial to the conceit that celebrity audiences are impression-able. Fantasy functions as a 'way in which identity is sutured together' (Hinerman 1992: 607), and as 'a necessary dimension of our psychical reality ... as the place of excess, where the unimaginable can be imagined'. Hinerman's small scale empirical research with Elvis Presley fans found that the escapist fantasies he offered up enabled them to withstand the traumatic events in their 'real lives'. The celebrity imaginary becomes a way to gather strength and resilience in the 'real' world. In Marsha Orgeron's work on fandom, they find:

> Fan magazine contests enabled and encouraged women to re-evaluate them-selves in response to the star system and to articulate their fantasies in tangible ways through their participation. Fan letters, which materialized when fans sought stars' studio addresses from magazine editors, also make material fans' desire to emerge from anonymity, to create a concrete existence for them-selves in relation to the star system. (2003: 79)

We found that fantasy was crucial to the way some of our respondents explored their fan relationship with David Bowie:

> *B5*: I would have liked to have walked around his mind for a while. I am sure several 30-something females will also say this but... I imagined myself as Sarah in Labyrinth a few times! He could keep my snotty little brother with pleasure. We would just dance in that snowglobe ballroom and maybe have a snog - this was the original Bowie fantasy.

> *B6*: I dreamed to become "someone" in art just to be validated by him. I wanted to talk with him about art and music and performance. As a kid I dreamed that Jaret could rescue me from the normal world where I didn't find my place and take me to his kingdom.

(Question 12. Did you fantasize about meeting David Bowie – or meet him for real?)

Both B5 and B6 regress to sharing a fantasy they both had about being taken to the magic kingdom in *Labyrinth* (Henson 1986), where Jareth (Bowie) is the Goblin King. For B5, this is in part a sexual encounter, where she gets to kiss Jareth/Bowie, while for B6 she is rescued from the ordinary world, transported to this magical kingdom where she now belongs. This role is a 'perfect fit' for Bowie since it connects and intersects with his 'alien' or 'Other' star image—a trickster figure (Grádinaru 2012; Stark 2015), caught between heaven and earth, a rule breaker who is mischievous.

Fandom is of course distinctly private, particularly when it comes to aspects of cherished possessions. Star and celebrity memorabilia are often a type of holy relic, invested with religious signification or higher-order iconicity by fans who purchase and then 'house' them in special places. For fans, an aura circulates around such memorabilia: an economy of the emotions is set in train. However, a commodity exchange value is also produced since these are not personally prized star possessions but are very often monetarised on auction sites.

At the personal level, no more is this true than when the item or items in question have a personal connection to the fan—a ticket to a first concert, an original rare poster, a signed autograph done at an event where they met the star or a drinking bottle flung from the stage with the star's own DNA wrapped around its opening.

The word possession is crucial to this relationship; one is not simply possessing the star-struck thing but their essence, their being-in-the-world. Their enchanted or charmed life is being co-located in the holy relic that is owned, cherished, touched and consumed by the fan. Memories are connected to it: life storied emanate from it. One can define this carnal and existential transference as celebrity contagion or 'the belief that a person's immaterial qualities or "essence" can be transferred to an object through physical contact' (Newman et al. 2011: 4). The material possession of a celebrity's personal item, then, captures their spirit and body, which through presence, touch, even/especially ingestion, possesses and changes or transforms the 'new you' who now holds it. Here, once public items become deeply private keepsakes and mementos:

> B7: One of my most cherished items is something I do not share with others because people are strange about such things. It is a drawing he did of himself sticking his tongue out like a nut. It is signed on the back to me with the caption " go on, laugh! Be well. " with his giant B and scribble of a signature. I also managed to save a hard copy of an email where he was telling me how his mother invented SETI. All in good fun. Plus a myriad of autographed albums, CDs, lithographs. Tour books, ticket stubs. Etc. two of my favorite things are from the Diamond Dogs tour. I have a necklace with a " dog tag " diamond shaped aluminium pendant that has the album info on it. And I have a big cardboard display of David as the Diamond Dog with the MainMan logo, etc. on it. A store promo prop. I asked the guy at Tower records if I could have it as he was going to toss it out.

B8: my brother is 15 years older than me and I was born in 1969, the record shop had to order the single in for him as they had not heard of David Bowie OR Space Oddity, I was just a few months old and my mother loves to tell me how she pushed me in my pram, down to the record shop to collect it when it came in…. she told me she couldn't have dreamed that the little baby in the pram would grow up to be the bigger Bowie fan out of her children! My brother stopped buying Bowie records in the late 70's, and gave me the single in the 80's, technically its been in my life longer than my teeth! It has been the one prize that has stayed with me no matter what, I simply could not part with it under any circumstances.

(Question 15: Do you have a cherished piece of David Bowie memorabilia?)

B7 has two distinct types of memorabilia: a private, very personal item that she shares with no one else and a collection of Bowie-related keepsakes that they have accumulated from concerts, events and 'scavenging'. The former, a self-portrait that David gave to them, inscribed with a personal message and signed, is guarded because of its personal, singular nature and kept private in case it is considered 'strange'. What we have here is the respondent sensing the uniqueness of the gift and the worry that it will be taken away.

B8 wraps a monumental familial life story around the buying of a record for her older brother, when they were still a baby. The record connects them to their mother who undertook the mission, and brother, and together to the life force that Bowie subsequently provided. These types of stories are memorial and event-based: they are everyday rituals and narratives of the self, providing a connection between child and adult, baby and mother, sister and brother.

Fandom and ageing very often sit on a vexed nexus: on the one hand, it is considered to be a young person's activity that when carried into later years can be seen to be shameful (Harrington et al. 2011: 584). However, as people age the stars they were connected to as young people age with them, providing a form of ontological continuity, and the material out of which seminal memories are often made during adolescent and young adult life. Paradoxically, as fans get older the stars they grew up with and were fannish about, connect them back to their youth, enabling them to feel young again. Laura Vroomen (2004) has identified the way mature female Kate Bush fans afforded them feelings of empowerment:

…claims to distinction on account of their 'feminine cultural capital', enabled by Kate Bush's blend of a 'masculine' musical virtuosity and a 'feminine' address, partly challenges the male domination of the popular music field. Furthermore, the women's articulation of popular music and a mature sensibility challenges the medium's youth ethos and offers an understanding of the way in which popular music returns its value for listeners through the long term. (2004: 1)

Tonya Anderson (2012) has studied adult Duran Duran fans who 'experience a euphoric empowerment from performing the same fannish activities they did as teens', where attending live concerts approximates a 'reclaimed youth' for adults who are approaching midlife' (2012: 239).

In our research, we found many of our respondents defining themselves as lifelong Bowie fans and marking their responses with how he provided them with narratives and experiences that they took with them from youth to adulthood.

> *B9*: I am a lifelong music fanatic. The first album I ever bought was Ziggy Stardust when I was 4 years old (1977). I still remember the store I bought it at, the record had such an impact on me. My older sister was a teenager when I was born and used to babysit me. My go to for being soothed when upset was she would put her headphones on me. I am told my favorites were Alice Cooper, Frank Zappa and David Bowie. I don't remember a time that his music was not a part of my life.

(Question 6. Please recall and describe what your first memory of encountering David Bowie is?)

> *B10*: Oh boy, where do I begin… Everything? He taught me many things that deeply influenced the kind of adult I became. He taught me that weird is not always a negative quality. Bowie introduced me to gender fluidity, and helped me figure out my own sexuality. I've known I was bisexual since I was about 13, but having been raised in a very heteronormative environment, I always thought there was something shameful about it. 5 or so years later, I came to terms with my sexual orientation, and I finally accepted it. I thought to myself, "If Bowie did it, it must be okay."

(Question: 8. What does David Bowie mean to you?)

Again, for both B9 and B10 we see a Bowie narrative being weaved into the fabric of their life stories: a chrononormative temporality that allows them to neatly map out the order of events, so that their selfhoods emerge as continuous forms of being-in-the-world (this is something that we further address in Chapter 5). Bowie fandom, then, has none of the shame of some other pop-orientated fandoms (Anderson 2012), to the contrary it seems to be a badge of honour, a higher-order attachment that is compelling. As Nick Stevenson also reasons,

> Bowie for the fans is representative of change and the passing of time.... Bowie is valued precisely because he can positively respond to change, and has done so in a way that is seen to be 'appropriate' for a man at his stage of life. He offers a model for how to grow old without shutting out new ideas and influences.... Bowie is valued as someone who could help you respond to change in your own life. (Stevenson 2009: 86)

Celebrities are first and foremost embodied individuals, intense molecular manifestations, and one of the key ways they affectively engage with fans and audiences is through the primary senses activated by sensorial-based aesthetics. This is not, however, a one-way mode of communication: these molecular manifestations occupy and move between celebrity and fan, between and across subjectivities and identities.

One can define this celebrity/fan relationship as *celebaesthetic* or one in which the individual and famous person face one another as experiential beings in a dynamic, relational structure of reversibility and reciprocity. Feelings and (their) affects move backwards and forwards, in and out, within and without the two identifying figures. There is a systolic/diastolic rhythm about these exchanges producing an intensification of bodily awareness, singular and combined. In this relational, cross-modal exchange through which the senses are activated, the body is the organ through which a communion—a shared experiential relationship—takes place.

This exchange relies on 'both synaesthesia (or intersensoriality) and coenaesthesia (the perception of a person's whole sensorial being)' (Sobchack 2004: 67). Put rather simply, celebrities and fans communicate with one another in and through; the activation of powerful emotions and senses; shared, heightened and proximate embodied awareness; and intense molecular manifestations that fill the body full of rapture and delight.

Too often a top-down framework is applied to both understand how star culture impacts upon everyday life, and to the interpretation of fan voices when they are indeed called upon to speak. Very often, when empirical research is carried out, the very responses that have been called upon are marginalised and re-framed, given a new theoretical 'voice' to capture what was supposedly there in the first place. While reading or making sense of audience responses is crucial, the tendency to dismiss the agency that is so palpably there, in the first place, is one of the failures of the work being carried out in this field. It is the relationship between the individual, the social and the cultural that calls for better alignment, as the rest of this book seeks to do. It is what Bowie would have wanted us to do.

REFERENCES

Anderson, Tonya. "Still Kissing Their Posters Goodnight: Female Fandom and the Politics of Popular Music." *Journal of Audience & Reception Studies* 9 (2) (2012): 239–264.

Bennett, Andy. "Wrapped in Stardust: Glam Rock and the Rise of David Bowie as Pop Entrepreneur." *Continuum* 31 (4) (2017): 574–582.

Bennett, Jane. *The Enchantment of Modern Life: Attachments, Crossings, and Ethics.* Princeton, NJ: Princeton University Press, 2001.

Bradley, Peri, and James Page. "David Bowie—The Trans Who Fell to Earth: Cultural Regulation, Bowie and Gender Fluidity." *Continuum* 31 (4) (2017): 583–595.

Cousineau, Phil. *The Art of Pilgrimage.* San Francisco: Conari Press, 1998.

Dyer, Richard. "Judy Garland and Gay Men." In *Heavenly Bodies: Film Stars and Society*, ed. R. Dyer, 141–194. London: Routledge, 1986.

Espiner, Tom. "'Bowie Bonds'—The Singer's Financial Innovation." *BBC News Online*, 11 January 2016. https://www.bbc.com/news/business-35280945.

Frith, Simon. "Music and Identity." In *Questions of Cultural Identity*, ed. Stuart Hall and Paul Du Gay, 108–127. London: Sage, 1996.

Gemp, Gary. "David Bowie Is: Gary Kemp and Jarvis Cocker Find Gold Dust, Memories and the Scribbles of a 15-Year-Old Genius." *Go London, Standard UK*, 2013. https://www.standard.co.uk/go/london/exhibitions/david-bowie-is-gary-kemp-and-jarvis-cocker-find-gold-dust-memories-and-the-scribbles-of-a-15-year-8538832.html. Accessed 22 September 2018.

Gradinaru, Ioan-Alexandru. "The Ways of the Trickster. Meaning, Discourse and Cultural Blasphemy." *Argumentum: Journal the Seminar of Discursive Logic* 10 (2012): 85–96.

Hanlon, Karen. "Heavy Metal Carnival and Dis-alienation: The Politics of Grotesque Realism." *Symbolic Interaction* 29 (2006): 1, 33–48.

Harrington, C. Lee, Denise D. Bielby, and Anthony R. Bardo. "Life Course Transitions and the Future of Fandom." *International Journal of Cultural Studies* 14 (6) (2011): 567–590.

Hellekson, Karen. "A Fannish Field of Value: Online Fan Gift Culture." *Cinema Journal* 48 (4) (Summer 2009): 113–118.

Hills, Matt. "Aca-Fandom and Beyond: Jonathan Gray, Matt Hills, and Alisa Perren (Part One)." *Confessions of an Aca-Fan*, 2011. http://henryjenkins.org/blog/2011/08/aca-fandom_and_beyond_jonathan.html. Accessed 22 September 2018.

Hinerman, Stephen. "'I'll Be Here with You': Fans, Fantasy, and the Figure of Elvis." In *The Adoring Audience: Fan Culture and Popular Media*, ed. L. A. Lewis, 107–134. New York: Routledge, 1992.

Hunt, Kevin J. "The Eyes of David Bowie." *Enchanting David Bowie: Space/Time/Body/Memory*, 175–195. New York and London: Bloomsbury Publishing, 2015.

Jacobs, Simon. *Saturn*. Spork Press, 2014.

Jenkins, Henry. "When Fandom Goes Mainstream." *Confessions of an Aca-Fan*, 2006. http://henryjenkins.org/2006/11/when_fandom_goes_mainstream.html. Accessed 1 February 2011.

Jenkins, Henry. "Fandom, Participatory Culture, and Web 2.0—A Syllabus." *Confessions of an Aca-Fan: The Official Weblog of Henry Jenkins*, 2010. http://henryjenkins.org/2010/01/fandom_participatory_culture_a.html. Accessed 23 June 2011.

Lothian, Alexis, Kristina Busse, and Robin Anne Reid. "Yearning Void and Infinite Potential: Online Slash Fandom as Queer Female Space." *English Language Notes* 45 (2) (2007): 103–111.

Newman, George, Gil Diesendrock, and Paul Bloom. "Celebrity Contagion and the Value of Objects." *Journal of Consumer Research* 38 (8) (2011): 1–15.

Orgeron, Marsha. "Making 'It' in Hollywood: Clara Bow, Fandom, and Consumer Culture." *Cinema Journal* 42 (4) (2003): 76–97.

Reader, Ian. "Conclusions." In *Pilgrimage in Popular Culture*, ed. Ian Reader and Tony Walter, 220–246. London: Routledge, 1993.

Sconce, Jeffry. "Trashing the Academy: Taste, Excess and an Emerging Politics of Cinematic Style." *Screen* 36 (4) (1995): 371–393.

Sobchack, Vivian. *Carnal Thoughts: Embodiment and Moving Image Culture*. Berkeley, CA: University of California Press, 2004.

Soukup, Charles. "Hitching a Ride on a Star: Celebrity, Fandom, and Identification on the World Wide Web." *Southern Communication Journal* 71 (4) (2006): 319–337.

Stark, Tanya. "Crashing Out with Sylvian: David Bowie, Carl Jung and the Unconscious," 2015. https://tanjastark.com/2015/06/22/crashing-out-with-sylvian-david-bowie-carl-jung-and-the-unconscious/.

Stevenson, Nick. "Talking to Bowie Fans: Masculinity, Ambivalence and Cultural Citizenship." *European Journal of Cultural Studies* 12 (1) (2009): 79–98.
Vroomen, Laura. "Kate Bush: Teen Pop and Older Female Fans." In *Music Scenes: Local, Translocal and Virtual,* ed. Andy Bennett and Richard A. Peterson, 238–253. Nashville: Vanderbilt University Press, 2004.

CHAPTER 3

Stories of Difference and of Awakenings

INTRODUCTION

In this chapter, we explore the way our respondents wrote and spoke about how David Bowie impacted upon their identity and sense of self, and the empowerment he often gave them through his representations and performances. Here, we find stories of difference emerging, either framed through culturally empowering narratives of gender and sexual transformation, or around discourses of outsiderdom and alienation, which our respondents suggested Bowie provided escape from and a 'home' to arrive in. We also find narratives of awakening and sublimation where Bowie—his body—gave people experiences that were heightened and charged, electrifying and liquefying their being-in-the-world.

Within the sociological and cultural studies traditions, identity is argued to be composed of who we think we are and how (we think) others see us (Woodward 2005). Identity always seems to be both a matter of two interacted ingredients. First, identity is a form of social agency whereby people exercise a degree of free choice about the way they self-present themselves to the world (what they wear, their body idioms and mannerisms); the way they choose to identify with a defined set of values and ideas such as monogamy, and the importance of self-independence; and the decisions they exercise to belong to certain fan groups or sub-cultures, sports teams and such like: a neo-tribal process (Bauman 2000).

© The Author(s) 2019
T. Cinque and S. Redmond, *The Fandom of David Bowie*,
https://doi.org/10.1007/978-3-030-15880-4_3

Second, identity is argued to be a matter of imposition, whereby certain identities are given or ascribed to individuals. People are classified on a daily basis as occupying certain subjectivities, embodying certain types of identity, because of their social class, gender, race, sexuality, occupation and age. These frameworks that identities sit within are called classificatory systems and they permeate every area of the social world. These systems are value-laden supposedly lessening the agency that one imagines one has: they are ideological constructs that interpellates people into various subject positions (Althusser 2008).

A sense of one's identity is therefore constructed from the dialogical relationship between individual autonomy and the labelling, regulating and manufacturing of identity through the significant others people interact with, the discourses found in the media, education and in bio-medical practices; and the wider cultural material out of which representations flourish. Identity is wrested over: it is a contested terrain. For this chapter, we see how Bowie occupies an almost sacred space, becomes a super significant Other, a father figure, shattering identity binary oppositions as he does so, opening up identity-based classificatory systems to new forces and challenging formations. We also see how Bowie emerged in maternal stories, as the first section of this chapter attests to. Finally, the chapter concludes with a turn to autoethnographic storytelling, drawing on the memories of Sean and his lifelong friends as they gathered together in Berlin.

My Mother

The gendered nature of fandom is a complex issue: the labour of fandom is generally gendered (Scott 2015) and often, if not completely, divided along gender lines, such as the female-teen fandom for K-Pop and the male fandom of motorsports stars. With the fandom of David Bowie, of course, we see gender lines blurred and recast. Nonetheless, gendered binaries do seem to emerge out of the stories told but with progressive politics and relationships built in. In the wider stories that the questionnaire responses fostered, we see, for example, how E2's 'Mum bought the tickets and she took me and my girlfriend because we were too young to go by ourselves', and for E3, 'My mother was a massive fan however and I grew up listening to him throughout my childhood'. P1 remembers, 'watching the ashes to ashes film clip when I was 5 with my mum', while P2 reminisces:

on the day he died, my 20-year-old son, who was away on holiday went and got a tattoo. He has "There's a Starman" on his leg. He came home and said "This is for you Mum".

In these responses, we see (*hear*) a feminine 'sonorous envelope' (Doane 1980) of the maternal voice sounding its way through the figure of their mother, providing our participants with a feeling of plenitude, or as a way to navigate their motherhood. As Joanne Lacey writes in relation to academic fandom:

> It is possible to extend Doane's image of the sonorous envelope… to a consideration of the maternal as a nostalgic metaphor in wider terms for fantasises of belonging, wholeness and safety. (2000: 38)

P2 is recounting the way her son was both able to understand their grieving but also to mark this grief on his body as a way of demonstrating his love for her. In this extended questionnaire response below, we also see how mother and daughter together create this maternal space of belonging in and through the figure of David Bowie. As Q2 writes:

> I was 10 when I first heard him. I had never heard music like that. It was fun. It was comforting during teenage years. Danced to it. Cried to it. He came with me through my life. My three grown children were born into my love of David Bowie. My 17-year-old daughter wrote this on Facebook the day he died.
>
> I'm sure you all know by now that yesterday David Bowie passed away. This was a man that was my Mum's hero. I have grown up watching Labyrinth, listening to Space Oddity, Fashion, Changes and so much more. I've watched videos of his concerts and I've heard stories of her going to his concerts and getting overwhelmed by being in the same room as him. My passion for music stems from my Mum's love of this man and his music. I was devastated to see people tagging her in news articles because this isn't just anyone to her. It should be treated as though someone who meant a lot to her died because that is exactly what has happened. You can never underestimate how one persons life can be moved and impacted by one artist. One song. One moment. So mum, I'm so sorry for your loss. I'm so appreciative of you introducing me to David Bowie. May he rest in peace.
>
> I have been in love with David Bowie most of my life X.
>
> (8. What does David Bowie mean to you?)

Q2 weaves their response around three intersecting themes: lifestorying and identity transitions; the role that David Bowie had in providing a safe haven, a happy place, for the raising of their children; and the particular memorial response their daughter made for Q2 on the day of his death (see Conclusion for an extended discussion of Bowie's death). Bowie is brought into the primal scene in this response, recast as the maternal voice that ushers, lullaby-like, Q2's children into the world, but he is also past tense, his death the stitch in time that connects beginnings and endings, birth and death, becoming an umbilical cord between mother and daughter. Q2's daughter does this publicly, in a Facebook post, that powerfully, beautifully, recognises the loss that Q2 is going through: in a sense, roles are being reversed, daughter becomes caring, knowing mother. But the post also offers more than this: Q2's love of/for Bowie has been passed on, it ignites the world of their daughter, and it has filled their world since they were born with music, with love. This is maternal bonding cast through the god particles of time.

OH FATHER

> *B11*: His rebel heart and gender bending bravery impacted my day to day identity claims I think he's always been there like a parent and his British sensibility felt like having a second Father.

In B11's response to the question (8), 'What does David Bowie mean to you', they draw upon a number of intersecting identity positions that they see in Bowie and which in turn shaped their sense of self. Bowie is thought to be an identity transgressor, breaking normative heterosexual binaries, opening up a space for B11 to experience and positively embrace their own liminal sense of gender. This is connected to Bowie having a British sensibility, and although this is not defined here, the respondent may be picking up on the camp nature of certain forms of British masculinity and of Bowie's various star images and one that, 'is not a natural mode of sensibility, if there be any such. Indeed the essence of Camp is its love of the unnatural: of artifice and exaggeration' (Sontag 1964). As Bowie's biographer, Nicolas Pegg, notes:

> Bowie was embracing the spirit of Camp according to its truest definition, which is not about sex but about the elevation of the aesthetic above the purely practical. Just so, David 's relentless habit of editing his personality,

appearance, vocabulary and frames of reference to present a succession of 'new 'Bowies, each fashioned for effect and exclusivity, follows the manifesto of Camp established by Oscar Wilde and Susan Sontag. Camp invested Bowie/Ziggy with a useful air of ironic detachment, placing the received image of the star on a pedestal aloof from the mundane reality of studio sessions, tour buses, and the wife and baby at home. (2009: 297)

A number of our respondents pick up on the 'campy strangeness' (C3) or 'captivating spectacle' (C4) of Bowie's various star images, which were seen to be portals to new forms of self-becoming and escapist fantasies where they could exist freely, free from the regulations and repressions of normative society:

> C5: *Labyrinth* was like the ultimate culmination of my childhood fancies and my departure into more mature adoration. I still recall hearing his voice in the trailer and snapping to attention, having recognized it from the albums I listened to near constantly. When I saw him, in those gray leggings, spiky hair and make-up, I was rather entranced, as he was both fantastic and threatening… I often joke that this was my sexual awakening, because for the first time in my mind realized what attraction actually was.

As was the case with B5, the architecture of desire that C5 draws upon here straddles the blossoming awareness of becoming sexually aware for the first time, and the sense that the adult figure who elicited it, Jareth/Bowie, was taboo: magical and dangerous, earthly and fantastic, all at once, something that we discuss further below.

This thread of perversion is something that emerges in Bowie's role as a father figure, the third identity facet that B11 notes above, and something that was briefly discussed in Chapter 2, where B2 also referred to him as 'Daddy' and a father. The sense that Bowie is a surrogate or fantasy father figure is also discussed by:

> B12: He was the best friend whom I've never met. He was like a Father, and he held my hand during difficult times. I love him.

(Question 8: What does David Bowie mean to you?)

> C1: Only fantasies. It was always low key, a meeting of peers. Comfortable, immediately falling into jokes and deep conversation. When I

started making music, it then grew to include him being interested
in my music. (I think I often saw the meetings as interactions I wish
I could have with my Father…ugh…admitting the "Father figure"
stuff outside my head feels odd…)

(Question 12: Did you fantasize about meeting David Bowie – or meet him
for real?)

> C2: He's been the most actively present male in my life. A
> muse, an encourager, someone I was sure would support the
> things that made me unique. At some point, this caused a
> shift from "artist/immortal/alien I was sexually attracted to" to
> "artist/immortal/alien who was my imagined Father figure." I knew
> he wasn't that, but his voice is often the one that surfaces when I'm
> about to go against my authentic self. I know he's "just a man," but
> he came to be God in my music Trinity, and music is the most impor-
> tant thing in my life. (Sorry, for a writer, I've been crap thus far at
> explaining what he means to me…)

(Question 8: What does David Bowie mean to you?)

One can make sense of these wish fulfilments through a number of lenses:
at the psychoanalytical level, the responses can be seen to be confirming and
challenging the Law of the Imaginary Father (Lacan 2001), since Bowie's
androgyny and queer-ness offers a different desiring sense of plenitude,
and a complex enactment of perversion (Leorne 2015). C2 seems to be
desiring her own father here and imagines Bowie as his literal voice, passing
on good advice when they are about to take the wrong course of action.
That *Father* becomes *God* in the very next sentence suggests a deification
of the relationship: Bowie is the ultimate or uber father figure, and one
who cannot be challenged.

It has been suggested that Bowie was also a 'lost child, deprived from
the Father figure who had taken care of him and taken him by the hand
through the tricky world of stardom' (ibid.: 116). That Bowie is imagined
to be caught in a fatherless state, while his fans see him embodying or
enacting rituals of masculine and fatherly perversion, suggests an identity
alignment—a story about fraught origins that embryonically connects fan
and star. There is desiring confusion in these responses, nonetheless, marking the respondents as grappling with what Bowie meant or came to mean

to them sexually: Bowie's fluid identity in turn produces liquid identity positions to reach out from.

The cultural sense that biological fathers have become figures of failure and that the patriarchal, nuclear family is in crisis is writ large across the popular and academic discourses of the age (Woodward 2015). Alongside the sense that structures of familial belonging are under threat is the argument that identities are more fluid and open and 'available'—a dichotomy of loss and founding that propels the position that people are ever more dislocated while never more able to adopt active subject positions. Identity is never fixed or unitary: it is, as Stuart Hall argues, multidimensional, fluid and always in process, 'a matter of becoming' (1997). For postmodernists, in fact, identity is now perpetually in a state of crisis because it is fractured and dislocated and the meta-narratives that used to give people sustenance are no longer believed in (such as religious faith in the West). People supposedly live in an age of postmodern angst, of identity dislocation. They no longer know who they are or what they should become, or what the world expects them to be. As Kobena Mercer suggests,

> In political terms, identities are in crises because traditional structures of membership and belonging inscribed in relations of class, party and nation-state have been called into question. (1994: 424)

D3 writes that they were caught up in this maelstrom of identity loss with Bowie the only figure able to provide the glue of belonging they cried out for:

> If there is a single message that carries through Bowie's life, not just his music, it's that we aren't by ourselves. This message resonates all throughout the "Ziggy Stardust" album in particular. I can remember singing along with this one in the bathroom, when I was overwhelmed by the pain and difficulty of adolescence… In my last year of high school, I was bullied relentlessly by one person in particular, to the point that I missed a lot of school. I was struggling with debilitating anxiety problems, and medicated to the point that when I discontinued, the brutality of withdrawal itself threw me into despair. I had weird hair and a weird body and weird taste in music, and nobody understood what I was about. And then there was Bowie.

(Question 8. What does David Bowie mean to you?)

Stars are always connected to vexing questions about identity, they 'articulate what it is to be human being in contemporary society; that is, they
express the particular notion we hold of the person, of the "individual"'
(Dyer 1987: 10). Chris Rojek suggests that stars, 'have filled the absence
created by the decay in the popular belief in the divine right of kings, and
the death of God' (2004: 13). In relation to Bowie, as we have seen with
all the responses so far quoted in this book, this identity confusion and
relocation of the self is seen to be empowering.

Nonetheless, this origin story is taken up in another way by our respondents; a number were introduced to Bowies music *through* their father:

C6: Lying on the floor of the flat with dad when I was 3 or so, watching lights
strobe as we listened to the Rise and Fall of Ziggy Stardust and the Spiders
from Mars. I remember wanting to be whatever that person was making
the music.

C7: Watching Labyrinth at about 4 years old. My dad then played me ziggy
stardust

C8: Generally, Jaret from The Labyrinth But I really fell in love later - I was
11, and my Father introduced me to Space Oddity.

C9: Listening "Let's Dance" on the radio when I was a kid with my Father.

(Question 6. Please recall and describe what your first memory of encountering David Bowie is?)

C10: The Rise and Fall of Ziggy Stardust and the Spiders from Mars. After
first hearing Space Oddity, my dad placed me this album from his record
collection. It remains a strong memory of me and my dad bonding over
a shared love of music. The songs also spoke to me and helped me emotionally during a period of time where I felt as an outsider.

(Question 7: What is your Favourite Album (s)?)

These memorialised events or micro-stories give a key role to our respondents' fathers, who introduced them to Bowie's music, in contexts that
suggest the ritual of bonding and of passing on one's artistic passions or
loves (Hesmondhalgh 2008). These fathers were passing on Bowie's legacy

in moments of curatorial intimacy and familial connection. C6 recalls the memory of laying on the floor next to her dad, under a disco ball, listening to the album Ziggy Stardust. C10 recounts the time where her dad chose her a Bowie album to share with them, a legacy gift at the time they felt they were an outsider in the world. There is a deep sense of the wonderment of such seeing and hearing, and of the closeness between child and parent being shared here. At our Melbourne 'migrant fan' focus group (also see Chapter 4), one of our respondents (AP) actually came in their Dad's place and recounted a similar story to the one outlined by C6. They had come to the focus group on his behalf because of his recent passing, and of them wanting to present him—his loves and passions—in what became a beautiful 'memorial' service. Similarly, in our Amsterdam focus group when asked where they had heard of Bowie's death, one respondent (C10) said on TV which they stayed glued to and 'it was like losing my Dad, it was devastating'. We return to death and David Bowie's passing in our Conclusion (Chapter 10) to the book.

The film *Labyrinth* is also crucial to these BowieSphere communions, as one can clearly see through the responses drawn upon so far, something we will now take up in more depth.

LABYRINTH

For a large number of our participants—26 in total—*Labyrinth* was the text that they were first introduced to Bowie. These participants were children or adolescents at the time, either watching the film at the cinema as part of the blockbuster event season, or at home on video/DVD, with their parents or older siblings, who were often Bowie fans. This is doubly interesting because Bowie is playing a sexualised fantasy character—a lustful Goblin King—within a children's fantasy film where he is inviting a young girl to love him, rather than a gender-bending, sexually perverse character within Bowie's own fantastical theatrical and musical works. Fact and fiction blur and conjoin here: his star image perfectly fits the role, and it is this conjunction which speaks to both fans who were children at the time, and those (adults) who watched the film because Bowie was performing (himself) in it. It is Bowie's 'always excessive star body', Rosalind Galt suggests, which in

> *Labyrinth* offers us the perverse spectacle of Bowie in leather outfits and makeup, casually wielding a black riding crop, and its mode of address sim-

ilarly invites the young viewer to respond sexually. Narratively, Jareth is the antagonist, but… the spectator's affective relationship to him is shot through with an erotics of power… his physical disruption is in excess of this role, as is demonstrated by fan response to the film, which is closely focused on the erotic effect of his costume and sexually provocative presence. (2018: 132)

C5 (see above) describes *Labyrinth* as the culmination of all their 'childhood fantasies' and where sexual 'attraction' was first noticed. Similarly:

> *C11*: My first memory of David Bowie was his performance as Jareth, the Goblin King in Labyrinth. I was instantly enchanted by this evil, but funny and charming antagonist. He was larger than life, sexy, strangely parental, and of course magical.

(Question 6. Please recall and describe what your first memory of encountering David Bowie is?)

> *C12*: During a particularly dark time, *Labyrinth* was my escape. The story, characters and music create an easy sense of escapism. Jareth resembled an older man who would fix things.

(Question 10. Considering your favorite David Bowie 'character' or 'performance', please give a reason for your choice.)

> *D1*: That would be *Labyrinth*. I was a child. He terrified me. And I don't just mean the cod piece.

(Question 6. Please recall and describe what your first memory of encountering David Bowie is?)

> *D2*: It is probably this one [holds a picture of Bowie as Jareth]; the first time I ever encountered Bowie was watching *Labyrinth* as a kid and I would have been really little, I was born in '82 so I was little watching it. I just love it. Whenever I think of Bowie, that is the image that I get. Partly I guess is also that I have connection to friends who also love *Labyrinth*, there is that sense of community, and the interaction and first sense of engagement that I had with him. It is such an awesome film, it is weird and bizarre and I love it. I also generally like weird and bizarre things, that has gone through my growing up. (Amsterdam Focus Group)

One can see how Bowie/Jareth occupies a pull/push effect on those watching him for the first time: he is occupying a liminal space for them, as the fantasy film does by definition, and as Bowie's star image impresses upon the text. Bowie/Jareth is an uncanny figure, both strange and familiar, creating a sense of the fantastic for our respondents or that hesitation between belief and disbelief in the magical Kingdom he rules over (Todorov 1975). That Bowie is over-sexualised, attractive and repulsive, desiring and dangerous, points to the way the fantasy film and his fantastic star image destabilise the text, bringing together in the same interstitial space opposites that should not meet. C11 sees the character as sexy and parental; C12 sees it as a space of escapism and yet Bowie is identified as the manly fixer of problems, a bare sublimation of the rule of the patriarch; D1 cannot bear to see Bowie's appendage as the thing that nonetheless terrifies them, while D2 defines the film/Bowie as both weird and bizarre but with cultish significance for their friends who share their love of the text together—a fan-gift community.

One can read the world of *Labyrinth* through a different register, however: as a barely coded recasting of queer and porn subcultures, as Rosalind Galt suggests:

> In the behind-the-scenes documentary Inside the *Labyrinth* (Des Saunders, 1986), Bowie admits that he sees Jareth as a reluctant Goblin King, adding, "One gets the feeling he'd rather be down in Soho or somewhere like that." Bowie plays Jareth as at home in a London neighbourhood known for gay subculture and sleazy sex clubs, piercing both Sarah's suburban world and the labyrinth's fantastical puppet-filled space. (2018: 133)

There is a fascinating and perplexing core/periphery, inside/outside mode of communication and form of identification being enacted in and through *Labyrinth* and Bowie's performance—different registers are in play, connecting to his various star images, binding the text at the same time as unravelling it. Bowie is always 'surplus value' (Dyer 1998), always on the verge of becoming queer, as our respondents variously identify with.

The Stars Are Coming Out Tonight

Alex Doty defines queer space as one of sexual instability in which, 'already queerly positioned viewers can connect with in various ways, and within which straights can express their queer impulses' (Doty 1993: 21). Judith Butler and Sue-Ellen Case have argued that queerness is something that is ultimately beyond gender—'it is an attitude, a way of responding, that begins in a place not concerned with, or limited by, notions of a binary opposition of male and female or the homo versus hetero paradigm usually articulated as an extension of this gender binarism' (quoted in Doty, XV 1993). In relation to David Bowie, Julie Lobalzo Wright suggests that:

> By creating a persona based on the unknown, he was able to experiment with gender and sexuality, particularly in terms of performing gender and sexuality outside of heteronormative culture… Bowie performed queerness, implying that there are multiple sexual identities and behaviours. (2015: 271)

There are two linking aspects to David's queerness: first, his various androgynous star images and flamboyant costuming and cross-dressing, his self-outing as bisexual (early in his career), his angular whiteness and his camp movements positioned him as a queer image (Auslander 2006). Second, he very often took on queer roles, entered visual spaces and storylines where gender and sexual binaries were undercut through the work of the mise-en-scene, character relationships and the communication of liminal desire. Films such as *The Man Who Fell to Earth*, *Merry Christmas Mr Lawrence*, *The Hunger*, and *Labyrinth* draw on both aspects, fusing the text with forms of border crossings and which 'display elements of a gay sensibility' (Wright 2015: 234). In relation to *The Hunger*, Deborah Michel (2007) suggests,

> They reflect a spectator position of perversely polymorphous sexuality. Here, the spectator's gaze might well be that of a heterosexual male, but it might also be a gay or bisexual male – or female – gaze which appreciates the images of both Miriam and John. This slippage of gender in the assumed spectatorial gaze and on the screen represents only the first in a series of border transgressions to come; masculine and feminine, sex and violence, animal and human, love and death, all shift uneasily like quicksand in this narrative.

We can see how Bowie was understood to be a queer figure, occupying an unstable identity space, through our respondents' comments. As we detailed in Chapter 2, Bowie introduced B10 to 'gender fluidity' and to have the courage to embrace their bisexuality. A7 commented that Bowie gave them 'a vocabulary for their sexuality' and that 'This is the guy who could be Major Tom, Ziggy Stardust, Jareth the goblin king, and give a remarkably understated performance of Nicholai Tesla'. Further,

3 STORIES OF DIFFERENCE AND OF AWAKENINGS

D3: Bowie made it okay to be an Outsider. He made it okay to be smart and interested in "strange" or obscure things. As I got older and started to sort out my sexuality (I was raised as an evangelical and didn't make peace with being bi until my mid-20s) Bowie made it okay to be queer. He introduced me to other artists that I love: Placebo, T Rex, Nine Inch Nails... He has helped me cope with the general experience of death salience; he has helped me to realise that self-expression can happen in a variety of ways, through your music, your actions, or your image, and that it's okay to reinvent yourself.

D4: Reflexivity of gender, dress androgynous, make up for man, great shows, dressing up, amazing songs that went along with me my whole life, great artist who is able to perform his death on a last album, icon,

D5: The reason that I chose this image is that it is all about the hair [the participant claims holding a picture of Bowie as Thomas Jerome Newton in *The Man Who Fell to Earth*] I just want to talk about the colouring of the hair as this is something that has always fascinated me about *this* Bowie hair in particular (I have a particular preoccupation with Bowie hair), the colouring of this hair is always sort of ... it is this sort of apricot colour which I can't imagine coming off very well on anyone else's head because it is so kind of ... there is a sort of brilliance in it – a kind of Quentin Crisp-type queerness about it...*about the colour* that I don't actually see in Bowie when he wears it. So I have been fascinated by that but the other reason that I am drawn to Bowie and hair is that I guess he is probably the first pop-star to change his hair in such radical ways that every time he changes it, it is a big part of the re-invention to see him in a different way. (Amsterdam Focus group)

D3 picks up on the theme of reinvention and self-expression, of remaking the self, which they see Bowie as embodying through his conscious and experimental play with image and self. D4 also alludes to this through the freeing idea of 'dressing up'. Of course, this can be read in two ways. First, dressed as Bowie, D3 and D4 are unravelling and revealing the gendered nature of the self, allowing them to resist and renegotiate what one is and can become. As Judith Butler argues, gender 'is not passively scripted on the body', but 'put on, invariably under constraint, daily and incessantly, with anxiety and pleasure' (1990: 128–141). The type of drag being referenced here 'reflects on the imitative structure by which hegemonic gender is itself produced and disputes heterosexuality's claim on naturalness and originality' (ibid.: 125).

Second, the comments reveal the way self-identity is caught up in a regime of individuated ownership. The 'possessive individual' (Abercrombie et al. 1986; Pateman 1988) is concerned with the ownership of the self that becomes 'a kind of cultural resource, asset or possession' (Lury 1996: 8). The possessive individual styles themselves in the same way as goods and services are styled: they measure their self-worth in terms of the aestheticisation of the self. However, here the remodelling of the self is centrally about resistance and renewal outside the forces of wanton consumer culture. As Nick Stevenson suggests,

> Many Bowie fans and Stardust clones have inscribed themselves with glitter and makeup as interpretative tributes to Bowie (see Cracked Actor for one documentation of this phenomenon); indeed, many girls' teen magazines from the 1970s included articles on how to apply make up like David Bowie (see T. Stark's "Because You're Young: How to Do Your Makeup like Ziggy Stardust"). (2015: 277)

D4 and D5 detail in different ways the way Bowie performatively offered or opened up spaces of gender and sexual play that they found intoxicating and liberating, drawing on aesthetics—born of the senses—as they do so. D5 revels in the colour and style of Bowie's 'apricot' hair from his performance as Newton in *The Man Who Fell to Earth*. Supportively, Julie Lobalzo Wright writes of this performance as decidedly alien and queer, reading Bowie's introduction in the film in the following terms:

> The following shot of Newton removing his hood is significant as it accomplishes two important elements of the film: highlighting the star image of David Bowie and Newton's queerness. By positioning the camera behind Newton, Roeg reveals one of the most identified aspects of Bowie's music star image at that time, his bright red hair. Newton's red hair is striking and distinctive as compared with every other person in the film... It is significant that Newton's red hair is part of his human surface, not his true alien body. The red hair acts as an obviously, visually queer marker, establishing difference that can be viewed publicly. (2015: 235)

Bowie's performances on stage and on screen mirrors, refracts and extends these types of impressions and readings. His hair has of course been an essential part of his image make-overs, each cut representing a new char-

acter, a new identity formation, providing the slippage between one body
and the next, which called into question the very materiality of identity.
Bowie fans would often be waiting to see what his new hairstyle would be
and for them it is hair they often notice first:

> D6: Bowie was electrifying! A bright pastel yellow suit and golden boy hair
> igniting the stage like a fire tornado whipping up a field.

> D7: Thin White Duke takes it for me, mostly because I love the look: it was
> classic styling in every way except for that amazing blonde-and-orange
> hair.

However, it is in seeing Bowie live where a new state of in-betweenness
emerges and where Bowie's performativity registers at a super-charged
level:

> D8: I was simply removed from consciousness of the rest of the world. In a
> crowd, I'm usually very aware of every other body that's touching me,
> their noises and movements and so forth. But he was very much all that
> existed. Like a pool of light in the dark stadium. (I was lucky enough to
> be within a few people of the stage.) I was, it's fair to say, transported.
> And then, for days afterwards, I was still giddily disconnected.

> D9: Yes, several times. I get very nervous and anxious waiting for him to come
> on. I want to cry when he struts on the stage. He is the absolutely epitome
> of cool.

> D10: I've seen him at Kooyong in Melbourne on a sweltering November
> evening, descending from the belly of the glass spider ... I was capti-
> vated from beginning to end. I also saw him again in Melbourne for the
> Reality tour... The consummate showman... He had the audience in the
> palm of his hands from beginning to end.

(Question 11: Have you ever seen David Bowie live in concert or on stage?)

While watching Bowie live, D8 seems to exist in a state of immanence and
transcendence—an inner and outer physicality—that shatters the confines
of their body lost in the transformative experience. Time and space seem to
collapse into one another as Bowie appears as a figure of the sublime, cut

free from physical reality, allowing D8 to feel giddy as the 'social' disappears before them at the wonder of Bowie performing on stage (see Chapter 6 for an extended discussion of seeing Bowie 'live'). Vivian Sobchack suggests:

> That as lived bodies we are always grounded in the radical materialism of bodily immanence, in the here and now of our sensorial existence – and this no matter how different our cultural situations or differently organized and valued modes of making sense. However, as lived bodies, we always also have the capacity for transcendence: for a unique exteriority of being – an ex statis – that locates us elsewhere and otherwise even as it is grounded in and tethered to our lived body's here and now. That is, our ontological capacity for transcendence emerges from and in our ontic immanence. This is an experience of transcendence in immanence. (2008: 200)

D9 verbalises their transcendence through the idea of wanting to cry when Bowie appears on stage, the 'scream' replacing language and discourse, becoming the sonorous mouthpiece through which their ecstasy is communicated. Such hysteria has of course a long history in pop music fandom: so-called 1960s Beatlemania was defined as, 'The ecstatic audience, breathing deeply in its rapt enthusiasm, can no longer hold back its shouts of acclaim: they stamp unceasingly with their feet, producing a dull and persistent sound that is punctuated by isolated, involuntary screams' (Lynsky 2013).

D9 ends their appraisal with the conceit that Bowie was the 'epitome of cool' while D10 draws on the metaphor of the showman charismatically creating an experience where the audience is in the palm of his hands. There is both the touch of the trickster and magician in such definitions, drawing threads back to his alien and fantastic star images. There is also the link to the idea that Bowie is a poseur or one who:

> insists on self-awareness, image, and surface and keeps in place the temporal and material positions of "original" and "copy," and ... functions within an interaction among creator, spectator, and the object of the gaze— an interaction that is already saturated with implications of power and desire. Importantly, to "strike a pose" is to stop the action of the body, to allow the viewer to become absorbed in visual pleasure and desire, and also to allow the poser the pleasure of inhabiting the object position. (Peraino 2012: 151–184)

Bowie's own star signification is in part built on striking poses, being a poseur, from one embodied image to another, whether it be Major Tom or the Thin White Duke. Bowie's posing is a form of subcultural resistance; it is predicated on gender and sexual subversion, opening up his pose to a nonbinary queer gaze. This posing offers fans another type of fan transcendence:

> *D11*: For me, Bowie represents transcendence from alienation. At the time that I discovered him, I was beginning to experience the onset of teenage depression. The music and aesthetic he created were a way out. His characters were alien and ethereal, at once rejected by society yet refusing to be earthbound and oppressed due to this rejection. He defied limitation and definition. He gave me hope.

This story of hope is one thread across a number of the responses we received. Bowie was seen to be a redemptive figure, embodying difference in ways that they felt allowed them to believe, take pride in their own outsider identities. As D13 poetically suggests:

> There is a video of Bowie performing "Heroes" - as himself, without snappy costume or makeup - at a charity event for 9/11 emergency responders that moved me to tears. It evoked the meaning of the song on a grand scale, the idea of hope and companionship and love, even in the context of a dark or uncertain (even doomed) future.
>
> (Question 10: Considering your favorite David Bowie 'character' or 'performance', please give a reason for your choice).

Bowie's body is crucial to these affective and effective identifications. His body was weird, 'an icon for any of us weirdos who always felt like maybe we were aliens, if not a sub species of the human: homo superior as "Pretty Things" says' (D12). The body is 'the medium through which messages about identity are transmitted' (Benson 1997: 123) and as Mary Douglas observes,

> The body is a model which can stand for any bounded system. Its boundaries can represent any boundaries which are threatened or precarious. The body is a complex structure. The functions of its different parts and their relation afford a source of symbols for other complex structures. We cannot possibly interpret rituals concerning excreta, breast, milk, saliva, and the rest unless we are prepared to see in the body a symbol of society, and to see the powers

and dangers credited to social structure reproduced in small on the human body. (2002: 373)

In reading the body as a cultural or social text; the site of a society's signifying practices; or as Douglas puts it above, 'a symbol of society', one gets to understand more about difference, the construction of otherness, cultural domination and resistance and the way that nature is used to efface the ideological processes that are at work in body politics.

Pierre Bourdieu is particularly interesting in this respect since he sees the 'meaning' of the body produced in a dynamic nature/culture framework. Bourdieu contends that bodily practices, and rituals and behaviours around the body, such as eating, act as vehicles for transmitting dominant cultural values. This, 'culture made body', plays out the actual social conditions and power relations of a society, and for Bourdieu, this resonates in terms of class differences/antagonisms. However, because such body idioms are represented as natural, essential, innate, they appear to be 'beyond the grasp of consciousness' and so are understood to be as nature intended and therefore without contestation (1977: 94). Star bodies can, of course, cross borders, as Bowie's does, and as Alison Blair outlines:

> Ziggy Stardust's gender---bending polysexualism brought homosexuality, bisexuality and cross---dressing to the fore of popular culture while at the same time emphasizing the 'alien', still relatively unspoken, nature of such practices in conservative society... Bowie's Ziggy Stardust... is the 'unknowability' of non---normative sexuality, laid out before us in its 'strangeness'—both the physical not---I, and the potential for radical otherness. (2016: 181)

Bowie's body is a site of both cultural dissent and aggressive agency, and functions as the sign of his unstable gender and sexuality. Bowies body is a site of resistance and resignification for many of his fans:

> *E1*: My proper introduction to Bowie was, well I was born in 1966, so I was 13 years old when I saw him perform on *Saturday Night Live* and I loved the music but again it was also the visual presentation, so one number he was in a dress, Klaus Nomi in a dress [check date of performance for accuracy here], that ruined my 13 year-old mind – in a very good way – and I remember his puppet-body was superimposed with his head and that too really blew my mind away and it was like here is this sort or authorization, permission if you will to do what you want, to be different,

and that ultimately led me to … (and I grew up in rural Indiana) and I craved deeply upon adolescence and since I carved escape from that, that area.

Vivian Sobchack suggests that 'our bodies escape' the cultural and ideological conditions in which they are produced (Bukatman 2009). For E1 the sense of an escape is twofold: they see the embodied metamorphosis that Bowie undertakes as somatic permission to do the same, and they see the resigning of the self as a way of escaping the confines of a space, a repressive location, to find a new home for their new body.

Sean also wanted an escape from that area he called home too, in Coventry, to Berlin.

Coventry, to Berlin

As we note in our Introduction to the book, one of the focus groups was conducted under different circumstances: it was composed of 6 of Sean's lifelong friends who had travelled from Coventry—their home town—to Berlin to rendezvous with him. Sean was in Berlin on a pilgrimage to visit a number of the locations that Bowie had resided in or worked from, and to gather his friends together to talk about their upbringing, to share memories, in relation to Bowie and his fandom. The method being employed here is one of the 'friendship group' or 'friendship cell', where participants are familiar with one another and with the subject matter being explored. As Jones, Newsome, Levin, Wilmot, McNulty, and Kline summarises,

> Pre-existing groups comprising people who know each other could be argued to have already passed through the early stages of the group process, thus facilitating the free expression of ideas. (2018: 99)

However, such friendship cells usually have an external moderator: for this gathering Sean acted as both facilitator and group member, with the intention that no 'outsider' was needed to drive the conversations—something the group had asked for, wanting the intimacy of their friendship to be the only binding needed.

The drawing on auto-ethnography here through the friendship cell extends and enriches our desire to triangulate our research method: one that deliberately moves across registers and approaches so that micro and macro, personal and cultural 'truths' are revealed.

This friendship cell was, in the main, quite a masculine gathering: all of Sean's friends were male, and the weekend it took place was surrounded by boozy nights out, dinners and a wider memorial framework as old stories were told and shared. All of Sean's friends came from lower working-class backgrounds and a number (2) came from immigrant backgrounds. Sean and one other friend had grown up in a highly deprived area of Coventry, and the Comprehensive, State school they all went to was also highly disadvantaged.

Their class position was something that was picked up on through the filters of single parenthood, low decile habitus, subcultural style and musical tastes. K1, for example, recalled dressing as a skinhead, and as a rockabilly, in their youth, the former conflicting with Sean's period as a mod. They recounted being taught to dance to the Lindy Hop and the Jitterbug on a Friday night at the Red House Pub, by their aunt, often while his mother worked long hours. These style-based, contextualised memories were tied to winning dancing competitions and familial frameworks: for K1 music was a class identifier and a marker of self-esteem.

In Paul Willis's class-based ethnographic study of 'bikers' and 'hippies', we see how class is imagined to shape musical tastes. The working-class position of bikers led them to like the simplicity and accessibility of rock and roll while the middle-class position of hippies led them to like more esoteric, experimental music (1978/2014). While these results are contentious, and which we will contest further below, when it comes to responses to Bowie in this friendship cell we see a dichotomy emerging between what was seen as accessible and popular mainstream music of the 1970s and 1980s, which the majority of Sean's friends liked, and the music of David Bowie, who was seen to be 'too out there' (K2D).

Nonetheless, Bowie's relationship to social class is not so easily class demarcated. Sean recounted how when feeling blue he would put on a Bowie record since it was outward looking, 'intergalactic', a musical form of enchantment, that allowed him to escape the concrete jungle he lived in. Similarly, K3JF spoke about how the album *Hunky Dory* provided a plethora of memories that was deeply cherished and held. These sentiments are not limited to these people: in a blog for the Centre for Working-Class Studies at Youngstown State University, Sarah Attfield writes from the perspective of a working-class girl who was educated to believe that she should have limited aspirations, and who wasn't encouraged to pursue intellectual or artistic pursuits. However, 'Bowie created a different dream' for her, one that fostered and fuelled artistic expression and a conscious play with identity and selfhood (2015).

K1 recounted a similar event at school where they were told by their Math's teacher they would 'end up on the dole with 7 kids'. K1 went on to talk about how Bowie was 'unconsciously apart of their background' growing up, and that he was a central part of the 1980s mixtape they played constantly in their work van, revealing the way music transforms us in unexpected and positive ways. K1 runs a very successful business and has been married to the girl he first dated in school for over 35 years.

The negative or challenging sentiments made about Bowie in this friendship cell were less to do with class positions than what was considered to be the 'shocking', confrontational gender of his star image in the 1970s, when they were all introduced to him. For K2, K4 and K5, it was Bowie's appearance on the countdown 'hit' television series, *Top of the Pops* (BBC), in the video to *Boys Keep Swinging* where he was first encountered. K2 playfully commented that you 'didn't know if he was a boy or a girl'; K4 called him a shocking site, a 'queer boy', while K5 suggested that his play with gender and sexuality was confronting at the time. All the friends, bar K3, went on to say that at the time they didn't feel as if they could openly be a fan of David Bowie because of fear of retribution, of being labelled gay or queer, locating their fear to the dominance of heterosexual scripts at the time. One can see how their comments marry with those of our other respondents who were gay or bi at the time, unable to 'out' themselves, utilising Bowie for the very things Sean's friends were fearful of.

One can also see how Bowie made Sean's friends uncomfortable since he directly challenged those scripts that they were used to seeing and identifying with. As all of Sean's friends went on to outline, however, they saw how Bowie was influential in transforming not only the representation of gender and sexuality but one's ability to identify with it. Although not commented upon here but taken up in the next chapter, such border crossings did have impact on migrant identities, as Samira Ahmed writes (2016):

> For many immigrant children growing up in south London suburbia – me included – David Bowie proved an unexpectedly powerful inspiration. My seminal David Bowie moment was the cross-dressing weirdness of his 1979 Boys Keep Swinging video: a conventionally good-looking white guy who chose to stand out, to attract hatred and ridicule. All the stuff second-generation immigrant children were desperate to avoid.

K5 and K6 were second-generation British Indians who didn't listen to much pop music at home. They nonetheless gravitated to anthemic popular bands such as Queen and Wham! For K5, George Michael was the pop icon he was most attracted to, and he talked passionately about what George meant to him. Bowie by contrast was too 'cultish', too 'shocking' to engage with. Of course, for Bowie fans it is difference, again, that mattered most:

> D12: During the teen years of conform and consume in the 80's, Bowie was the voice of "fuck that, it is boring and a waste of time." Bowie was a big influence on my immersion into different literary and artistic modes of expression.

K3 in one sense was the outlier, since his connection to Bowie was heartfelt and memorial, linking him to the way respondents quoted earlier in this chapter were connected back to their fathers in and through Bowie's music, as he was. K3 recalled how his father passed on his musical favourites, including Jimi Hendrix, and how the album *Hunky Dory* was their shared, prized possession. Fondly remembering the track Kooks, which 'takes him somewhere special', K3 felt Bowie's death the most.

One of the prime conversations that emerged in this friendship cell was how collective *and* personal music was, how one song heard could transport you to a very specific place and memory. This manifested in two ways. Each friend weaved in stories of what the Two-Tone movement meant to them growing up in Coventry; how key members of the band *The Specials* lived in their neighbourhoods and how their songs such as *Ghost Town* (1981) and *Too Much Too Young* (1980) captured the realism of their working-class lives. Secondly, each friend spoke about how a song acted as transportation device in hearing it again, to a fabulous memory once lived. As DeNora writes, 'Music [acts as] a device or resource to which people turn in order to regulate themselves as aesthetic agents, as feeling, thinking and acting beings in their day-to-day lives' (1999: 62).

The memorial work undertaken in this friendship cell continued to develop out of two strands: the first, a conversation about how we pass on musical memories to our children, again connecting back to the responses we analysed earlier in this chapter, where fathers were seen as conduits of this curatorial transmission. K5 said that 'if we were to conduct this group in 30 years' time with our children they would be recounting how their dad's had played them Wham, Bowie, and Spandau Ballet all day long'.

The second continued the conversational strand of old friends gathered together remembering their live stories together, through music, dance and style. At the very end of the focus group, K1 broke down as he talked about how he had felt he had missed seeing his son grow up due to work commitments. If a moderator had been in place, this may not have taken place and the need to express may never have been met, nor the friendship and love that was extended to him countenanced.

We sat in a small circle, like we were back at school, or holed up in one of our bedrooms, or sat in the old car we bought as kids, until late on school nights. Such ease, such familiarity, such intimacy. We breathed memories. We laughed continually. We told tall stories. How did I get here, from Coventry to Berlin? Bowie had brought us back together.

References

Abercrombie, Nick, Stephen Hill, and Brian S. Turner. *Sovereign Individuals of Capitalism*. London: Allen & Unwin, 1986.

Ahmed, Samira. "To Suburban British-Asian Kids Like Me, David Bowie Was an Unexpected Hero." *The Guardian*, 12 January 2016. https://www.theguardian.com/commentisfree/2016/jan/12/suburban-british-asian-kids-david-bowie-hero. Accessed 5 July 2018.

Althusser, Loius. *On Ideology*. London: Verso, 2008.

Attfield, Sarah. "David Bowie: Creating a Middle-Class Dream for a Working-Class Fan." *Working-Class Perspectives*, 3 August 2015. https://workingclassstudies.wordpress.com/2015/08/03/david-bowie-creating-a-middle-class-dream-for-a-working-class-fan/. Accessed 16 July 2018.

Auslander, Philip. "Watch That Man, David Bowie: Hammersmith Odeon, London, July 3, 1973." In *Performance and Popular Music: History, Place and Time*, ed. Ian Inglis, 70–80. Hampshire: Ashgate, 2006.

Bauman, Zygmunt. *Liquid Modernity*. Cambridge: Polity, 2000.

Benson, Susan. "The Body, Health and Eating Disorders." In *Identity and Difference*, ed. Kathryn Woodward, 121–166. London: Sage, 1997.

Blair, Alison. "Marc Bolan, David Bowie, and the Counter-Hegemonic Persona: 'Authenticity', Ephemeral Identities, and the 'Fantastical Other'." *MEDIANZ: Media Studies Journal of Aotearoa New Zealand* 15 (1) (2016): 167–186.

Bourdieu, Pierre. *Outline of the Theory of Practice*. Cambridge: Cambridge University Press, 1977.

Bukatman, Scott. "Vivian Sobchack in Conversation with Scott Bukatman." *E-Media Studies* 2 (1) (2009). http://journals.dartmouth.edu/cgi-bin/WebObjects/Journals.woa/xmlpage/4/article/338. Accessed 6 April 2017.

Butler, Judith. *Gender Trouble: Feminism and the Subversion of Identity.* London: Routledge, 1990.

DeNora, Tia. "Music as a Technology of the Self." *Poetics* 27 (1) (1999): 31–56.

Doane, Mary Ann. "The Voice in the Cinema: The Articulation of Body and Space." *Yale French Studies* 60 (1980): 33–50.

Doty, Alexander. *Making Things Perfectly Queer: Interpreting Mass Culture.* Minneapolis: University of Minnesota Press, 1993.

Douglas, Mary. *Purity and Danger: An Analysis of Pollution and Taboo.* London: Routledge, 1966/2002.

Dyer, Richard. *Heavenly Bodies: Film Stars and Society.* London: Macmillan, 1987.

Dyer, Richard. "Resistance Through Charisma: Rita Hayworth and Gilda." In *Women in Film Noir*, ed. E. Ann Kaplan, 91–99. London: BFI, 1998.

Galt, Rosalind. "David Bowie's Perverse Cinematic Body." *Cinema Journal* 57 (3) (2018): 131–138.

Hall, Stuart. "The Work of Representation." In *Representation: Cultural Representations and Signifying Practices*, ed. Stuart Hall, 13–69. London: Sage, 1997.

Hesmondhalgh, David. "Towards a Critical Understanding of Music, Emotion and Self-Identity." *Consumption, Markets and Culture* 11 (4) (2008): 329–343.

Jones, Chandria D., Jocelyn Newsome, Kerry Levin, Amanda Wilmot, Jennifer Anderson McNulty, and Teresa Kline. "Friends or Strangers? A Feasibility Study of an Innovative Focus Group Methodology." *The Qualitative Report* 23 (1) (2018): 98–112.

Lacan, Jacques. *Ecrits: A Selection.* London: Routledge, 2001.

Lacey, Joanne. "Discursive Mothers and Academic Fandom: Class, Generation and the Production of Theory." In *Cultural Studies and the Working Class*, ed. Sally Munt, 36–50. New York: Cassell, 2000.

Leorne, Ana. "Dear Dr. Freud—David Bowie Hits the Couch a Psychoanalytic Approach to Some of His Personae." In *David Bowie: Critical Perspectives*, ed. Eoin Devereux, Aileen Dillane, and Martin Power, 111–127. London: Routledge, 2015.

Lobalzo Wright, Julie. "David Bowie Is the Extraordinary Rock Star as Film Star." In *David Bowie: Critical Perspectives*, ed. Eoin Devereux, Aileen Dillane, and Martin Power, 230–244. London: Routledge, 2015.

Lury, Celia. *Consumer Culture.* Cambridge: Polity, 1996.

Lynsky, Dorian. "Beatlemania: 'The Screamers' and Other Tales of Fandom." *The Guardian*, 2013. www.theguardian.com/music/2013/sep/29/beatlemania-screamers-fandom-teenagers-hysteria. Accessed 11 April 2018.

Mercer, Kobener. *Welcome to the Jungle.* London: Routledge, 1994.

Michel, Deborah. "The Proprietary Cinematic Gaze in Tony Scott's the Hunger." *ACIDEMIC Journal of Film and Media*, 2007. www.acidemic.com/id97.html. Accessed 23 May 2014.

Pateman, Carole. *The Sexual Contract.* Cambridge: Polity, 1988.

Pegg, Nicholas. *The Complete David Bowie*. 5th ed. London: Reynolds & Hearn, 2009.

Peraino, Judith A. "Plumbing the Surface of Sound and Vision: David Bowie, Andy Warhol, and the Art of Posing." *Qui Parle: Critical Humanities and Social Sciences* 21 (1) (2012): 151–184.

Rojek, Chris. *Celebrity*. London: Reaktion Press, 2004.

Scott, Suzanne. "'Cosplay Is Serious Business': Gendering Material Fan Labor on Heroes of Cosplay." *Cinema Journal* 54 (3) (2015): 146–154.

Sobchack, Vivian. "Embodying Transcendence: On the Literal, the Material, and the Cinematic Sublime, Material Religion." *The Journal of Objects, Art and Belief* 4 (2) (2008): 194–203.

Sontag, Susan. "Notes on Camp." In *Camp: Queer Aesthetics and the Performing Subject: A Reader*, 53–65. Ann Arbor: University of Michigan Press, 1964.

Stevenson, Nick. "David Bowie Now and Then: Questions of Fandom and Late Style." In *David Bowie: Critical Perspectives*, ed. Eoin Devereux, Aileen Dillane, and Martin Power, 280–294. London: Routledge, 2015.

Todorov, Tzvetan. *The Fantastic: A Structural Approach to a Literary Genre*. Ithaca: Cornell University Press, 1975.

Willis, Paul E. *Profane Culture*. Updated edition. Princeton: Princeton University Press, 2014.

Woodward, Kath. *Questioning Identity: Gender, Class, Nation*. London: Routledge, 2005.

Woodward, Kath. *The politics of in/visibility: Being there*. Palgrave, 2015.

CHAPTER 4

Lazarus Rises: The Migrant Fandom of David Bowie

INTRODUCTION

In this chapter, we focus upon the ways that 'migrants' in Melbourne have used David Bowie to story and make sense of their arrival to Australia, often as refugees or as people looking for a better life. In relation to identity and belonging, some recent work on music fandom has imposed a meta-frame on the empirical method, substituting voices for a top-down analysis and interpretation (see Groene and Hettinger 2015; Lowe 2003). To repeat, our approach is to instead draw upon auto-ethnography and to allow our fellow fans to 'story' their own responses, in an attempt to get beneath the modes of feeling that music fandom ignites—situated within the narratives that people construct as they talk these stories. We argue that Bowie's alternative and outsider status resonates keenly with people who find themselves 'strangers' in a new land. Lyrically, musically and in terms of star representation, Bowie becomes the figure through which migrants navigate themselves through new cultural and social environments. Here, we also find that migrant identity readily intersects with sexuality, gender, class and age concerns, something we pick up on and develop in the course of the chapter. This chapter thus builds on the storied work undertaken in Chapter 3, where identity—both lost and becoming—is seen to flow across the ripples of Bowie's star image.

The auto-ethnographic approach we are explicitly utilising for this chapter draws upon Ruth Finnegan's sociological method (1997) and

© The Author(s) 2019   67
T. Cinque and S. Redmond, *The Fandom of David Bowie*,
https://doi.org/10.1007/978-3-030-15880-4_4

the affective turn within star and celebrity studies (see Redmond 2014), whereby writing oneself into identification and desire is centred and encouraged rather than marginalised. The storying the self approach to empirical research draws on a,

> Model of the self as 'storied' and of culture as both moulded and moulding through the personal stories of individuals ... It extends the idea of 'culture' and media beyond the organizational structures of, say, the culture industries, broadcasting or the published media, into the everyday modes in which we express and construct our lives in personal terms, telling our own stories. (Finnegan 1997: 69)

The emphasis on 'writing the personal' (Probyn 2011) has also been central to the epistemological and political interventions of popular culture theorists and those interested in 'hearing' the stories of the marginalised and politically disenfranchised. Connected to this approach is the recognition that researchers also have stories to share and in a way that democratises the empirical process—no one story is more important than the other—and through shared storytelling, experiential equivalences and 'clusters' emerge. Through storying the self, we find out about how people directly experience their own, often marginalised, subject positions.

As we outlined in our Introduction, for this book we adopted the focus group method for these various reasons: we intended for it to be a participatory space, where participants could openly share their stories. However, our Focus on migrant identity in relation to the fandom of David Bowie sets the discussion in a cultural and social context that has not been explored by other fan scholars or through a story-framed empirical method. This migrant study is unique in both Focus and method.

Migrant Method

By way of background to this study, Australia until the 1950s had defined itself largely as a 'new Britannia' emulating the 'empire' in the southern hemisphere (Langer 2001). With post-World War II immigration, however, the 'monoculture' of Australia changed towards an official notion of 'multiculturalism' or multi-ethnicity (Jupp 1996). The terms 'multiculturalism' or 'multi-ethnicity' are now frequently referred to in policy documents as 'cultural diversity'. Moreover, the terms 'multicultural' and 'ethnic' become imprecise when they are only associated with people from non-English-speaking backgrounds (NESBs) because English speakers in Australia form various ethnic groups, for example, the English, Irish or Welsh, but so do the many aboriginal communities. According to Gillard (2002), the term 'multiculturalism' was first used in Australia under the Whitlam-led Labor government (December 1972–November 1975) as part of its policy for Australia to move beyond its 'White Australia' heritage and beyond the assimilation policies which had governed the initial years of post-war migration. The constitution of Australia's population was changing with migrants coming increasingly from non-English-speaking nations such as Italy, Greece and Germany rather than from the English-speaking countries of England, Scotland, Ireland and Wales as had occurred in the past. By 1976, the national census revealed that one in five persons in Australia was born overseas and at least another one in ten had parents who were born overseas (Ethnic Television Review Panel 1980: 10). The most recent 2011 Australian Bureau of Statistics (ABS) Census recorded data indicating that where initially most migrants were born in countries in North-West Europe, followed by a number born in Southern and Eastern Europe. The proportion of the overseas-born population originating from Europe has now been in decline in recent years, from 52% in 2001 to 40% in 2011 (ABS 2013). Moreover, recent arrival data reflect the increasing number of people born in Asian countries:

> Recent arrivals accounted for 47% of the total Indian-born population in Australia and 35% of the total Chinese-born population. In contrast, only 11% of the total United Kingdom-born population were recent arrivals.

> Data reveals that Country of Birth groups which increased the most between 2001 and 2011 were India (up 200,000 people), China (176,200) and New Zealand (127,700). The largest decreases were seen in the birth countries of Italy (less 33,300 people), Greece (16,500) and Poland (9,400) according to the ABS (2013).

Almost half (49%) of longer-standing migrants to Australia and 67% of recent arrivals spoke a language other than English at home. New migrants to Australia came from almost 100 countries, and, in one way, a multicultural society can be understood to be one which is based on mutual respect and recognition of difference, having a commitment to the core values of Australian democracy and a desire to maintain harmony in the wider community (Jakubowics and Newell 1995: 130–131). An alternative argument posed by Rex (1996: 15), however, sees multiculturalism as the means by which society is organised so that ethnic groups are incorporated and dominated by others, where these ethnic groups would otherwise be separate societies not bound by the state.

For the purpose of this chapter, clarity around the term 'migrant' is justified in due consideration of its complexity. We in no way want to create another work that might be seen to commodify 'the other'. On culture and cultures, and the notion of 'otherness', the important work of Edward Said (1978) presented the argument that the (postcolonial) West writes about and describes a version of the East in order to dominate it. In the Australian context, Seneviratne (1992) has argued that the Special Broadcasting Service (SBS)—a media organisation established initially for new migrants to the country—pursued an elitist and monocultural outlook as demonstrated in news and current affairs programming and employment policies marked by cultural superiority. As a consequence, 'serious viewers' or 'cosmopolitans' (usually the well educated in upper-income brackets) are able to enjoy, indeed revel in, 'ethnic' culture—but from a distance. This act, Hage (1995) claims, supports ideological domination within the nation.

What is not distinguished in the argument above, however, is that the term 'cosmopolitan' can refer to a group which, in Australia, includes people from various ethnic backgrounds because they too are often with secure socio-economic status having come to Australia for 'the better life' and also curious about the activities and interests of other communities. Our intention with this paper is not to 'revel in' a version of 'ethnic fandom' and popular music culture but to allow fans to story their own 'becoming'. In undertaking the primary research, our aim was to discover the important ways that participants use(d) David Bowie to 'story' and make sense of their identity within Australia's particular cultural and social circumstances. Our aim was to learn how the fans feel (or felt) about the work of David Bowie, leading us towards a richer understanding of how they have negotiated their own identity amidst a contemporary Western media culture that largely marginalises and marginalised the 'alternative'.

Four Melbourne-based adult participants, who self-identified as recent migrants to Australia or from a post-war migrant family, and as fans of David Bowie, formed the focus group, which took place in metropolitan Melbourne in 2016, not long after his death. Our findings here are based on this focus group session, and as we note in our Introduction, they remain a 'pilot' in the sense that further groups and with a wider diversity of participants are necessary to further test the conclusions we draw out here.

The focus group participants were recruited from our network of peers. This was to ensure that individuals had appropriate interest in the research topic and were willing to participate. The focus group included us, and we were active in the discussions that took place. The focus group was composed of two males and four females with a modal age of 40 years and lasted for approximately one hour. Participants were invited to respond to open questions and visual stimuli (laid out on the table) about David Bowie's music and the role it plays (has played) in their lives. Participants were also asked to bring a special piece of memorabilia (see Chapter 5 for further discussion of fan memorabilia) that they were invited to speak to, but not compelled to discuss. The focus group was again audio-recorded and transcribed.

The focus group was organised around questions designed to enable the participants to 'story' their fandom in relation to migrant identity and identity politics more generally (given the way that subjectivity is always involved in intersectionality). The session began with asking each of these participants why 'they were here today' and 'what it was about David Bowie they so identified with?' The conversation then continued with specific framing around how Bowie helped them each navigate their migrant identity, with each participant drawing upon a memory, event or series of events to story his impact on their lives. During the session, we played softly a compilation of Bowie's music and introduced visual stimuli—colour photocopied images of David Bowie from various decades and periods—and asked our participants to choose one that they felt they most identified with and to talk through their choice. The participants were then asked to story their self-chosen piece of Bowie memorabilia, linking it to their own (migrant) identity. Finally, we asked participants about how Bowie's recent death impacted upon them, and why they felt he was such an important figure (for migrants).

We listened to the transcripts four times and made notes on each occasion, looking for clusters of themes that repeated themselves and which were drawn upon by all respondents either directly or in terms of supportive commentary and affirmative gestures. We found that there were four clusters of articulating or intersecting stories in relation to migrant identity, and we now structure our chapter according to these clusters. Migrant identity was understood and addressed in terms of: (1) identity difference; (2) family and community; (3) grieving and healing; and (4) resurrection.

1. The Difference in Me

[s]ubjectivity includes our sense of self. It involves conscious and unconscious thoughts and emotions which constitute our sense of 'who we are'... We experience our subjectivity in a social context where language and culture give meaning to our experience of ourselves and where we adopt an identity. (Woodward 1997: 39)

As Woodward notes directly above, and as we have outlined earlier in this book, we come to take up an identity position in situational and temporalised contexts, which involve conscious and unconscious processes, and yet which are actively enacted within language and culture. Identity is never fixed (Hall 1990) and is involved in a range of intersections including class, sexuality, gender, ethnicity, age and nationality. Often identity 'is most clearly defined by difference, that is by what it is not' (Woodward 1997: 2) and becomes of importance 'whenever one is not sure of where one belongs [or] is not sure how to place oneself among the evident variety of behavioural styles and patterns' (Bauman 1996: 19).

For our focus group participants, the question of difference and not (quite) belonging was central and centrally tied to their migrant status and the role that Bowie had in both mitigating their sense of ethnic and cultural 'otherness' and providing an audio-visual arena in which they could validate their 'alien' identity through song, lyric and performance. Bowie made 'weird cool' (ID), and:

> In Adelaide, as a little working-class migrant girl, I was on the outside to the Anglo private school thing, but also on the outside to my own Italian community... he spoke on the border, through ambiguity...and enabled me to cherish not fitting in. (MP)

The sense that migrant identity involved alienation and exclusion from white Australia, as well as providing a conformist and claustrophobic environment to grow up in, was an often-repeated position. Our participants were caught by and yet resisted a number of cultural binds, as: outsiders within outsider migrant families; outsiders within conformist and religious migrant families; or outsiders to Anglo-Saxon, white embodiment. As AN revealed:

> I was very against the Greek upbringing, I didn't have any Greek friends, it was really conservative and oppressive. I hated being dragged to these fucking

Greek dances… Bowie, his music, was a way of opening up a different path for me which said creativity, I didn't want to be the same as everyone else…

Similarly, ID reflecting on his own perceived oriental features and sense of ethnic otherness, as a child at school, shared:

> I already felt weird. I was already the 'Chinese Kid' in a private primary school where everyone else was white … and yet there was no race I felt I belonged to, no race I identified with, I was expunged from other races, I was having weird sexual thoughts because of my abuse, and I was also escaping into the grotesque and there was Bowie who encapsulated all that.

In different ways, each of the participants made reference to being (like) matter-out-of-place—their migrant status a signifier of mutancy, detritus and dirt. The Italian community, for example, considered MP's father, effeminate, and his own perceived border crossing resonated with Bowie's androgyny. The common word drawn upon was 'alien' in relation to both their sense of self and Bowie's star images. This alien otherness was felt to be a pejorative, a not-belonging and also a lived experience to be embraced and championed. For AN, the alien became the comforting norm, and the everyday became their version of alien living. Bowie was the regenerative force that enabled the reversal of these normative binaries—he gave the participants a way of experiencing what idealised counter-cultural life could be. As Frith (1996: 123) writes:

> But if musical identity is, then, always fantastic, idealizing not just oneself but also the social world one inhabits, it is, secondly, always also real, enacted in musical activities. Music making and music listening, that is to say, are bodily matters; involve what one might call social movements. In this respect, musical pleasure is not derived from fantasy – it is not mediated by dreams – but is experienced directly: music gives us a real experience of what the ideal could be.

Ghassan Hage (1997) argues that migrant home building is an active and conscious process of re-settlement, centred on the production and consumption of food and associated design and cultural practices. This home building combines the cultures of origin with the new setting and is as much about making place as remembering the space that one came from. For our participants, the migrant home was a haven or a prison, and sometimes both, its duality comforting and confronting. For AN, her Greek parents supported her desire to resist conformity, the strictures of Greek culture, and so Bowie's music filled the house and was welcomed. Similarly for AP, her dad shared with her cultish figures, such as Bowie, and embraced the transgressions that he embodied. Their 'home building' together involved horror film nights and music video binges, away from the traditional Greek community she/they were also connected to.

For ID, the home he remembers is his own private hell. Conforming and relatively strict, the space was also the site where they suffered sexual abuse. Bowie was played to both hide the fact that this was taking place and was also the music that allowed our participant to soar beyond its earthly terror:

> There was this weirdness emerging in me that was actually imposed by external sexual forces and no form to discuss it ... All my drawings became very creepy. I drew monsters, hairy beings and I drew a lot of aliens. Escaping to the aliens is exactly what Bowie did and was an escape past his abuse.

Bowie is very often considered to be an artist one escapes in and through. His music reaches towards the stars and is engaged in alternative universes and grotesque histories, and his own liminal and transgressive images enable him to be written on and over (see Chapters 3 and 6 for further fan responses to his live performance). In terms of identity, he allowed our participants to both find alternative selves within and in opposition to migrant identity and rise above the damage they encountered within everyday life.

2. Family Matters

Controversial social commentator and knight errant, David Bowie, struck a chord with fans dissatisfied with the prevailing established narratives growing up. For those feeling isolated or oppressed or closed off from wider society, Bowie afforded a portal to possibilities unknown (again, see Chapter 3 for a detailed discussion of this). Imaginings garnered from the screen and sounds of 'the seductive' presented a desirable visual and sonic 'other' world, a tapestry consisting of the alluring *leit-motiv* of (post)modernity. Bowie was a vehicle for social influence (Cinque et al. 2015; Devereux et al. 2015) and a central means by which our focus group participants, as young teens growing up in Australia, observed and evaluated themselves. Moreover, in the bosom of family (variously understood and experienced), Bowie provided a means to 'new' thinking at critical junctures, adding shape to their world-views. For AN:

> Bowie was a way of processing all the other shit that was considered 'norm' and that was oppressive around me. He became my way of putting stuff together and saying 'no! *this* is my world; *this* is the stuff I love and if that is 'grotesque', then so be-it!

Many fans came to Bowie's work very early in their lives, and the same was found to be true within the migrant focus group. Bowie 'reached out' to them shrewdly expressing 'life-threatening ideas' (ID)—what it might mean to exist 'outside' certain norms so that they came to an understanding of their particular distinctiveness being challenged by the (then?) dominant oppressive characterisations of gender, race and ethnicity (see Klein 1983) that they were being faced with and where 'Bowie made it OK' (ID). Parts of a society wherein they might not 'fit', Bowie provided a space for them to inhabit, where they were content to be different and, even able to push back upon, the accepted culture around them. For MP:

> I found Bowie at 12 or 13 and he was just the epitome of masculinity, the way I thought it was amazing, softly spoken and elegant – and here, I had also grown up with an uncle and a father who were similarly very different to the mainstream masculinity whether 'the typical Italian' or 'man's man' and for me, Bowie just spoke of ambiguity, of never knowing quite where you fit …

And when 'seeds are planted the vine flourishes' (ANON):

> My parents emigrated from Ireland to the UK. I grew up initially in an Irish community; a catholic upbringing and quite a masculine one too. My Dad was a masculine man, not a 'bruiser' in any way but quite tough and I had this conservative, forceful upbringing. But for me, Bowie presented a figure beyond this sort of doctrine – a heavenly embodiment that I loved; I absolutely adored it. I didn't know at the time what it was, no idea, but the visceral connective response to Him I have kept all my life and it has steered me right in terms of my identity politics. (ANON)

For the participants in our migrant focus group, 'Bowie-inspired' creative activities were also important to their emerging personal identity and to their well-being growing up in a family and/or community with which they were at times, at odds. While sometimes creativity can be negative when 'darkly' motivated, for example, a torturer might be creative, but his/her creativity makes the world a worse place (see Gaut 2010), this facet was not found to be the case for our participants—indeed, participants' own creativity was personally valuable and instrumental. Noted above ID, as a young teen trying to 'escape the grotesque' originating from his abuse, would draw aliens personified by Bowie as Ziggy Stardust and later Thomas Jerome Newton in *The Man Who Fell to Earth* (Roeg 1976). AN hand-sewed outfits inspired by the Diamond Dog, Halloween Jack, to enrage her family, especially her Greek father (who was disowned by her grandfather for not having a son) but that enthralled her sisters:

> I introduced my sisters to non-Greek music and I always went for the non-traditionally Greek things in music and fashion for example. I was very against the conservative and what I saw then as oppressive Greek upbringing …

Encouraging and fostering their creative spirit was understood by participants to be imperative to making sense of the world into which they had emerged or, in certain situations, the events forced upon them. For years growing up, MP crafted scrapbooks that she filled with images taken from popular music magazines of David Bowie:

> I always felt like I was on the outside of the prevailing 'Australian' culture *and* the Italian community both. My parents were anti-Catholic [Italians are commonly Catholic], not homophobic [Catholics are required by Biblical decree, to be homophobic] and they encouraged me to be a strong, strident, feminist, and; I was brought up differently to the 'typical' nuclear family. I had two Mums and two Dads and I was brought up in a community. I had a gorgeous childhood – and then I went to school where I found that my life was considered 'different' or 'alien' and everyone else was living the so-called normal life. I was given labels like 'neglected' and even 'abused' which certainly was not the way I was brought up. Then at 12, I found David Bowie and I keenly remember a picture of him and Angie holding their son Zowie [MP finds the image in one of her scrapbooks]. And I thought 'WOW', you could get families that were queer, that you could get families that don't live up to the norm and that this was another possibility.

What became apparent from participant comments was that in mainstream Australian society growing up, there was a seeming lack of overt 'vision' for the ways in which people might live together harmoniously in the larger community while simultaneously being able to maintain, rather than diluting or losing, a strong sense of personal core values or identity. They did not, however, 'give in' to this. For our participants, the use of key rituals, symbols and articles of belief allowed the then dominant cultural 'norms' and/or practices to be resisted through drawing on an alternative, an 'alien', so that they might question and explore the validity of the representation of lifestyles and values circulating at the time. As noted above, this was especially true for participants resisting the stereotypes of 'family', 'masculinity' and ethnic identity. For three of the participants, Bowie and his music afforded the cultural means of functioning effectively within their communities without feeling required to necessarily change their cultural allegiances or personal identities. For AD and MP, Bowie was an exploratory foray into new possibilities that moved in tandem or journeyed alongside other media of personal cultural significance rather than a retreat into a separated enclave. What is at stake then for the individual is far more than supporting imprecise notions of unrestricted freedom of choice (to rock and popular music for instance) and the personal significance for such that lies therein. It concerns nothing less than how (and by whom) our dreams have been shaped.

3. Grieving and Healing

> There is no binary division to be made between what one says and what one does not say; we must try to determine the different ways of not saying such things, how those who can and those who cannot speak of them are distributed, which type of discourse is authorized, or which form of discretion is required in either case. There is not one but many silences, and they are an integral part of the strategies that underlie and permeate discourses. (Foucault 1990: 27)

As we outline in our Introduction, the focus group method is in one sense 'an incitement to discourse' (Foucault 1990: 17), organised to reveal the unspoken and to hear the silences that may remain. It is also an intervention into dominant discourse: a way of cracking open the capillaries of power nodes that circulate within everyday life. Celebrity culture is itself a discursive set of practices and processes involving confessional and gossip modes and modalities of communication. On the one hand, celebrity talk can be argued to reinforce the politics of the neoliberal self and commodity culture. On the other, it can be argued to reveal inequalities and to challenge and counter-normative behaviours and relations. Joshua Gamson sees celebrity gossip as involving an audience who reject the vertical (top-down) relationship between celebrity and consumer for a horizontal one involving a collective or shared evaluation of the famed figure under the spotlight (Gamson 1994: 177–178).

This was very much the case with our focus group—we found participants commenting on each other's responses, offering words of encouragement and support and using 'echo' and reinforcement strategies to align their thinking and emotional investment. Words such as 'icon', 'alien', 'elegant', 'liminal', 'boundary testing' and 'border-crosser' were the most often used phrases, becoming a way of not only defining Bowie but also the shared investment in him. A collective and empowering 'voice' emerged through this celebrity talk: that in its sharing and hearing became a liberating tool of identification and a form of progressive social cohesion. As previously discussed, migrant identity became a shared badge of resistance and transcendence. However, we not only found that in talking about Bowie—in sharing stories about how he impacted on the participants' lives—was he a figure of 'togetherness', but that in the 'conversation' that took place, a healing processed emerged or was sought. As AP shared and AN responded:

> I was always a Bowie fan, like my first record was a David Bowie record, which my Dad bought for me when I was two. It was Let's Dance. And my Father passed away really recently, and he was a really big Bowie fan. A month ago, like a couple of days before David Bowie. There was this weird thing that kind of happened with the mourning, that kind of fused to the point that the song was playing on the radio when he took his last breath was Space Oddity…weird sense of symmetry. And I thought my Dad would have really liked to come along…
>
> AN: well he is here…

The sense that AP (and AN) re-materialise her father is a powerful one: we are party here to a ritual of grieving for both a loved one just lost and the shared subject of their affection and bonding. This is grieving and healing emerging in the same collective place—a place of new communion. AP is in part dealing with her grief by being here; a mechanism to deal with her dad's death; it may ultimately work to support social cohesion. However, one may also see celebrity mourning as anti-structural and grieving as a carnal response to loss and which open up mourners to doubt and confusion, rather than closure and cohesion. This can be seen as ritual of philosophical questioning and phenomenological experience.

Each of our participants used and uses Bowie at crisis or critical points in their lives (also see Chapter 3). Bowie embodied a particularly transgressive and transcendent form of agency which was drawn upon to both garner support for the identity positions they were seeking to take up or which offered a life-affirming way of overcoming obstacles. Both AN and MP migrated to Bowie to normalise and ratify their difference. MP revealed how as a child at school she struggled to talk in public and so used David Bowie to overcome her shyness and sense of strangeness and alienation from other children who would mark her out as different: 'nah, you don't have a TV, we know your house ...'. For MP, Bowie was a gateway to self-actualisation:

> By the time I got to year 10 I still couldn't read out loud properly, couldn't do a presentation ... The first time I ever did a presentation at school and managed to get through it was speaking about David Bowie. Such a strategy of diversion...

For ID, the question of grieving and healing was connected to the sexual abuse he suffered. Bowie was employed to hide the abuse but also became the voice, the melody and the star image that allowed him to escape his abuse and abuser and overcome the deep traumas he faced. Nonetheless, for ID, Bowie was also the vehicle through which a darker side of self-realisation emerged:

> (Holding up an image of Ziggy) I was in a psychiatric hospital, under observation, at the age of 17... thank God for David Bowie... personally speaking, the staring, insanity of the man...there is no other escape than madness... I spent my 18th birthday in a psychiatric hospital.

For our participants, Bowie embodied a particularly transgressive and aggressive form of active agency, and self-empowerment, and yet was also a conduit of/for understanding suffering in the face of conformity and abuse. For AN:

> For me, it wasn't an escape ... he became a way of processing all the other shit that was norm and oppressive around you ... this is my world, the stuff I love, and if it means it is grotesque or horrific or alien or whatever the hell it was, then bring it on.

ID: That in itself became a kind of anchor.

One can argue that celebrity talk also works as a ritual of refusal to patriarchal norms, and it offers one an 'anchor' in a sea of complex, messy and unequal identity positions. Bowie acts as a nautilus for our participants—a sacred shape; perfect symmetry, ultimately capable of resurrection ...

4. Lazarus Rises: Resurrection

> Now a man named Lazarus was sick ... "Our friend Lazarus has fallen asleep: but I am going ... to wake him up" ... "Did I not tell you that if you believed, you would see the glory of God?' ... When he said this, Jesus called in a loud voice, "Lazarus, come out!" The dead man came out [of his tomb], his hands and feet wrapped with strips of linen, and a cloth around his face. (John 11: 1–44)

The story of *The Death of Lazarus* is about demonstrating publicly the wonder and power of God through the miracle of a dead man raised to life. In his video for the song Lazarus, created during a time in which he faced his own sickness (cancer), Bowie linked spiritual belief and death by depicting the metaphoric Lazarus bearing linen superposed around his head, perhaps pitting his faith upon his own spiritual and/or physical resurrection—or, is he in fact '*The Exile Symbolised*' on earth with his covered eyes replaced by useless plastic buttons:

> Son of man, you are living among a rebellious people. They have eyes to see but do not see and ears to hear but do not hear ... (Ezekiel 12: 2)

If read in this way, it is certainly an important religious statement, but it is also one with implications for being far from 'salvation'. We might present the provocation then that while seeking his own (our) 'resurrection' through grappling with the esoteric, David Bowie acted concurrently to restore belief (life) to those suffering. One participant found accord with this statement:

> After everything that has happened I've been thinking a lot about how one person can have such an incredible impact on society in their life. I haven't been able to stop thinking about his death and because of that, his life and what he did. (AN)

While David Jones ('Jones' remained his legal surname) pursued a single dictum of exploring life's depths, he did so via the mercurial 'Bowie' and associated characters, using different metaphors and metonyms at various times for different purposes (Cinque 2015). Throughout a rebellious biography involving resurrection moments, his rise and fall and rise again trajectory acted as a contextual frame. As Redmond (2013: 377) argues: 'his process of renewal means that Bowie constantly kills himself, an artistic suicide that allows for dramatic event moments to populate his music, and for a rebirth to emerge at the same time or shortly after he expires'.

Reflecting upon his final expiration, when asked about the profound response to his death by people of all ages from around the globe, across popular culture and the avant-garde, AN commented that:

> On one hand it was the music and also how he performed as a musician – it really tested boundaries. So there was the message (for want of a better word) that was sent out that reached people that way (his music and his persona), but beyond that he was a cultural presence in cinema. He represented things in terms of identity in the media, testing sexuality, individuality, and creativity. So his impact crept out beyond the music – it wasn't like he was a great musician alone and that was the end of it. (AN)

For a number, *his* struggles suffered (depicted in his art) have help(ed) to create an existential understanding. An important study undertaken by Stever (2011) found that fandom could assist individuals to overcome difficult life events by reconnecting with their feelings allowing them to: 'rejoin … the social world' (2011: 3) after long periods of isolation (ibid.)—much like Lazarus emerging from the tomb or Bowie 'living on' in digital form or the individual finding purpose anew:

> My Dad came to Australia from Greece when he was 15. He was actually helped to learn English by listening to Bowie albums because Bowie's diction was very, very good. He bought me my first Bowie album. So, he was a big Bowie fan. When he passed away and where the song playing on the radio was 'Space Oddity' that was weird and a kind of symmetry that is always something that I have associated with Bowie. (AP)

> I am so glad that we did this today [refers to the Focus Group]. After the news of His death it brought everyone together and has opened up another whole dimension for me. (AN)

One participant was able to find an escape from this great loss:

> When Bowie died, my little ones who live overseas were coming to visit the very next day. Normally, I would be pretty morose and down about it, thinking about Bowie's death and what it meant and I would have locked myself away – but my children arrived at 8 O'clock the morning following his death – this let me forget not Bowie, but to live on. In a sense his death (a perfect death) came at a perfect time for me. (ANON)

In a heightened ideological sense, with regular recurrence David Bowie's works have engaged with the suffering of everyday life while synchronously tendering renewal so that the pain of living unequally in the world might be evaluated, worked through and extinguished. Through his body, whether his intent or no, our own life events are explained or justified in ways that let us keep going.

CONCLUSION

> ...identities are never unified and, in late modern times, increasingly frag- mented and fractured; never singular but multiple constructed across differ- ent, often intersecting and antagonistic, discourses, practices and positions. (Hall 1990: 223)

In this chapter, we have demonstrated the way David Bowie has positively impacted upon migrant identity and how notions of the self and selfhood move across sheets of belonging and estrangement—themselves connected to age, gender and sexuality. What we have seen emerging from these con- versations—from this ship of stories—is not only the way stardom impacts upon everyday life, but also the way identities are forged, shaped and lay- ered in dynamic points of intersectionality. As we have suggested, Bowie's own shape-shifting identity and liminality became the art, sound and the flesh that our participants were able to utilise to empower and enrich their own lives. Lazarus rose and continues to rise within them.

While in this chapter we have extracted clusters of themes, the talk that emerged merged them—so that in one 'story' from one participant, the themes of family/community; sexuality and gender; ethnicity and differ- ence; and personal renewal or 'resurrection' rose up together like the most beautiful song, like the most liberating sounding. That our participants deftly, unconsciously, wrapped the complexities of their lives around Bowie, tells us the way in which memory is enacted and active agency manifests in the world. Our work demonstrates the way fandom is decidedly private and continues to be beautifully communal. The talk of David Bowie not only allowed our participants to share how, why and when he mattered, revealing secrets and privacies rarely shared before, but in the telling and the hearing new understandings emerged—the participants saw their histories and herstories in a new light. Further, in the sharing, friendships emerged as stories aligned.

Of course, in a contemporary Australia, where certain 'types' of migrant are left to waste away in detention camps, these stories of migrant belonging are particularly relevant and important. These ships welcome those who arrive on boats.

For Toija and I, who are two lifelong David Bowie fans, the organisation of the focus group and its running, happened only a few weeks after Bowie's death. Our participation in the focus group, then, was not only to do with exercising our preferred research method, but also so that we could share our stories with everyone else—at a time of great sadness and some personal need.

REFERENCES

Australian Bureau of Statistics (ABS). "Cultural Diversity in Australia: Reflecting a Nation: Stories from the 2011 Census." Catalogue No. 2071.0, 2013. http://www.abs.gov.au/ausstats/abs@.nsf/Lookup/2071.0main+features902012-2013. Accessed 18 February 2016.

Bauman, Zygmunt. "From Pilgrim to Tourist—Or a Short History of Identity." In *Questions of Cultural Identity*, ed. Stuart Hall and Paul Du Gay, 18–36. London: Sage, 1996.

Cinque, Toija. "Semantic Shock: David Bowie!" In *Enchanting David Bowie: Space/Time/Body/Memory*, 197–214. New York: Bloomsbury, 2015.

Cinque, Toija, Christopher Moore, and Sean Redmond. *Enchanting David Bowie: Space/Time/Body/Memory*. New York: Bloomsbury, 2015.

Devereux, Eoin, Aileen Dillane, and Martin Power (eds.). *David Bowie: Critical Perspectives*. Vol. 6. Abingdon: Routledge, 2015.

Ethnic Television Review Panel. "Programming for the Multicultural/Multilingual Television Service: Objectives and Policies." Third Report of the Ethnic Television Review Panel, 6 February. Canberra: Australian Government Publishing Service, 1980.

Finnegan, Ruth. "Storying the Self: Personal Narratives and Identity." In *Consumption and Everyday Life*, ed. Hugh Mackay, 65–112. London: Sage, 1997.

Foucault, Michel. *The History of Sexuality: An Introduction.* Trans. Robert Hurley, Vol. I. New York: Vintage, 1990.

Frith, Simon. "Music and Identity." In *Questions of Cultural Identity*, ed. Stuart Hall and Paul Du Gay, 108–127. London: Sage, 1996.

Gamson, Joshua. *Claims to Fame: Celebrity in Contemporary America.* Berkeley: University of California Press, 1994.

Gaut, Berys. "The Philosophy of Creativity." *Philosophy Compass* 5 (2010): 1034–1046.

Gillard, Julia. "From 'White Australia' to Whitlam: Migration and Multiculturalism in Australia." Paper Presented at a Conference to Mark the 30th Anniversary of the Election of the Whitlam Government, *The Whitlam Government as Modernist Politics: 30 Years Later.* Old Parliament House, Canberra, 2–3 December 2002.

Groene, Samantha L., and Vanessa E. Hettinger. "Are You 'Fan' Enough? The Role of Identity in Media Fandoms." *Psychology of Popular Media Culture*, 20 April 2015. http://dx.doi.org/10.1037/ppm0000080.

Hage, Ghassan. "The Limits of Anti-racist Sociology." *UTS Review* 1 (1) (1995): 14–21.

Hage, Ghassan. "At Home in the Entrails of the West: Multiculturalism, 'Ethnic Food' and Migrant Home-Building." In *Home/World: Space, Community and Marginality in Sydney's West*, ed. H. Grace, G. Hage, L. Johnson, M. Langsworth, and M. Symonds, 99–153. London: Pluto Press, 1997.

Hall, Stuart. "Cultural Identity and Diaspora." In *Identity: Community, Culture, Difference*, 222–237. London: Lawrence and Wishart, 1990.

Jakubowics, Andrew, and Kerie Newell. "Which World? Whose/Who's Home?: Special Broadcasting in the Australian Communications Alphabet." In *Public Voices, Private Interests*, ed. Jennifer Craik, James Baily, and Albert Moran, 130–146. Sydney: Allen & Unwin, 1995.

Jupp, James. "Understanding Australian Multiculturalism." Centre for Immigration and Multicultural Studies, Australian National University, Australian Government Publishing Service, Canberra, 1996.

Klein, Hilary. *All the Women Are White, All the Blacks Are Men, But Some of Us Are Brave.* Edited by Gloria T. Hull, Patricia Bell Scott, and Barbara Smith. New York: The Feminist Press, 1983.

Langer, John. "Media Democratisation in Australia: What Is It, Who's Got It, Where to Find It, How It Works (or Doesn't)—Part 2." *Screen Education* 26/27 (2001): 68–85.

Lowe, Melanie. "Colliding Feminisms: Britney Spears, 'Tweens', and the Politics of Reception." *Popular Music and Society*, 26 (2003): 123–140.

Probyn, Elizabeth. "Glass Selves: Emotions, Subjectivity, and the Research Process." In *The Oxford Handbook of the Self*, ed. S. Gallagher, 1–10. Oxford: Oxford University Press, 2011.

Redmond, Sean. "Who Am I Now? Remembering the Enchanted Dogs of David Bowie." *Celebrity Studies* 4 (3) (2013): 380–383.

Redmond, Sean. *Celebrity and the Media.* London: Palgrave, 2014.

Rex, John. "Transnational Migrant Communities and Ethnic Minorities in Modern Multicultural Societies." In *Ethnic Minorities in the Modern Nation State*, 96–113. London: Palgrave Macmillan, 1996.

Said, Edward. *Orientalism.* New York: Pantheon Books, 1978.

Seneviratne, Kalinga. "Multicultural Television: Going Beyond the Rhetoric." *Media Information Australia* 66 (1992): 53–57.

Stever, Gayle S. "Celebrity Worship: Critiquing a Construct." *Journal of Applied Social Psychology* 41 (6) (2011): 1356–1370.

Woodward, Kathryn. *Identity and Difference.* Vol. 3. London: Sage, 1997.

CHAPTER 5

Bowie Contagion

INTRODUCTION

In this chapter, we explore two interlocking themes: first, the way memories are called upon to manage and imagine fans' relationship to, and identification with, David Bowie. Second, the chapter examines the way that David Bowie memorabilia contextualises and provides anchor points for fan identifications, becoming a 'home' or 'contagion' of treasured objects that are embodied and self-narrated. As Hoelscher and Alderman suggest, 'people now look to this refashioned memory, especially in its collective forms, to give themselves a coherent identity, a national narrative, a place in the world' (2004: 348–349).

We will look at two forms of memory, personal and collective, private and communal, although as our work suggests, memory shifts, folds into itself, so that it is very often personal and shared, private and collective, as soon as it is 'told'. As Crane suggests, 'lived experience and collective memory "interpenetrate" each other through autobiography, the self-conscious memory of individual members of a group' (1997: 1377). The chapter takes the position that:

> We are conglomerations of past everyday experiences, including their spatial textures and affective registers. Memory should not be seen as a burden of the past, rather it is fundamental to becoming, and a key wellspring of agency, practice / habit, creativity and imagination, and thus of the potential of the performative moment. (Jones 2011: 875–876)

© The Author(s) 2019
T. Cinque and S. Redmond, *The Fandom of David Bowie*,
https://doi.org/10.1007/978-3-030-15880-4_5

The chapter examines memory as recollection and as spatial, textural and temporal coordinates that shape a fan's often lifelong connection to David Bowie. The memories drawn upon and evoked are nostalgic, desiring, affirming and ritualistic. Cherished objects are seen to be affective forms of belonging, connected to people, places and feelings that rear-up as soon as the item is remembered and/or touched.

The chapter also draws upon the way Time (capital T) acts a form of contagion, both linear, striking the event beats of Bowie fans as they recall their life stories; and irregular and viral, spreading out to impact (infect) the multiple fragments that occupy peoples' recollections and remembrances. Here, Time is all at once and no Time at all.

REMEMBERING LISTENING TO DAVID BOWIE

When it comes to understanding the role that memory plays in the fandom of David Bowie, we see a number of repeating themes. First, in recalling David Bowie, fans draw on both nostalgic refrains and affective stories of the self. For the fan, this looking backwards is both a travelogue into their past but also a resurrecting remembrance that ignites their present and presence in the world as they reflect on it today. As Annette Kuhn suggests, memory work is a temporal puzzle which in solving allows one to '[patch] together reconstructions out of fragments of evidence' (Kuhn 1995: 4). In response to the question (8), What does David Bowie mean to you? K2 responds,

> There isn't an emotion or feeling that isn't represented by his music. His contributions to music and film are like place holders in my memory. Often times, when I'm feeling especially nostalgic, his presence overlays the memory. Though he was always changing, he was one of the few constants in my life.

This is a beautifully complex and poetic answer: K2 is suggesting that Bowie's music provides a soundtrack or score to not only the memories they hold of him, but of major and minor life moments, like a sonic, melodic glue that adheres their sense of self together. As Van Dijck suggests, 'like photographs or diary entries, music has a mnemonic function; listening to records helps inscribe and invoke specific events, emotions, or general moods' (2006: 359). K2 also suggests that these memories are nostalgic, creating an affirmative sense of their past and of Bowie's role in it. Finally, K2 is pointing towards the way we see ourselves as often caught or buffeted by seas of change, and for them, it is figures such as changeling Bowie that provides chrononormative certainty. In this retelling, there is not only a self-conscious and self-reflective externalisation of interiorised feelings but a recognition that music provides a 'human resource through which people can enact their lives with inextricably entwined feeling, thought and imagination' (Finnegan 2003: 188).

In Answer to Question 6, 'Please Recall and Describe What Your First Memory of Encountering David Bowie Is?', H4 Writes that

> Although his music seemed ever-present through older brothers and sisters, my first memory on a personal level is November of 1980 when I saw him perform on Broadway in The Elephant Man. I was 16 years old and went with my sister and a friend. I knew he was Bowie, I understood the significance, but at the point, I was not a fan. The moment he appeared onstage it was as if I were struck by something. I remember there was silence at first – just the image of him on that stage as he went through the physical movements to transform into his character. He had such a presence, almost an aura I could physically feel. He was so larger than life, so incredibly captivating. That was the moment I became a fan and it hit me like a ton of bricks.

In this loving remembrance, where collective memory is quickly replaced by personal memory, H4 creates an affective narrative out of their first encounter with David Bowie who becomes in the retelling, 'sensuous imagery that evokes memory of the senses' (Totaro 2002). There are embodied textures and materials being drawn upon to evoke the memory—silence, stillness, being struck by something, movement, aura, bricks—and the words used by H4 suggest they are moved by their own recollections here. H4 draws on the ideas of aura or presence to layer the recollection with what might be termed a double ghosting—remembering the aura she once saw fills them with the glow of it again. As Megill writes, 'memory is an image of the past constructed by a subjectivity in the present' (1998: 56). There is also, of course, a returning to a moment of youthful nostalgia and the reconnection to 'first' desires and longing. Bowie is exalted love interest here but also a sublimated one: the response is coded erotica.

In Chapter 4, we saw how MP kept a scrapbook of the popular music magazine photos and spreads that she had selected and kept as a teenager, linking the keepsake to their identity as an alien and alienated Other. At the focus group they attended in Melbourne, they produced the scrapbook and shared the photos and their associated memories with everyone present. Not only was this a scrapbook to ignite the recalling of personal memories, it was a sensorial or textural series of leaves turned over as they recalled their youth. As each page was delicately turned and gently caressed, the curatorial work was not simply chronological or historical but part of the very substance through which their embodied memories flooded. Certain photos of Bowie were dwelled upon, held in higher esteem, and certain memories they solicited provoked smiles, wistful pauses and animated descriptions. The pages themselves were carefully set and ordered. What MP had done with their scrapbook was apply emotional design principles to it: the dream book was not just a treasure trove of memories but an affecting and affective design brief, so that it had to be seen, touched and felt in its entirety. There is a co-mingling of emotion and affect here, where 'emotion is the conscious experience of affect, complete with attribution of its cause and identification of its object' (O'Sullivan 2001: 126). MP draws upon emotions to express the inexpressible, to find a lightning rod to ground feelings that are beyond words. Affect in this context is, as Simon O'Sullivan argues:

> the molecular beneath the molar. The molecular understood here as life's, and arts, intensive quality, as the stuff that goes on beneath, beyond, even parallel to signification. (ibid.)

In our numerous focus groups, we found there were moments where participants were lost in affect, found themselves unable to speak as they tried to recall Bowie-inspired memories or the fact of his death. For example, in the London focus group, the participants struggled to express how they felt when they had heard of David's death, and further, one of the participants (Q1) spoke of how they wandered, in a daze, to those sites in London they knew were connected to Bowie. Their bodies escaped the discourses that normally account for feeling and affect and for moments in time, it was their vibrating, intensified silences and failure to express in words that 'spoke' for their sense of loss and mourning. In the Melbourne, London, Amsterdam and Lisbon focus groups, there were instances where tears were shed, both a private response to a memory being recalled and a collective or shared response to memories that resonated with everyone. The most powerful and challenging of these, as we outline in Chapter 4, were when ID recalled their sexual abuse at the hands of a perpetrator, with Bowie's music becoming the escape room for them.

Of course, as we also noted in Chapter 4, in finding David Bowie, MP found a way of finding value and meaning in their non-orthodox family:

> … I had a gorgeous childhood – and then I went to school where I found that my life was considered 'different' or 'alien' and everyone else was living the so-called normal life. I was given labels like 'neglected' and even 'abused' which certainly was not the way I was brought up. Then at 12, I found David Bowie and I keenly remember a picture of him and Angie holding their son Zowie [MP finds the image in one of her scrapbooks]. And I thought 'WOW', you could get families that were queer, that you could get families that don't live up to the norm and that this was another possibility.

This book has so far made much of the father role that Bowie has played in fan's lives. However, for MP, Bowie is an *alternative* father figure, someone who queers normal patriarchal familial relationships, offering up the family to new possibilities. The memory being shared here is about how Bowie helped give place and space to new identity formations. For many of our respondents in looking back at their fandom, it was either a pivotal life moment or the awakening of sexual desire. For example,

> H5: Changes was sampled in Confessions of a Teenage Drama Queen when I was thirteen. I didn't think much of it back in the day. Then I threw myself headfirst into The Rise and Fall of Ziggy Stardust and the Spiders From Mars, and I didn't think much of it either. Then it returned over and over again in my head, like a haunting memory, until eventually I found myself addicted to listening to him.

> H6: I had a crush on a friend who I found out was a huge devotee. So I 'schooled up' on DB's back catalogue - i was about 16 - and I was hooked on the music and the man. Didn't get anywhere with the friend but it left me with a lifetime of pleasure and obsession. This would have been around the time of the 1978 tour. Seeing 'Boys Keep Swinging' on Countdown was also a big early memory in 1979.

> H7: My first memory of Bowie is no doubt ambiguous and confused with other memories, but I recall seeing graffiti on a wall: 'ashes to ashes, funk to funky, sex is best without a dunky' (condom) I knew this was a reference to a Bowie lyric and it confirmed my sense that he was 'grown up', adult, taboo, shocking.

(Question 6: Please recall and describe what your first memory of encountering David Bowie is?)

Memory work here is being conducted in a really interested fashion: Bowie is connected to transgression, to the taboo and, for H5, to a form of hauntology. The participants are recalling the 'shock' that they felt when first hearing and/or seeing him and at the same time are connecting the memory to sexual hopes and hopeful advances. These are now playful memories, drawn from the standpoint of adults looking back on what they see or sense as their rites of musical and sexual passage (see Chapter 3 for further discussion of fandom and desire).

In Tonya Anderson's ethnographic investigation of adult female fans of '80s heart-throbs Duran Duran, we find that 'their teen idols stirred their first sexual desires' and 'that it is possible the notion of a first crush may have instigated the formation and continuance of their fan attachment'. Further,

> Paradoxically, and as the case study data reveals, today this attachment has less to do with sex and more to do with memory and a nostalgic identification with one's 'teen' self… because it approximates a 'reclaimed youth' for fans who are approaching or have reached midlife, as many Duran Duran fans have. (2012: 240)

Over 68% of the respondents to our questionnaire were aged 40 or over, and one can see how fan identifications often hinged on both memories of youth and of life stories being framed and cohered, narrated and understood in terms of Bowie's music, films and live performances. For example,

> *H8*: His music was a consistent presence in my life. There will never be another like him. What a great man.

> *H9*: Life … I have been a fan since 1969. He has seen me through my teenage angst and through personal difficulties as an adult.

> *H10*: David Bowie provided the sound track to my life. His music helped shape the person I am and helped me accept my kookishness. I was and am happily the black sheep, whereas once it bothered me greatly.

(8. What does David Bowie mean to you?)

H11: Catlin Moran's obit in The Times last week got pretty close for me - she described how she felt that Bowie's lyrics were aimed at her and that he was speaking directly to her. For all the (perhaps slightly over-sensitive) confused teenage souls of the world, he understood us. He encouraged us to carry on. He encouraged me to create and to be the person that I wanted to be.

(14. What description best sums up David Bowie for you?)

Again, in these responses, we see an imagined chronology of the self, and identity material being constructed through Bowie's work and pronouncements. The personalisation of the encounters—he sings to and for me—is coupled with a subcultural recognition that he was attuned to a wider group of outsiders, teenagers on the margins of society (Tait 1993). As David Hesmondhalgh observes in relation to popular music more broadly, 'it represents a remarkable meeting point of the private and public realms, providing encounters of self-identity (this is who I am, this is who I'm not) with collective identity (this is who we are, this is who we're not)' (2008: 330).

There is a great deal of emotional connectivity, and positivity to these responses, which we find repeating across the questionnaire and focus group responses, something that might be attributed to the older age of the responses. As Harrington et al. note,

… the 'bulk of evidence … points to no real declines in the capacity for emotion across the adult years; if anything, older adults sometimes express more acute emotional experience than younger adults' (Magai, 2008: 383–4). In addition, this meta-analysis finds that there are 'increases in the level or frequency of positive emotion and declines in negative emotion broadly across the adult years' (2008: 388), that 'adults become increasingly skilled emotion regulators over the lifespan' (2008: 378–9), and that our later years in particular are characterized by heightened emotional mastery and complexity. (2011: 12)

Overall, then, it is understood that the very process of ageing brings with it an 'increasing appreciation for the affective aspects of life and social relations', something we pick up on in relation to the memorabilia our respondents spoke about and shared with us.

CHERISHED OBJECTS IN TIME AND SPACE

Memorabilia is centrally defined as the collection and curation of objects because of their associations with memorable people or events. Celebrity memorabilia relates to items, objects and artefacts that are connected to a famous person, which are highly prized by the owner and which also can have commercial value. We can think of personal celebrity memorabilia as types of 'cherished possessions' or,

> Those objects that are experienced as extraordinary and emotion-evoking rather than as merely functional; owners of such treasured objects are generally unwilling to sell them for market value or otherwise dispose of such objects. (Belk 1991: 18):

Such items, keepsakes and mementoes can stir reminiscence, something that has been termed 'reminiscentia' because they possess the 'special aptitude for arousing a reminiscent state of mind' (Casey 1987: 110). Both F12 and F13 engage in reminiscentia:

> *F12*: I still have my ticket from the Starplex show in Dallas in 1995. I keep it in my wallet all day everyday and have since then. You can't actually *read* it anymore, mind you! Other than that, my brother bought me "Space Oddity" on vinyl just a few weeks ago, a few days before Bowie's death. Inside the album jacket, there's a really nice poster reprint from his early days. I can imagine me hanging that up on my wall.

> *F13*: I have one of the balloons that were released into the air during the Aragon Ballroom performance that I attended. I also have one of the David Bowie promotional posters from the Torhout concert. Both of these are reminders of the concerts, but also of that time in my life.

(15. Do you have a cherished piece of David Bowie memorabilia?)

For F13, a balloon and concert promotional poster are not just exalted pieces of nostalgia but the doorway through which they can recall wider life memories. The keeping of the (deflated?) balloon of course not only 'presents' them at the concert but embodies something of the spectacle and transcendence of the live event itself. For F12, the concert ticket that they carry around in their wallet is no longer legible but its significance remains: that it is kept in a wallet, like a partners or child's photograph, and can be easily accessed and 'touched', suggests that it remains a happy object Ahmed (2008), a piece of memorabilia that they store not away from sight but in plain sight. For both F12 and F13, these mementoes combine the two drivers of keeping cherished possessions: they are objects of affection and the material through which favourite memories are activated and which become the plasma, the heart and lungs of their own identity maintenance. As Rochberg-Halton suggests

> Valued material possessions…act as signs of the self that are essential in their own right for its continued cultivation, and hence the world of meaning that we create for ourselves, and that creates ourselves, extends literally into the objective surroundings. (1984: 335)

When it comes to celebrity memorabilia, the phenomenon of magical contagion is important since it is a 'form of magical thinking in which people believe that a person's immaterial qualities or essence can be transferred to an object through physical contact' (Newman and Bloom 2014: 3705). The possession of Bowie memorabilia was very often an empowering sense of magical contagion:

> G3: yes. I have a feather boa. I wore it to the Astoria and threw it up to him on stage - he put it around his neck and sang "Drive in Saturday". I asked for it back from a security man as the show ended and I still have it.

(15. Do you have a cherished piece of David Bowie memorabilia?)

For G3, the feather boa now has Bowie's DNA embedded in its materiality: that he touched it, wore it, sweated into it, at a live concert they were in attendance, carries the contagion from them to Bowie and from Bowie back to them. In this imagined sensory exchange, Bowie also has an imprint of them on his neck and shoulders. That Bowie chooses to pick it up off the stage and to wear it implies an experiential connection for G3. As Torben Habermas argues, objects can play a 'critical role in the process of internalization; significant others can be brought into a psychological presence via the symbolic meaning of a treasured possession' (quoted in Kroger and Adair 2008: 8).

At the London focus group, this was played in two instances: FL recalled daring to touch the Union Jack Coat that Bowie had worn for *Earthling* (1997) while visiting the *David Is* V&A exhibition. They described the fabric of the coat and of later posting the fact on Facebook, as if they had almost touched David Bowie directly. Second, FX described receiving a signed jacket from the Serious Moonlight tour, it arriving at their hostel while studying at University. FX then proceeded to get the jacket out of the bag they had with them, creating gasps around the room, and said to everyone present, 'you can put it on if you like'. Each of the participants then got a chance to try it on, in a communal sharing setting.

In Newman and Bloom's (2014) study of auctioning celebrity memorabilia, they found that the death of a celebrity 'produces a grief reaction and increased sacralization of related goods'. Further, they find that:

> People's expectations about the amount of physical contact between the object and the celebrity positively predicts the final bids for items that belonged to well-liked individuals (e.g., John F. Kennedy) and negatively predicts final bids for items that belonged to disliked individuals (e.g., Bernard Madoff) … These effects are driven by contagion beliefs: when asked to bid on a sweater owned by a well-liked celebrity, participants report that they would pay substantially less if it was sterilized before they received it. However, sterilization increases the amount they would pay for a sweater owned by a disliked celebrity. (2014: 3705)

Bowie Contagion works in similar ways for G7 and G8:

> *G7*: Yes my signed album and the photograph and video footage of me with bowie getting the autograph. It is my pride and joy framed and permanently on display and talked about when visitors see it

> *G8*: I have a tattoo of Bowie/Aladdin Sane on the inside of my right forearm. This way, he will live on forever on me

(15. Do you have a cherished piece of David Bowie memorabilia?)

G7 keeps a photograph on display of Bowie signing one of his albums. Captured in a photo together, the keepsake is indexical and evidential, a Stadium: there they stand together it signs, fan and star, ever present in time and space. The photograph also acts as a Punctum or 'that accident which pricks, bruises me' (Barthes 1981: 27). Punctum is the rare detail that attracts a viewer/reader to an image, and 'its mere presence changes my reading, that I am looking at a new photograph, marked in my eyes with a higher value' (ibid.) For G7, the Punctum is autobiographical and the 'autograph' cuts through the past materiality of the image, bringing it constantly into life/light for them. For G7's friends, who see it proudly displayed on the mantelpiece, the Punctum is the realisation that G7 shares the same space with 'David Bowie', and the autograph is authentic, marking the image with its autographic and biographic impressions. The importance of the personal autograph was mentioned by a number of our participants when it came to the question of cherished possessions:

> *F14*: Personal autograph dedicated to me and my wife

> *F15*: Loads and loads of things but probably, my most cherished would be the very first autograph, from that first meeting at the March Hare in 1989.

> (15. Do you have a cherished piece of David Bowie memorabilia?)

One can see how having David Bowie autographing a photograph or object would carry such significance for his fans: it is again a form of contagion and requires Bowie to write something especially meaningful for the person in question. What one has in one's possession, then, is the lines made by Bowie's own hands and a message that is singular and unique to the person it is written for, making them feel 'special', as if they have a special connection to him. We saw in Chapter 2 how B7 prised the signing of a drawing that Bowie had done of himself especially for them, commenting on 'his giant B and scribble of a signature'. Bowie is here drawn into the fan-gift economy, to a degree given equal status while remaining exalted. B7 writes as if they are part friends while still showing how Bowie exists as a star figure for them.

The idea of the memorabilia gift is also taken up by H8:

> A present that my boyfriend bought for me for our first Christmas together is a print of David Bowie smoking a cigarette. The print sits up on the shelf in the living room in a place of pride.

> (7. What is your Favourite Album (s)?)

Cherished possessions are either locked away, kept in a box or trove, and only taken out on special occasions, or else they are proudly displayed, often in a designated special place, such as this example that H8 offers us here. Such forms of visibility are connected to wider domestic cultures where cutlery, crockery, vases and ornaments are either locked away or proudly displayed. They are of course also connected to fan cultures and the way that special objects are both private and public, kept secret, or shared in and among the fan community for approval, for bonding and for celebrating (Hills 2003). These are valuable items: both personally and commercially speaking since the rarity of the piece often accrues it great value in the neo-liberal marketplace.

For G8, the item she shares knowledge of is of a tattoo of Bowie as Aladdin Sane: given its location, on the forearm, this will likely be often visible, a proud marker of her fandom. However, the artwork also draws Bowie into the very lining of their skin: co-locates her identity to his, his body to hers, a different form of contagion since while this is only replication or inscription, the sense that Bowie lives on/in her is powerfully observed.

Other memory and object work revealed by our participants centred around the prized possession of certain record albums:

> G2: I have a ragged vinyl of Ziggy Stardust- I'd seen a copy in the only vinyl shop I knew at the time, but I could never afford it. one day it was gone, and I feared I'd never get my hands on one. I asked the owner, and he got mine from his attic, and I only had to pay 5 euros. it doesn't even play very well, it's a bit scratched, but I love it to pieces.

> G6: that is a hard one. My Man Who Sold the World vinyl. When I put it on, it transports me.

> F7: All his albums in vinyl. Those were the cherished objects, the doors to his imaginary worlds, the things that took me to other places.

> F9: Many badges, some rare-ish records and many many magazine clippings. I also have a framed Bowie that I got for my 21st and all of my memories.

> F16: Only the albums, and I think I may be keeping the receipt from my purchase of Blackstar (on the day of release) as a reminder of the emotions and thoughts that prevailed for the two days when that album was unburdened by the knowledge of his death.

(15. Do you have a cherished piece of David Bowie memorabilia?)

Will Straw (1997: 15) has argued that record collecting is distinctly homosocial and masculine and that the 'valorising of the obscure is linked to trash fandoms generally, and the consequent discourse surrounding these is a feature of the homosocial world of young men' (Shuker 2004: 313). However, 58.3% of our respondents identified as female and 25.8% as bisexual or gay suggesting, as Shuker (2004) also does, that record collecting is a much more complex process, especially when tied to fan identifications.

G2 outlines a lovely story of how they came to own a copy of Ziggy Stardust, the story behind the purchase a part of its magic. What we hear and see in the recollection is the record, worn out, playing unevenly on the turntable as they 'love it to pieces'. G6 and F7 link the record to personal transportation and unfettered freedom, where the record—Bowie's voice and music—gives them existential flight. F16 comments that they have kept the receipt for the Black Star album in part because it's both memorial and mausoleum combined: Bowie's voice was already dead when they heard it, a heartbreaking call to ghostly sound and vision. In many ways, our respondents created a contagious archaeology of time out of their shared memories, something we will now go onto discuss.

A Contagious Archaeology of Time

Stars and celebrities operate within and across two time continuums. In so doing, they actualise the way time is generally experienced and contested in what are the uneven liquid streams of the modern age. On the one hand, stars and celebrities exist as the embodiment of linear time or time which is ordered, regular and sequential. This is time with a goal, moving forward with purpose, like the hands of an immaculate timepiece. Stars and celebrities are central to what has been defined as the neoliberal temporal imaginary, which, as Claire Colebrook argues, is linear and spatialised; it is that of a subject 'for whom time is the passage towards complete actualization' (Colebrook 2009: 11; 2012: 21). This 'chrononormativity' contends that we all share the same metered time (Freeman 2010), which we move through 'as though it were composed of successive points that drop away once we pass by' (Neimanis 2014: 117).

Stars and celebrities carry and are carried within discourses that suggest life is made up of a series of sequential stages—one after the other, which we all move through. These stages—child, tween, teen, youth, twenty-something, etc., suggest a deepening of experiences and challenges as one moves through the corridors of life's greater journey. These are also often signalled as moral stories, since if (when) a celebrity goes off the rail at a certain 'stage', their transgressions are used to teach us a lesson about the need to keep on the straight and narrow. This rise-and-fall trajectory is contingent on linear time and creates the conditions for us to experience time as forward moving and with moral speed humps. Drew Barrymore, Macaulay Culkin, Miley Cyrus are all examples of this staged transgression. Closely related to the stages of life trope, stars and celebrities undergo rites of passage (event) moments—where we see them at the prom, passing their driving test, getting married, having their first child, cheating and getting divorced. While these are often heightened and spectacular events, they nonetheless demonstrate the ordinariness of the ritual and of the natural-ness of the moment in time it captures—these are rituals and events we all (must) pass through. Culturally speaking, while rites of passage events are more fluid in their actualisation, they nonetheless become a point in time that dictates that which follows and eventuates in someone's life.

On the other hand, stars and celebrities are also constituted out of, and constituents for, what has been termed thick time heavy with a present-past (Colebrook 2012). In this conceptualisation, time is always an embodied becoming, full of the memories and encounters of what once was. Thick time is not something we are simply 'in' or which we progress 'through' but is rather inaction: a series of intersecting horizontal and vertical layers and sheets we are wrapped in and shaped by, and which is contingent on the spaces, things, objects we are in contact with. Thick time is space and place, thing and human, in dynamic and reverberating relationship. It is, as Neimanis describes, 'made by material agents, including, but not limited to us, in collaboration' (2014: 118). The conceptualisation of thickened time has been taken up by new materialist feminists and queer theorists (Freeman 2010), for example, to demonstrate the possibility and potentiality of time unwound and being constantly remade, always lived and always becoming.

Our respondents' relationship with David Bowie (un)hinges on both these conceptions of time: he is the figure at the centre of the linear stories that fans recall when reflecting on their life and identity, and he is a figure that collapses and recasts the clock of chrononormativity because of the way his multitude of star images exist on top of one another and can be mixed and re-mixed in anti-narrational ways. Time is very often rendered contagious, freely carrying the memories of the past backwards and for-wards. Bowie offers his fans not just a fixed and forward-moving linearity, then, but a way to experience a radical archaeology of time. We now go onto look at both these conceptions of Time.

LINEAR TIME IN CONTAGIOUS SOUND AND VISION

For our respondents, Bowie was remembered in terms of first encounters and event moments: they recall hearing and seeing him for the first time, and they draw upon heightened biographical stories in which Bowie appears as a positive architect of blossoming selfhood. As we highlight in Chapter 3, and above, the recollections that our respondents have of first contact with David Bowie are often familial, with father and mother pivotal, and siblings crucial, in his appearance and sounding in the home or car, or at a special event. Also central is the thread that first impressions became life-long attachments, with Bowie providing a linear way for our respondents to remember major and minor events in chronological order. For example,

> Z1: Hunky Dory. Because it is does not have a bad track. And I have great memories of listening to it as a teenager. Then later on when I first met my adopted son, who was 13 months old, my husband and I played him Kooks - dancing around our kitchen with our boy in my arms - because it sums up what we feel about him, and our attitude to parenting. 'If the homework brings you down then we'll throw it on the fire and take the care downtown' is our anthem along with the line 'we believe in you, so take a chance on a couple of kooks hung up on romancing'.

> Z2: I was just 4 years old and visiting family. I remember hearing music filtering through the door of my cousins' room and felt drawn to go in to hear it better. They were listening to the Aladdin Sane album and I danced and danced for hours. The draw to the music that day led to a lifetime of appreciation for Bowie.

> Z3: I was 12 and I bought Aladdin Sane. Couldn't stop looking at the cover. Listened to it and it was all over. I was hooked.

> Z4: When I saw his appearance on Top of the Pops in 1972 singing Starman, I was fascinated by both the song and of course David. I got the Ziggy album straightaway. That was the start of a lifetimes appreciation of his work. Z2

> Z5: 13 years old - my friend at school loved David Bowie - I remember watching The Hunger and being transfixed by it. We shared love for John Lennon and David Bowie and often used their identities to wrap around ours - a preferred identity.

> Z6: See Ziggy on TV in the UK in 1972 and thinking I want to meet this
> wonderful character/alien/man. That was in Black and white at the time,
> so when I did see the full colour images my jaw dropped. He started to
> scare in the most enchanting way. I developed a life-long intrigue with
> his writing, performance, singing and personas since.

For Z2, a landscape of remembrance is recalled: a family visit, music pouring out from behind a closed bedroom door, discovery and then the reverence of dancing and dancing to Aladdin Sane. Z1 charts this introduction as life-changing and life-lasting. Similarly, for Z3, and Z4, both the image of the Bowie and the songs themselves provided them with a connection that lasted for all their life. Bowie's transgressive, border crossing Aladdin Sane and Starman clearly resonates with them, as does the enchanted music, which becomes a sonic envelope they carry with them for the duration of their lives. Z3 seems to be arrested by the Aladdin Sane Bowie album cover, holding them in its strange spell. Z6 picks up on this, recalling the shock that they felt when they saw Bowie for the first time in colour.

Shock and fear are usually identified as two negative emotions or reactions but here are seen to be positively transformative: perhaps liberating the docile body from its governed instrumentality. Z5's recollection of watching *The Hunger*, a vampire film, draws also on this theme of pleasurable distaste. One can situate these reactions within the notion of disgust which can be understood to be a gatekeeper emotion; a technique or mechanism that is used to propel or keep at bay that which threatens one. Disgust can also be understood as an anti-democratic force that opens up the body to new experiences and sensations that are usually repressed or denied expression. Disgust can be understood to be a border crossing emotion, a particularly hyper-charged form of affect, a type of 'beyond' normal experience that cuts one free from language and a stable or simply known subjectivity.

This aural–visual alignment—hearing Bowie strangely, while strangely seeing his animalised, hybrid self—allows fans to enter an enchanted world where his hybridity opens up new otherworldly spaces to exist in and new liminal identity positions for people to 'try on' and embody (Frith 1996; Bennett 1999). This is much less a conscious remaking of self than a sensorial leap into welcoming aural–visual textures.

One can make the argument here that while David Bowie can be seen to be pivotal to the respondents stages of life maturation and is the crux at many of their ritualised events, he does so to undermine the patriarchal and heterosexual script and to offer bonds of communion which go against the grain of dominant ideology. He allows one to experience the stages of life through a resistant aesthetic—through rites and rituals that are simultaneously enchanted and 'realistic'. Simon Frith (1996: 123) writes:

> But if musical identity is, then, always fantastic, idealizing not just oneself but also the social world one inhabits, it is, secondly, always also real, enacted in musical activities. Music making and music listening, that is to say, are bodily matters; involve what one might call social movements. In this respect, musical pleasure is not derived from fantasy – it is not mediated by dreams – but is experienced directly: music gives us a real experience of what the ideal could be.

The 'ideal' that our respondents find in David Bowie is the counter-ideal: the one that celebrates the marginal, ignites the heart of the lonely and fuels the fires of counter-culture resistance and self-renewal and alien selfhood that is hopeful.

What is striking about the responses we received is the sense that Bowie was an ever-present, even when his star image may have waned in terms of popular, public appeal. Our respondents don't dwell on his absence or absences, his failures and missteps, but create a living tissue of memory as they recall him. That said, one can also see how Bowie fandom also exists as a quivering labyrinth: where Time is everywhere and nowhere, here and there, this place and that place, a series of intersecting layers. This is contagious Time that spreads out virally.

BowieViralTime

One can make sense of the way our respondents remember David Bowie through reference to a form of escapism from materialist life and linear time, into an exquisite hinterland where time stretches out. Such forms of time unwound readily produce an 'unheimlich (uncanny) feeling of being disrupted or torn out of one's default sensory-psychic-intellectual disposition' (Bennett 2001: 5). When listening to, and/or watching David Bowie, fans often felt re-mobilised, enraptured, cut free from the physical and psychological limitations of place, space and body, and are exhilarated as a consequence (also see Chapter 6). Bowie's music—the alien figure that creates it—provides an escape from the limiting confines and regulatory conditions of everyday life, where his fans exist in a transcendental habitus.

As we saw in Chapter 2, A2 defines this experience as magical and what they understood to be the very definition of out-of-body rhapsody. In this long, and affecting confessional, D3 outlines the way that Bowie sets his time, place and body free:

> If there is a single message that carries through Bowie's life, not just his music, it's that we aren't by ourselves. This message resonates all throughout the "Ziggy Stardust" album in particular. I can remember singing along with this one in the bathroom, when I was overwhelmed by the pain and difficulty of adolescence...
>
> In my last year of high school, I was bullied relentlessly by one person in particular, to the point that I missed a lot of school. I was struggling with debilitating anxiety problems, and medicated to the point that when I discontinued, the brutality of withdrawal itself threw me into despair. I had weird hair and a weird body and weird taste in music, and nobody understood what I was about. And then there was Bowie. With an orange shaggy haircut that he invented, his mismatched eyes, white skin painted over his thin limbs... Playing this weird, fearless, deep, cryptic music. Ziggy Stardust told me:
>
> > Oh no, love, you're not alone.
> > You're watching yourself, but you're too unfair.
> > You got your head all tangled up, but if I could only make you care!
> > Oh, no, love! You're not alone,
> > No matter what or who you've been,
> > No matter when or where you've seen.
> > All the knives seem to lacerate your brain,
> > I've had my share, I'll help you with the pain,
> > You're not alone.

D3's response here is a fantastic accumulation of thoughts, pronouncements, layered over one another. While there is an attempt to formulise a linear narration, charting adolescent milestones and life-lessons, what we have instead is the insertion of the past into the present, as the tense subtly shifts or reverberates in the prose and as the lyrics to the song that were first heard 'then' are 'recalled' (sung?) in the present. Reality is clouded by medication, withdrawals, low self-esteem, and yet is recuperated through the figure of Bowie. Further, the strangeness that Z15 feels as a teenager seems to carry forward into the present, cracking open the sediments of Time.

We can also see how Bowie enters the dreams and anxieties of his respondents, collapsing or conjoining the conscious with the unconscious, real time with the fantasies and traumas of dream time. A number of our respondents begin to suggest that BowieViralTime occupies numerous physical, psychological and dreaming and waking states way beyond the earthly. For example,

Z16: I have met Bowie a 1000 times in my dreams and each time it felt so real! I remember one vivid dream where I asked him about his own baby boy & why he had called him Zowie, we talked for what seemed like hours about all things family & loss (I had just lost my baby daughter that week) we listened to Kooks & I cried with him for my loss & it felt so real & he understood I'm sure I was just mad with grief but Bowies words seem to calm me.

Z17: Indeed, at my most freaked out period in my twenties, I believed his alien force was descending upon me and I was directly communicating with David Bowie, who walked in from another universe. So cliched, so predictably ordinary, this fantasy: nevertheless, an indication of our collective belief in the man. His uncanny power to light up our imaginations as if from another planet. Was it accident or design that associated him with outer space and astronauts?

Z18: I was 8 years old and I dreamt that I had a gathering of musicians at my home. Marc Bolan, David Bowie etc. David Bowie came into my room to see my records and posters. He liked my collection and kissed me on the cheek. As he was wearing make up, I went back to the lounge room with a blue lipstick kiss on my cheek. Everyone was so surprised and shocked yet I felt great to be weird and different. I have been a dedicated fan since that dream.

Z19: in my early twenties, I had a masochistic dream, which manifest images connected to the words: "all the lies that would lacerate your brain", and interpreted it from a place of polymorphous perversity only Bowie could signify. But more obviously, there have been many dreams in which I attend a Bowie concert and then he seeks me out to tell me I alone understand him. As I reach to others to join the experience, he gently and politely (as was his way) stops me and tells me it is myself alone he has come to see, that I understand his art as no one else does. It is a meeting of minds and feels quintessentially spiritual: like the feeling of meditation, of prayer and erotic satiation all in one. The narcissism behind this is laughable, but in dreams the profundity of this meeting with the shaman feels like eroticism to the power of one hundred.

(Question 12: Did you fantasize about meeting David Bowie – or meet him for real?)

For Z17, there is, of course, a science fiction element here, where David Bowie is the Alien Messiah, translating the figure of the outsider to messianic and outer-worldly propensities. Z16's reflections on a dream in which she mourns the loss of her baby, with David Bowie confident and counsellor, is profound, granting him presence at the most intimate of times, while Z19's masochistic dream returns us to the theme of perversity and self-love, where they become equal to Bowie. Z18's innocent dream that ends up with Bowie kissing her on their cheek is sublimation and sweet recollection. Nonetheless, together they create a re-conceptualisation of Time, each recollection infecting the other, as these Time contagions blur and conjoin. This is a form of VirtualTime.

When fans search online for images and stories of their favourite star, the search engine throws up the many moments of their star images. These starry images are not ordered in a linear fashion at all but are subject to algorithms and real-time events that might change or effect what images are presented before them. Set in a sea of accumulations, the star or celebrity appears with all their stages and rituals set freely before them.

This is not, then, linear time but all of time at once. All of time at once is the past meeting the present, the present visiting the past and the past-present, present-past touching the hands of the future. Matter and materiality are of course important here. Karen Barad (2007) writes of 'intra-active becoming as indicative of a collaborative, productive, and open-ended relationship between time and matter' (178). In the here/now and there/then, montage of celebrity faces the screens materially contain and maintain and sustain the 'living present'. So is true of the photo albums that fans keep and the memories they store and share of David Bowie: each time we revisit them, re-tell them, something else is highlighted, remembered, lost or forgotten. Each time a new layer of 'you, 'me' or 'I' emerges, one's selfhood sits upon the one before, and the layers before you weave themselves into your (now) updated biography. When one thinks of David Bowie, recalls his music, performances, importance, a whole interconnecting cosmos of possibilities opens up before one. This changes every Time.

The thick time of stars and celebrities ultimately exist as personal and intimate carriers and conveyors of dynamic temporality—this is not a temporal imposition, which clocks us in and out, but one fashioned out of the self as it is really lived in the world. Thick time is shared with, in, through and across places, spaces, people, memories, mementoes and keepsakes. In relation to the fandom of David Bowie, this thick time personalised involves memorial and material work, archiving and rituals, actions and reactions, talk and walking, hearing and seeing—rhythmically beating out the endless possibilities of the world—the enchanted world—where there is life on Mars.

REFERENCES

Ahmed, Sara. "Sociable Happiness." *Emotion, Space and Society* 1 (1) (2008): 10–13.
Anderson, Tonya. "Still Kissing Their Posters Goodnight: Female Fandom and the Politics of Popular Music." *Journal of Audience & Reception Studies* 9 (2) (2012): 239–264.
Barad, Karen. *Meeting the Universe Halfway*. Durham, NC: Duke University Press, 2007.
Barthes, Roland. *Camera Lucida: Reflections on Photography*. London: Macmillan, 1981.
Belk, Russell W. "The Ineluctable Mysteries of Possessions." In *To Have Possessions: A Handbook on Ownership and Property* [Special issue], ed. F. W. Rudmin. *Journal of Social Behavior and Personality* 6 (1991): 17–55.
Bennett, Andy. "Subcultures or Neo-tribes? Rethinking the Relationship Between Youth, Style and Musical Taste." *Sociology* 33 (3) (1999): 599–617.
Bennett, Jane. *The Enchantment of Modern Life*. Princeton: Princeton University Press, 2001.
Casey, Edward. *Remembering: A Phenomenological Study*. Bloomington: Indiana University Press, 1987.
Colebrook, Claire. "Stratigraphic Time, Women's Time1." *Australian Feminist Studies* 24 (59) (2009): 11–16.
Colebrook, Claire. "A Globe of One's Own: In Praise of the Flat Earth." *SubStance* 127 (41) (2012): 30–39.
Crane, Susan A. "Writing the Individual Back into Collective Memory." *The American Historical Review* 102 (5) (1997): 1372–1385.
Finnegan, Ruth. "Music, Experience and the Anthropology of Emotion." In *The Cultural Study of Music*, ed. Martin Clayton, Trevor Herbert, and Richard Middleton, 181–192. London: Routledge, 2003.
Freeman, Elizabeth. *Time Binds*. Durham: Duke University Press, 2010.

Frith, Simon. "Music and Identity." In *Questions of Cultural Identity*, ed. Stuart Hall and Paul Du Gay, 108–127. London: Sage, 1996.

Hall, Stuart. "The Neo-Liberal Revolution." *Cultural Studies* 25 (2011): 6.

Harrington, C. Lee, Denise D. Bielby, and Anthony R. Bardo. "Life Course Transitions and the Future of Fandom." *International Journal of Cultural Studies* 14 (6) (2011): 567–590.

Hesmondhalgh, David. "Towards a Critical Understanding of Music, Emotion and Self-Identity." *Consumption, Markets and Culture* 11 (4) (2008): 329–343.

Hills, Matthew. *Fan Cultures*. London: Routledge, 2003.

Hoelscher, Steven, and Derek H. Alderman. "Memory and Place: Geographies of a Critical Relationship." *Social & Cultural Geography* 5 (3) (2004): 347–355.

Jones, Owain. "Geography, Memory and Non-representational Geographies." *Geography Compass* 5 (12) (2011): 875–885.

Kuhn, Annette. *Family Secrets: Acts of Memory and Imagination*. London and New York: Verso, 1995.

Kuhn, Annette. "Memory Texts and Memory Work: Performances of Memory in and with Visual Media." *Memory Studies* 3 (4) (2013): 298–313.

Kroger, Jane, and Vivienne Adair. "Symbolic meanings of valued personal objects in identity transitions of late adulthood." *Identity: An International Journal of Theory and Research* 8 (1) (2008): 5–24.

Megill, Allan. "History, Memory, Identity." *History of the Human Sciences* 11 (3) (1998): 37–62.

Neimanis, Astrida. "Speculative Reproduction: Biotechnologies and Ecologies in Thick Time." *philoSOPHIA* 4 (1) (2014): 108–128.

Newman, George E., and Paul Bloom. "Physical Contact Influences How Much People Pay at Celebrity Auctions." *Proceedings of the National Academy of Sciences* 111 (10) (2014): 3705–3708.

North, Adrian C., and David J. Hargreaves. "Music and Adolescent Identity." *Music Education Research* 1 (1) (1999): 75–92.

O'Sullivan, Simon. "The Aesthetics of Affect: Thinking Art Beyond Representation." *Angelaki Journal of the Theoretical Humanities* 6 (3) (2001): 125–135.

Rochberg-Halton, Eugene. "Object Relations, Role Models, and Cultivation of the Self." *Environment and Behavior* 16 (3) (1984): 335–368.

Shuker, Roy. "Beyond the 'High Fidelity' Stereotype: Defining the (Contemporary) Record Collector." *Popular Music* 23 (3) (2004): 311–330.

Straw, Will. "Sizing Up Record Collections: Gender and Connoisseurship in Rock Music Culture." In *Sexing the Groove: Popular Music and Gender*, ed. S. Whiteley, 3–16. London: Routledge, 1997.

Tait, Gordon. "Re-assessing Street Kids: A Critique of Subculture Theory." In *Child and Youth Care Forum* 22 (2) (1993): 83–93.

Totaro, Donato. "Deleuzian Film Analysis: The Skin of the Film, Off-Screen." 2002. www.horschamp.qc.ca/new_offscreen/skin.html. Accessed 1 August 2011.

Van Dijck, José. "Record and Hold: Popular Music Between Personal and Collective Memory." *Critical Studies in Media Communication* 23 (5) (2006): 357–374.

CHAPTER 6

Being There/Being Him

INTRODUCTION

Throughout his career, David Bowie's artistic compositions drew upon an exhibitionistic image, deliberation and virtuosity in performance. Experiencing David Bowie live in concert, one quickly appreciates his grasp of affective presentation (as we saw in Chapter 3). Bowie does not just create silent awe in the majority of his fans. Rather, his fans find exuberant wonderment in special live encounters. Fans deliberately fashion personal meaning, taking particular joy in his markedly emotive spectacle. In this chapter, we firstly unravel the nature of David Bowie's performances towards a specific purpose of exploring the ways that fans themselves have metaphorically and physically 'performed David Bowie' in professional and socio-sympoietic entanglements, or in the domestic and the most personal of ways. Here, we explore the means by which fans adopt, transcode and extend various Bowie star images or personae. In the sections that follow, we will meet these performances through the fans' recollections, individually and in focus groups, of their real life and 'live' encounters seeing and 'being' David Bowie.

While reference is made to the musician, recording artist, public performer, actor, artist as 'David Bowie', it is clear that on another level David Jones never changed; he just exercised different metaphors and metonyms at various times for different purposes and different performances. By that is meant that through the overarching 'Bowie' (the actor's actor), the creative work becomes a metathesis for life's grit. Jones used Bowie to

© The Author(s) 2019
T. Cinque and S. Redmond, *The Fandom of David Bowie*,
https://doi.org/10.1007/978-3-030-15880-4_6

move on stardom's stage. In a 1973 interview for the BBC1 news programme, Nationwide, he explained that: 'I am very much a character when I'm onstage ... that's what "Bowie" is supposed to be about'. Indeed, he employed the trope of artist in the mould of Giacomo Puccini's Rodolfo in the opera *La Bohème*. Rudolfo is a talented but starving poet who lives in a sparsely furnished single-room garret along with his friends: the painter, the philosopher and the musician. The interesting parallel to be drawn here is that Bowie was simultaneously all of these characters, imaginatively paradoxical, hungering not for food but creativity. Artistically, Bowie has appeared to build from inside, that is, from an internalised backstory and from vulnerabilities for dyadic reactions.

In acting himself, Michael Chekhov (1985) developed the use of the 'Psychological Gesture', an acting method for expressing the essence of an archetype (to love, to take, to desire, to hurt and so on) and found that genuine actors hold within themselves the aptitude to inhabit the internal process of performance. For Chekhov, action from internal thought becomes an artistic frame the actor uses to make the gesture initially without the physical body or via 'intangible means of expression'; an inner energy of the feeling body for later translation into an outer expression (Petit 2010: 64). Waldrep (2004: 110) writes that Bowie 'transposed the conventions of one ancient art form onto a relatively new one' as a rock performer. Feeling the results of Bowie's many performances, J1 told us that from their perspective:

> David Bowie was a consummate performer. He chose what parts of his life he shared, but when he opened up, you felt like you knew everything about that part of his life. It felt like he knew exactly how to control his messaging.

For this respondent, through his choices and measure, David Bowie's performances were seemingly controlled intimacies that left them raw. Drawing on this thread, David Bowie embodies the symbolic complexities of art and culture signalling exotic and aesthetic strangeness in critically important aural and visual ways that so many fans have found appealing. For KX in our study, the creative intrigue for them was that:

> Bowie could write songs inspired by Nietzsche and he could do an elaborate piece of performance art showcasing the fluidity of identity and attract hordes of screaming fans. He was a relentless autodidact who poured every strange idea he encountered into his art.

(Question 6: What does David Bowie mean to you?)

LIVE PERFORMANCE AND THE RESONANCES
OF THE FEELING BODY

David Bowie's live performances especially have generated particular artistic and narrative frames that have enchanted his audiences. His characters over time such as Ziggy Stardust, Aladdin Sane and the Thin White Duke for example offer templates that emerge and re-emerge as aspects of personality that fans themselves have drawn upon and replicated in their self-reflexive journeying through life. Gramsci is correct when he defends that: '[t]he starting point of critical elaboration is the consciousness of what [and who] one really is' (Gramsci 1971: 324). A participant in our study, J2, confessed to us that:

> Bowie was an early influence on being authentic and creative. To hell with the riches, what does an artist have to say? And I learned to continue being creative and to always look for new ways to express myself and create art. Though I became a writer and stage performer, my first love has always been music and Bowie was a first love of my first love.

Their light shined powerfully through these words so that we appreciate deeply that fans are active stakeholders in their 'becoming'; ruminating as much on the circumstances of their own making as on the professed subject of their attention who inspired their continued focus, even love. As a result, the affects of Bowie's own creative practices have themselves been transposed many times over onto and by his fans—with good reason.

The linguist, Zoltán Kövecses (2002: 60), in contemplating classical literature has argued that one's ability to understand conceptual metaphors could actually save the individual's life (as it did for Oedipus from the Sphinx). This is because metaphors allow for: 'the representation of nonimmediate experience ... making sense of the world, enabling making inferences from the representations used, and allowing for productivity and creativity' (Kövecses 2015: 46). Against this background, made palpable is that David Bowie's own use of metaphor and metonym throughout his visual and sonic creations largely freed him from the constraints of merely describing the world. Bowie's artistic metaphors are able to simultaneously describe what 'is' and what 'is not', therefore, giving rise to a tension in what might be perceived as real. Metaphors consequently amplify our comprehension of reality. It is through producing and maintaining multiple tensions that metaphor is able to articulate that which is inexpressible. Ricoeur has argued that metaphor has the capacity to: 'make sense with nonsense, to transform a self-contradictory statement into a significant self-contradiction' whereby metaphor might give the impression that it is: 'the solution of an enigma' (Ricoeur 1991: 78). It is without doubt that David Bowie makes sense despite the seemingly contradictory nonsense.

This position by extension sees Bowie's use of metaphor and metonym to have afforded him and his fans both possible re-evaluations of the world, in new ways, by breaking the association between language and things to discover the important spaces between. Bowie' own lyrical and visual assemblages have allowed fissures to be created with new and multiple meanings rendered possible and valid for his fans, providing them in part with an interpretative framework for inner contemplation and outer presentation in daily living. Many fans attest to this, finding themselves drawn to the enigma of Bowie's deeply evocative presence on a personal level. Responding to this notion for how they have performed in their everyday, participant K1 stated that for them:

> He was the ONE above all that made me see the potential of a creative life, that it could make you extraordinary, that one could play with words and identities and make a life from it, that there was spirituality within the creative life.

Threaded throughout some fifty years of David Bowie's experiential phenomena are hints towards a mutuality between constitutive factors that consequently afford possibilities for positive individual experiences and in forming and performing an 'identity' through Bowie. Enmeshed within affective arrangements are what Fuchs (2016: 197) argues are two emotion components of bodily resonance. The first is: 'a centripetal or affective component, i.e. being affected, "moved" or "touched" by an event or person through various forms of bodily sensations'. An example of this form might be perspiring or blushing or an elevated pulse rate in response to one's 'object of desire'; a meeting with a star or seeing them in real life such as the stirring memory recalled by a survey participant KL:

> I was standing feet away from him, right opposite him and it felt as if we were dancing together. He smiled at me and made eye contact so many times over the course of that night. It was the best night of my life.

The recollection of KL above depicts an encounter of undeniable transcendence as they interacted with David Bowie in a moment felt to them as
akin to the intimate movements shared shyly between lovers. For them,
this 'meeting' for just a moment in time has remained long embedded in
the recesses of their heart and is felt keenly still. Another participant in
our study, BK remembers experiences of David Bowie live in concert as
intimately inspiring a certain aesthetic submission:

> I was able to see David Bowie twice in concert. The first time was at the Rock
> Torhout/ Rock Werchter Concert in Werchter, Belgium in July 5, 1997. I
> was 13 years old at the time. My family was taking a European vacation,
> ending with a visit with family friends that had moved to Belgium. I found
> out that the Torhout concert that was the same time as our visit. My mom
> spent hours on the phone trying to get tickets. It was an amazing show. It
> was a huge arena, much like the Lollapalooza concerts that I had attended
> in the States. But the energy of this show was different and the attitude was
> more relaxed. Bowie's performance was amazing, but I was much farther
> from the stage than I would have liked. I later saw David Bowie perform at
> the Aragon Ballroom in Chicago on October 17, 1997. The venue is very
> small and intimate, which totally changed the feel of the show from Tourhot.
> I was able to stand in the front row and actually touched David's hand when
> he reached down into the crowd. This show is probably my favorite that I
> have ever attended. It is what I judge everything else by.

These recollections by the fans KL and BK confer momentary physical
connections, intimate movements, sight and touch with/of Bowie that for
them was real, poignant and remains long-standing. Such moments are
often individually felt by fans but also shared with close friends in a sort of
communion of cultural significance. From another fan, KJ's stories in time,
they made multiple pilgrimages to meet David Bowie, driving many miles
to see him or to chat in person (see also Chapter 9). In specific detail they
told us:

> *KJ*: I've met David about 12-13 times. One time, on the 19th September
> 2002, David was on the Parkinson chat show and, with many other fans,
> I was in the audience. After the show, a few of us waited on Wood Lane at
> the BBC entrance for David's car to pull out so we could shout 'thanks'
> and wave. It was quite a while before the car eventually came, and there
> was only seven us there. But it stopped. Erik got out of the front passenger
> seat and opened the back door for David to get out. He thanked us and
> shook all our hands. There have been other meets, another was at the

docks in Southampton when he got the QE2 back to NY after the tour in 2002. We went to give him a send-off and got autographs and photos.

From the first aspect of being intimately moved via bodily sensations, the second 'emotive component' of affective arrangements here implies a propensity to move the body towards a craved object as forcible action through specific tendencies of movement including physical (desirous) approach and being-with 'it'/them or others for enjoyment (Fuchs 2016). Together these arrangements experienced frequently across time and space, always charged with affective qualities, have lured fans to bodily resonate and render the affective aspects of engagement more salient as noted above. Similar such instances are found when fans share their thoughts and emotions in fan clubs (both online and offline—a motif of fandom studies explored further in Chapter 8) as well as in live encounters at concerts or chance encounters with their object of desire. When we asked participants in our survey: 'Have you ever seen David Bowie live in concert or on stage?' (Q 11), for what the experience meant to them, special memories of encounters were evoked:

> *K8:* Twice, in his late career - the *Heathen Tour* and *Reality Tour*. The first performance was especially memorable because he played through the whole *Low* album, one of my favourites. My head was buzzing and trying to soak it all in. Couldn't believe I'm hearing those songs live. The second time his performance was cut short by health problems, which made the closing number ('The Man Who Sold The World') very powerful.

> *K9:* Yes, only once at Wembley for the *Reality Tour*. He played 25 songs and I was so impressed by his respect for the fans in playing the big hitters as well as new material ... I remember being so proud to be a Bowie fan, knowing that he genuinely respected us enough to put on an incredible show.

In accord with the suasory arguments of Fuchs (2016), resonances were felt in these fans as if they were intercorporeal as individuals collectively experience and consequently respond to others that they are in physical contact with or close proximity to in a given situation. Often special live encounters fervently shared in unity with others become important for what they might mean, not only to themselves, but the broader fan community. As participant K10 recalls of the first time, they saw David Bowie live in concerts:

The first was in 1972. I was a wide eyed 10 year old kid with an equally wide eyed 32 year old mother. She used to take me to all kinds of concerts but this, this was so different. It was performance art infused by music. We couldn't talk about it for a few days afterwards. When we could it was about the ideas, the costumes, and the huge girl crush I decided I had on Mick Ronson. Each time I saw him after that on every tour was so different, yet so reassuring that he was David. The last time I saw him was on the Reality Tour. I miss him so very much.

Suggestive here is the possibility to attribute a certain intrinsic teleology to the bio-system itself. Overarchingly, this is not, however, an attempt to break the individual and their experiences down into isolationist parts. Instead, we trace the arc of Plessner's philosophical anthropology with its emphasis on the intimate proximity of the individual to the fundamental layers of meaningful behaviours within the interactive context (Plessner 1970). As Loenhoff (2017) convincing demonstrates (and taken up further below), there is an important interplay between the individual in milieu-specific contexts and one is not constituted as a singular entity (nor mind versus body) adrift from such sociocultural forms. Rather, we possess a 'transactional body' affording an exchange or interaction with others. Surprising reflections of corporeal experiences and sensations were registered by fans when they were asked (Q 11): 'Have you ever seen David Bowie live in concert or on stage?':

> K5: I saw him in Cardiff on his *Glass Spider Tour*. I started off the day getting myself ready, i.e. Aladdin Sane make-up etc. Waited patiently through the other bands hence David slides down the Spider and everything is a blur. I cried throughout most of his performance.

> K6: Yes. *Reality Tour* 2004, Sydney Entertainment Centre. I was 19 and had only recently moved out of home. I had no money, but I went and bought a ticket for my best friend. We stood and yelled and sang and cried and practically floated home afterwards and declared to my flatmates that I could now die happy.

> KP: Yes, firstly, the *Serious Moonlight Tour*. My passion for his music had diminished by then but I was blown away. It was the perfect pop gig. Secondly in 2002, I think at Old Trafford cricket ground in Manchester. It pissed down all day. Bowie had played the whole Low album at previous gigs, I was praying he'd do the same in Manchester. He came on a-la thin white duke (white shirt, black trousers and waistcoat), walked to the right apron

of the stage, looked to the sky and raised his arms in a pose reminiscent of the Heroes cover and instantly, the clouds parted, the sun came out and the rain stopped. Seriously.

The haecceity of David Bowie is impossible to define for his especial individuation and the emotions he inspires, but his impact is most certainly felt by his fans. For some, he is sensed as being somewhat god-like, able to command the natural elements—and in some ways he does do this when his fans shed tears of joy, burst with song and render themselves to utter jubilation during such live encounters. A certain reformation occurs within them when such shared experiences in awe become more than mere entertainment. K7 told us that they had seen David Bowie live in concert several times and for them:

> *K7*: I was in awe at seeing him after 12 years of solitary experience. Hearing Heroes live that night put me in some kind of a trance. I saw him in London in 1997 at a tiny gig. Me and my girlfriend - now wife - were so wound up by The Motel that he noticed from the stage. We saw him in Vienna in 1999 and several times on the Heathen and Reality tours in 2002-4. We once experienced him playing the complete Low album live, in Germany in 2002. A gig of three and a half hours, if I remember correctly. He always managed to engage the audience and create an experience that would live in the memories of the audience.

What the fans here refer to is the affect of the concert event channelling fan energy. Without doubt, the key is David Bowie's magnetism, variously perceived, for why he is so deeply identified with and loved by his fans. The strength of aesthetic appreciation or adoration can conversely reduce fans to a state of speechless resignation. One fan, TB explained to us that even though they chanced upon David Bowie as an 'everyday man' simply going to a music performance, they became so shy on actually encountering him:

> I met him once briefly at a Mick Ronson concert. David and Angie Bowie came up to the seats I was sitting into see the gig from the audience. Angie Bowie thought we were in her seats and struggled past me. They then sat just behind me for the whole gig. I met him in the interval but couldn't speak!

The delightful examples above suggest that live moments 'experiencing' Bowie, be it in a trance-like state, yelling, screaming, crying, being 'blown away' or standing in awe, were felt by the participants in our study to resonate in their entire bodies. The body is, however, a complex system and emotions are relevant to the circulation of Bowie's affect-producing music, visual work and creative performances.

Ratiocinating from a slightly different theoretical perspective now, research by Nunn and Biressi (2010: 49–50) found that the economies of affect and intimacy now structure public life and authenticity in the public sphere, demanding and compelling performances of emotion and intimacy, or 'emotion work'. The authors proposed that stars and celebrities are actually emotional labourers whereby the tensions and dilemmas at the heart of celebrity emotional labour critically foreground the affective terrain which all individuals are forced to negotiate in the public realm in order to be regarded as socially successful. Useful to this understanding is the definition of 'emotion work' as proposed by sociologist Arlie Hochschild (1979, 2003) which is work requiring the artist to perform the 'right' feeling and ultimately even 'feel' the right feeling according to the rules of the setting and often in the service of commerce (Nunn and Biressi 2010: 50). The ideology of intimacy and the primacy of emotion in performing authentic and normative subjecthood means that frequently the celebrity figure performing emotion is at the high (visible) end of a spectrum of emotional conduct (Nunn and Biressi 2010). In other words, 'ideology of intimacy' has formed the conditions in which the celebrity now labours as an emotional subject in the public realm. This ideology operates via the conviction that social relationships are considered to be 'authentic' or 'real' mainly by virtue of their commitment to the 'inner psychological concerns of each person' (Sennett 1974: 259). Not surprisingly then, some understand Bowie's live performances to have been tightly choreographed, and professionally controlled experiences, as Mackay (1984 in Thomson and Gutman 1996: 195) recounts of Bowie performing live in the 1980s:

> Carefully timing the removal of his jacket. Selecting the right moment to casually roll up the sleeves of his shirt. Nonchalantly loosening his tie. In earlier rock eras, these movements might have been in the heat of the moment. But not now. Not for Bowie. He's in control.

As noted above, research into rock music performance and audience response reveals that the production of affect is of critical importance in negotiating the seeming authority and legitimacy of the music. In the context of contemporary challenges to 'authentic' productions of affect, it becomes reasonable to consider that fans come to experience authenticity of intent. On emotion here, and not with little allusion to Michael Chekhov's 'Psychological Gesture', Bowie has explained the influence for his own music and image arising from the artistic traditions of music theatre: 'I want to portray emotions symbolically' (Gore 1997: 46–47). The 'stylistic gesture' as Bowie referred to drawing emotions such as the sharp vicissitudes of love, desire/despair or anger is aimed at calling forth feelings in fans and the listening/viewing audience in contrast to luring 'the audience into the emotional content of what you are doing' (Gore 1997: 46–47).

What is worth underscoring at the same time though is that David Bowie was mercurial. It is equally the case that he has been disingenuous frequently and some of his public statements ostensibly ironic. Setting this aside, one can indeed see that Bowie's work over time has used a kind of metonym of emotion in order to mobilise the emotion of listening and viewing bodies and without doubt, this has channelled affect into positive, critical contemplation and politic action in many of his fans. For example, L5 recalled for us their personal and emotional story when asked the question: 'Please recall and describe what your first memory of encountering David Bowie is?' (Q 6). They articulated a story of painful childhood memories, but stressed to us that positive healing swirled amongst their 'becoming' a mature adult through their fandom:

> Listening to him while reading alone in England. When I began living in the States, I immersed myself in all things Bowie and hid away from the other kids who teased me for being different. He helped me get through a lot of hard times. He let me feel all right, while feeling like a freak.

David Bowie has himself emotively embodied certain identity positions that are alien, alternative and transgressive via metaphor and alter egos as we saw in Chapter 3. This has demonstratively allowed an atmosphere of strangeness to rise up about him that resonated with kindred speculative souls. As survey respondent D3 told us and recalled for emphasis here:

> *D3*: With an orange shaggy haircut that he invented, his mismatched eyes, white skin painted over his thin limbs, playing this weird, fearless, deep, cryptic music, Ziggy Stardust told me: Oh no, love, you're not alone … Bowie made it okay to be an Outsider. He made it okay to be smart and interested in "strange" or obscure things … he has helped me to realize that self-expression can happen in a variety of ways, through your

music, your actions, or your image, and that it's okay to *re*invent yourself [emphasis added].

The narrative of Bowie's physical body circulated predominantly as one of translucent androgyny, but also that he is 'cyborg', characterised by a sense of otherworldliness that drew many to him. For feminist author and Professor of Humanities and Media Studies, Camille Paglia (1990: 368), David Bowie in the 1970s was the 'classic modern android' when his 'skull-like face seemed coldly artificial'. The affect of his controlled and haughty mask-like mannequin style for many Bowie-boys and Bowie-girls was sexually and/or fashionably desirable and therefor imitated. Ziggy Stardust was the perfect metaphor for 'the outsider' to be drawn upon by his fans and other marginalised creatures as they (re)imagined their own respective destinies. For Nicolas Roeg's character of Thomas Jerome Newton in the film *The Man Who Fell to Earth* (1976), his performative 'look' made the perfect alien outer-body. In some ways, Bowie's 'alien' appearance also symbolised a certain anti-humanist position that begged off being part of the pre-constituted and structured society that he then inhabited should the limits to what one could 'be' or 'do' beyond the normative bounds remain.

One certainly understands that Bowie's image has not remained static over time. His various characters might quickly be recognised as denoting 'change' as being inevitable, be it growing up/growing old, but this can be tolerable and even interesting. In our study, a number of participants told us that they had a sense of wanting to be like Bowie from their earliest years. This was not in terms of literally changing places with him, but adopting his particular creative/intellectual approach or 'essence' that they had experienced and which seemed to them to be powerful. When asked: 'Please recall and describe what your first memory of encountering David Bowie is?' (Q 6), KS1 and C6 recalled that:

> *KS1*: We always had music playing … I remember hearing Space Oddity on the radio. Was instantly in love with this idea. As a 9-year-old in the early 1970s with a huge imagination, this alien singing over the airwaves made everything seem possible.

> *C6*: Lying on the floor of the flat with dad when I was 3 or so, watching lights strobe as we listened to The Rise and Fall of Ziggy Stardust and the Spiders from Mars. I remember wanting to be whatever that person was making the music.

Drawn by the creative world, David Bowie emerged as someone who thought deeply and wanted to be the author of his own star image and a number of fans aimed to do the same or at least aimed for self-improvement, be it intellectual, creative and/or socio-economic (see Chapter 7). Bowie wanted to be seen as an 'auteur' and through particular metonyms of emotion he successfully mobilised reaction and channelled affect into action via his visual and sonic creativity. Bowie provided a star image as an interpretative framework for inner contemplation, simultaneously subverting the creative cultural industry from which he emerged. This confirms him as an empowering figure and disruptive agent whose work underlines the early intertextual writing of Richard Dyer in *Stars* (1979): that the value of stars and their art affords consideration for the ways we understand ourselves and others.

Fans Being Bowie: The Flourishing of the Earthly Ones

As we have discussed, our stars provide us with narrative frames or ways to understand and interpret the world around us. Consider too, the ideas of French philosopher, historian and postmodern theorist Michel Foucault (2005, 2013), who argued that we should actively and critically question 'widely deployed' discourses of the grand narratives such as sex, race, nationality, class, gender, age, mortality and sanity, among other 'categories' or ways of classifying people, opinions, information and events. He posits that we should create a world that looks different. From this position then, we are insisting on cuts in the structure of culture to unravel the syntactic knots by locating and emphasising personal story frames. In this section, we are newly contemplating the impact on fans of David Bowie's creative output, the inspirations and actions that spring from and around him, for the extent to which his creative works have represented a template for others to follow. We look to how fans have gradually intertwined experiences of him into their own emerging and personal sense of self, their own aesthetic self-invention. As theoretical physicist and philosopher, Karen Barad (2007: xi) emphasises '[e]xistence is not an individual affair'. Feeling some mental-emotional configuration with Bowie to their own identity construction, participant KS in our survey wrote:

> *KS:* David Bowie provided the sound track to my life. His music helped shape the person I am and helped me accept my kookishness. I was and am happily the black sheep, whereas once it bothered me greatly.

In the thickness of now, a time of the media's tentacular materialities, stars and celebrities are indeed central for their parts in the process of socialisation whereby certain mechanisms position particular values, issues and attributes as being important, desirable, neutral or normal. That is, our ideas and beliefs are established, managed and maintained through a number of social institutions; broadly, one of which is the media, and more personally our chosen stars and celebrities. Other operational 'socialising agents' or 'social agents' include one's family, friends, peers, education, religion (as we have discussed in Chapters 3 and 4); but they do not lead in a direct way to a transparent world because reflexively: '... knowledge spirals in and out of the universe of social life, reconstructing both itself and that universe as an integral part of that process' (Giddens 1990: 15–16). Sometimes they play an important part without us realising it.

Like Derrida's 'text', Bowie might be understood as referring to: 'history, the world, to reality, to being, and especially ... to the other' wherein reality always appears: 'in an experience, hence in a movement of interpretation' (1988: 137). Following a Derridean (1978) through-line, individualisation with its range of sociocultural variables and perceptions and the constant dispersal of ideas is impactful for an optimistic epistemology regarding consequent affective behaviours and the touching of feelings that move us emotionally. In our Amsterdam focus group during the *3rd International Celebrity Studies Conference: Authenticating Celebrity* (28–30 June 2016), recalling the words of participant E1 (see Chapter 3), who remarked in response to the questions: 'What does David Bowie mean to you?' and 'What sort of role did he play in your social and/or private life?':

> I was 13 years old when I saw him perform on Saturday Night Live and I loved the music but again it was also the visual presentation, so in one number he was in a dress, Klaus Nomi in a dress and that ruined my 13 year-old mind – in a very good way ...

As it was for E1 above, having one's 'mind blown' is dramatic for conceptual shifts in and escape to, new thinking and being. Gilles Deleuze (2008) suggests that the only way to think about knowledge (old and new) and guiding principles for behaviour is through conceptual creativity. The inventions of concepts for thinking have to be produced and this cannot be done without the massive intervention of communication. Linguistically, this works well for Derrideans because everything hangs on the 'text'. To better grasp conceptual processes of aesthetic self-invention then, an apposite starting point finds anthropologists such as Elizabeth Fisher (1979) rightly sensing that initial cultural inventions would have included some form of container to hold gathered materials or products, some type of sling or carrier. This premise became a conceptual zone for Ursula K. Le Guin's (1986: 151–152) theory of storytelling via the narrative frame of the 'carrier bag' and this akin to a vessel or 'thing' in Heidegger's (1967) philosophical conception. Here, one uses its literal functioning (the container into which we place items for safe keeping) as a metaphor for storing the intangible 'things' that might be precious, their carriage, then taking them out of the carrier bag to be shared. At the same time, the notional carrier bag container is one from which our creative thoughts and actions might also emerge:

> [I]t is a human thing to do, to put something you want, because it's useful, edible, or beautiful, into a bag, or a basket … a net woven of your own hair, or what have you, and then take it home with you, home being another, larger kind of pouch or bag, a container for people, and then later you take it out … and share it or store it up for winter in a solider container or put it in the medicine bundle or the shrine or the museum, the holy place, the area that contains what is sacred.

The theory is fluid and the movement of 'things' into/out of the 'container' non-linear. The Bowie 'carrier bag' is the concept of something into which we might safely add; such as our own fears, ideas, perceptions, identity politics, creativity and so on. That which might be useful or beautiful or even difficult—the socio-emotional 'trinkets' we pick up along life's path. The carrier bag (the 'net woven of our own hair', the thing of our own choosing) holds everything together until we are ready to empty the contents and reveal our selves. From it emerges a certain 'becoming'; the creation of something more solid through his initial/our consequent imagining. Placed on the shrine, in the museum or holy place intrinsic for/of ourselves. Indeed, there are 'seeds to be gathered, and room in the bag of stars' (Le Guin 1986: 154).

Upon this ideational journeying, our participants responded when asked in the survey (Q 8): 'What does David Bowie mean to you?', that:

> K2: Bowie is the soundtrack on which my soul operates. There isn't an emotion or feeling that isn't represented by his music. His contributions to music and film are like place holders in my memory. Often times, when I'm feeling especially nostalgic, his presence overlays the memory. Though he was always changing, he was one of the few constants in my life.

K3: He means the art itself. The most complete man that ever lived here, that truly translated art into life in the shape of music, lyrics, performs, acting, painting and helped a lot of artists that I love into music like Nine Inch Nails and Placebo.

K4: He has had an impact on everything: art, music, fashion, theatre, TV, movies, sex and gender.

Bowie traversed creative elements of visual arts and music that consequently forged reactions in these fans within the lived experience of criss-crossing events in their own lives. For K2, Bowie's music touched every important facet of their existence, indeed creating a personal soundtrack that played alongside their everyday. For them, music was placeholder to which they might emotively return for succour or comfort and also relive important times. Other fans were assisted to build from within, locating strength of spirit to push troubled times away and forge confidently ahead. Participant KT recalled the enshrined 'holy place' that they created out of their love bounded by poverty when we asked if they had seen Bowie live in concert:

KT: No. I was too young and didn't have the money when he came to my country. So I just cut every newspaper about the show and glued it on my bedroom wall.

For others, carving out the fane is through confronting life's existential terrain by being him:

K15: I'd note that his many personas helped me embrace my own multi-facedness and also offered a variety of templates for me to examine my own aesthetics and ideas against. Each speaks to a different piece of who I am.

A young participant some twenty years of age spoke about the impact of David Bowie for them during a focus group session in Japan. When asked: 'how did you become a David Bowie fan?':

TS: Well, first of all, my mother is a big Bowie fan since she was a high school student in the 1970s. When I was an elementary school student she was listening to Bowie and so I was listening to Bowie too and in 2004 there was a concert for the *Reality Tour* in Budokan [Nippon Budokan indoor arena in Chiyoda, Tokyo, Japan] and I went there with my other and it was of course, a brilliant concert! Our seat was not so good, maybe at the back on the second floor, but I remember when Bowie came to the stage I thought that he was staring at me. He had such a presence that I was shocked! "Oh my God, this is the rock star", everyone stood up and was shouting and singing. For the first time I understood what a rock star is. His aura was so big. From then I started to make my music. Bowie inspired me ... my life.

Becoming their own 'version' of David Bowie, participant TS subsequently formed different bands over the years with some success and happily teaches music at a college having decided to make music a lifelong pursuit. Bowie's music was also a personal touchstone between this son and his mother. In the interview, TS recalls being very young when the pair went to this fist Bowie concert; a shared joy they tearfully recalled. They had proudly brought with them to the focus group treasured keepsakes of Bowie concert memorabilia to show and share. At a deeper level, we might consider this early 'mothering' (real/metaphoric) and sharing of values and interests to have produced the circumstances in which TS musically flourished (see also Chapter 3). David Bowie has acted conceptually as a 'carrier bag' for important 'things' that his fans could identify with so that, metaphorically or literally, they might perform 'as Bowie' in their day-to-day compelled by the urge to demonstrate their fandom or by the deeper need for connection to a like-minded other.

It is not surprising that fans often frequent conventions such as overtly identifying with Bowie by simply wearing a T-shirt to denote one's 'tribe' of interest to full immersion in the Bowie persona through costume and dressing up. David Bowie has acted for many as a store for ideas, emotions or sensibilities to be drawn upon in key life moments, and our fan participants recalled being entranced by his performance during the live concerts they attended:

T77: Madison square garden, the Glass Spider Tour, he held my hand. Sang right to me. I was dressed exactly like him in gold space suit mouthing all the words.

T8: I could never get enough of him ... I travelled to Holland, New York and Las Vegas to see him and wore various costumes! I walked around as Ziggy in Holland!

As GG, a huge Bowie fan recalls from their college years during an interview in New York for this study:

GG: I dressed up Friday, Saturday and Sunday in the same outfit [as Aladdin Sane] for three different events ...

Participant BB who took part in our London-based focus group recalls of her fandom during the 1980s:

> BB: I went through a period when I dressed in suits; shirts and ties, just for a laugh really. It is all about finding one's feet. I think that's something that I've always carried through and appreciated; being alternative and different. I think it's for people who are not afraid and a lot of the reason that they are not afraid is because of their own Bowie experience or having him in the world and sort of changing things while they are growing up.

Of the same point in time, during one of the focus groups held in Berlin, two participants discussed how Bowie's image evoked cultural significance:

> K1: We'd watch Top of the Pops and he'd come on and he was a really striking figure.

> K2 adds: When you look back on it, you've got David Bowie and it's a man wearing make-up and what followed was Adam Ant wearing eye-liner and costumes on stage and it just exploded. People expressed themselves a lot more.

Creatively, the recent work of Will Brooker involved research chronicled over a twelve-month period focused on David Bowie's life and career by re-enacting important Bowie images and behaviours. Brooker embarked upon an immersive experience of Bowie's various phases across a forty-year history via costumes, make-up, performances and including dietary regimes (incorporating the famous red peppers and milk, but energy drinks replaced the cocaine of this 1975 LA period). In an interview for *The Atlantic* (Kornhaber 2016), Will Brooker said that his work was part scholarly research and part performance art. What emerged from the experience was a close study of David Bowie's star image through his recurring patterns and motifs, raising important questions about the identity politics of stardom. The authors of this book observed Will's first public appearance as David Bowie for his project. We had organised the *Stardom and Celebrity of David Bowie Symposium* in Melbourne, Australia (17–19 July 2015) to run in conjunction with the globally touring *David Bowie Is …* exhibition at the Australian Centre for the Moving Image (ACMI) and had invited Will to be a keynote speaker. We consequently organised radio interviews and accompanied him 'as David Bowie' and experienced the significant public curiosity in his approach to 'being' him.

For his fans, David Bowie was the prime artist provocateur imbued with his own essence of art-form fusions, vision and sound; he depicted the dialectical tension between art and commerce, of genuine acts associated with risk and will which has inspired many. As we found in our international fieldwork and from the many fan responses, this was something that a number of fans have emulated in various ways and to different degrees in their own lived experiences.

Conclusion

Precisely because there is 'no definitive David Bowie' means that multiple interpretations are rendered possible. David Bowie has, therefore, afforded fans with reflexive resources that are held in/drawn from their imaginary 'carrier bag' for a multitude of ways of 'seeing' as they attempt to sustain across their contemporary lives a coherent self-identity. There is an additional flow 'within/without' whereby Bowie seems to be felt from within the body by resonating with/in his fans, and; without as fan perform in tributes, wear costumes, dress up, form ideological affinities and engaging in overarching joyful celebration. We found participants who were 'acting out'/coming out, taking critical thought and turning it into their lived practices as well as making personal sense of things or developing critical self-awareness about their history, identity and place in the world. This all ironically yet consciously placed against the background of the temporality of existence and the incompleteness of being. David Bowie's legacy is a star image that continues to performatively guide the listening/viewing audience to question the world and remains fundamental to fans—then and now—for the purposes of, in ideal circumstances, positive and purposeful identity formation—for taking on a leading and independent role in the curation of the self and for being more than we might have been.

References

Barad, Karen. *Meeting the Universe Halfway: Quantum Physics and the Entanglement of Matter and Meaning.* Durham: Duke University Press, 2007.
British Broadcasting Corporation (BBC). Nationwide, News Program, 5 June 1973.

Chekhov, Michael. *Lessons for the Professional Actor*. From a collection of notes transcribed and arranged by Deirdre Hurst du Prey; Introduction by Mel Gordon. New York: Performing Arts Journal Publications, 1985.

Deleuze, Gilles. "What Is the Creative Act?" In *Two Regimes of Madness: Texts and Interviews 1975–1995*, ed. David Lapoujade and trans. Ames Hodges and Mike Taormina, 312–324. Cambridge, MA: MIT Press, 2008.

Derrida, Jacques. *Writing and Difference*. Translated with an Introduction and Additional Notes by Alan Bass. Chicago: University of Chicago Press, 1978.

Derrida, Jacques. "Afterword: Toward an Ethic of Discussion." In *Limited Inc*, trans. Samuel Weber. Evanston, IL: Northwestern University Press, 1988.

Dyer, Richard. *Stars* (1979). London: BFI Publishing, 1998.

Fisher, Elizabeth. *Women's Creation: Sexual Evolution and the Shaping of Society*. Garden City, NY: Anchor/Doubleday, 1979.

Foucault, Michel. *The Hermeneutics of the Subject: Lectures at the Collège de France 1981–1982*. Translated by G. Burchell. New York: Macmillan, 2005.

Foucault, Michel. *Archaeology of Knowledge*. Translated by A. M. Sheridan Smith. New York: Routledge, 2013.

Fuchs, Thomas. "Intercorporeality and Interaffectivity." *Phenomenology and Mind* 11 (2016): 194–209.

Giddens, Anthony. *The Consequences of Modernity*. Stanford, CA: Stanford University Press, 1990.

Gore, Joe. "Changes 2.1: New Digital Stimulation from David Bowie and Reeves Gabrels." *Guitar Player*, June 1997, 46–47.

Gramsci, Antonio. *Selections from the Prison Notebooks of Antonio Gramsci*. Edited and translated by Quintin Hoare and Geoffrey Nowell Smith. New York: International Publishers, 1971.

Heidegger, Martin. *What Is a Thing?* Translated by W. B. Barton, Jr., and Vera Deutsch, with an analysis by Eugene T. Gendlin. Chicago: H. Regnery, 1967.

Hochschild, Arlie Russell. "Emotion Work, Feeling Rules, and Social-Structure." *American Journal of Sociology* 85 (3) (1979): 551–575.

Hochschild, Arlie Russell. *The Commercialisation of Intimate Life: Notes from Home and Work*. Berkeley, CA: University of California Press, 2003.

Kornhaber, Spencer. "Life as Bowie: Thoughts on David Bowie from a Professor Who's in the Middle of a Year Spent Impersonating Him." *The Atlantic*, 15 January 2016. https://www.theatlantic.com/entertainment/archive/2016/01/david-bowie-will-brooker-interview-professor/424386/.

Kövecses, Zoltán. *Metaphor: A Practical Introduction*. Exercises written with Szilvia Csábi, Réka Hajdú, Zsuzsanna Bokor, and Orsolya Izsó. New York: Oxford University Press, 2002.

Kövecses, Zoltán. "The Conceptual System." In *Where Metaphors Come From: Reconsidering Context in Metaphor*, 31–48. New York: Oxford University Press, 2015.

Le Guin, Ursula K. 1986. "The Carrier Bag of Fiction." In *The Ecocriticism Reader: Landmarks in Literary Ecology*, ed. Cheryll Glotfelty and Harold Fromm, 151–152. Georgia: The University of Georgia Press, 1996.

Loenhoff, Jens. "Intercorporeality as a Foundational Dimension of Human Communication." In *Intercorporeality: Emerging Socialities in Interaction*, ed. Christian Meyer, Jürgen Streeck, and J. Scott Jordan, 25–50. New York: Oxford University Press, 2017.

Nunn, Heather, and Anita Biressi. "'A Trust Betrayed': Celebrity and the Work of Emotion." *Celebrity Studies* 1 (1) (2010): 49–64.

Paglia, Camille. *Sexual Personae: Art and Decadence from Nefertiti to Emily Dickinson*. London: Yale University Press, 1990.

Petit, Lenard. *The Michael Chekhov Handbook: For the Actor*. New York: Routledge, 2010.

Plessner, Helmuth. *Laughing and Crying: A Study of the Limits of Human Behavior*. Evanston, IL: Northwestern University Press, 1970.

Ricoeur, Paul. "Word, Polysemy, Metaphor: Creativity in Language." In *A Ricoeur Reader: Reflection and Imagination*, ed. Mario J. Valdés, 65–85. Toronto: University of Toronto Press, 1991.

Sennett, Richard. *The Fall of Public Man*. New York: Norton, 1974.

Thomson, Elizabeth, and David Gutman. *The Bowie Companion*. Cambridge, MA: Da Capo Press, 1996.

Waldrep, Shelton. *The Aesthetics of Self Invention: Oscar Wilde to David Bowie*. Minneapolis, MN: University of Minnesota Press, 2004.

CHAPTER 7

Aca-Fans on Tracing Bowie Stardom
for Being and Becoming

INTRODUCTION

The cumulative scholarly explorations of David Bowie, his volume of works and the nature of fandom in general have led us towards this nuanced look into *aca-fandom* in relation to Bowie for this chapter. The starting point for critical elaboration is the participants in our study who regard themselves as fans and academics both. These individuals can be understood to represent not only a subgrouping of fandom, but of academia as well. Using the notion of the 'aca-fan' (Hills 2002, 2012; Jenkins 2012), these academics *in propria persona* are growing in number and significance for their distinct scholarship in the academy that critically delves into the nexus between popular culture and fandom. Here in this chapter, the comments of aca-fans are critically drawn upon so that we might work towards a deeper understanding of the particular personal/professional experiences of these David Bowie fans who are also academics for what their fandom has contributed to their professional practice, being and becoming. For this, we convened focus groups wherein aca-fans could openly and intimately tell their respective stories, a *story-sharing* built in and around the affects brought to bear through David Bowie fandom for them personally in relation to their professions. In this chapter then, we critically consider the ways that David Bowie is significant for aca-fans, especially for the unique impact he has had upon their consequent writing and creative careers, towards a richer perception of Bowie fans themselves.

© The Author(s) 2019   131
T. Cinque and S. Redmond, *The Fandom of David Bowie*,
https://doi.org/10.1007/978-3-030-15880-4_7

The approach then for this chapter is to aim its searchlight at the impact on aca-fans' individual emotional and creative development attributable to their fandom for how this lead subsequently to active professional agency. Participant LGM, a New York opera singer and writer commented that for them:

> *LGM*: Bowie was an attitude, an appreciation, a hunger for a particular style of life and part of its grit. You see, most New Yorkers are from somewhere else - they have decided to have a different life so they move here. I felt David Bowie had an energy level for, and interest in, people and all things and as a performing artist I connected with him!

We could approach David Bowie's impact for the respondent LGM here through the metaphor of a Culture Media, from the perspective of a special medium that supplies essential nutrients for microbial growth. Here, Bowie's impression for his aca-fans is aligned to the preservation, enrichment or resuscitation that such Culture Media afford micro-organisms when they are faced with being damaged or less productive (or less creative) due to exposure to certain harmful environmental factors (i.e. socio-emotional harms in this human context). In the first instance, David Bowie has allowed his aca-fans (indeed all his fans) inspired opportunities to conceive of ways forward, forging a personal creative approach to life (sometimes a new one with a fresh start as it was for LGM above) and emotional growth that we so desperately need, yet many are so often deprived of.

But he is even more than this auto-biochemistry for a number as we will see in this chapter wherein confessional comments run beneath our modes of story-sharing, and thoughts are expressed at times as memories solemnly whispered. For MTS, a Professor of Sociology and Cultural Studies in Tokyo, and Bowie fan, told us that for them:

> *MTS*: When I was young living in Japan, Bowie seemed like a typical upper-class British person and also a little crazy which I loved, but in Japan, for our age group, things which I loved that had a certain sonic aesthetic, music—typically Western—was not appropriate to talk about. I was certainly influenced by his [Bowie's] fashion and music. I later went to study in London, buy my records there. Bowie offered me an unusual and different direction to follow—a different aesthetic I took to my approach toward writing about art, culture, music and more, both privately and professionally.

What MTS allows us to sense is that there is something of a reciprocal relationship where aca-fans actively invest in the ideas of David Bowie that flow into and swirl around their own, while conversely affording Bowie with audiences to perform to and engage with. The result is that as David Bowie's creative work circulates and various stories about him—his 'myths'—become a kind of currency of value within popular media and in public commentary. We could look to the notion of 'productive consumption' as a useful way to describe this 'movement of cultural commodities and their proliferation of value beyond consumption by understanding any cultural form is dependent on a co-creation of value by both the artist and the artist's audience/consumers' (Marshall 2017: 564). We can see this especially through the passionate productive consumption of fans buying records or CDs, dressing up like Bowie as one special 'character', to writing their own fan-fiction, scholarly works and pursuing creative passions—all the while David Bowie is both artist and the muse. Not least, however, is that David Bowie is someone so much more than a mere entertainer for many fans. Indeed, as explored in Chapter 6, he acts as a 'carrier bag' akin to a vessel or 'thing' in Heidegger's conception for a container into which fans 'place items for safe-keeping' (meant here as investment of time, actions, thoughts, questions and emotions) for storing the intangible 'things' that seem precious and their carriage. The liquescency of the un-fixed notional vessel is that it is one from which creative thoughts and actions might also *emerge* when aca-fans carefully untangle and purposefully take them out of the carrier bag to be shared at appropriates times.

ALL-TOO-HUMAN: FRAMING ACA-FANDOM WITH EMOTION, INSPIRATION AND MOTIVATION

As we noted in the introduction to this book, we have relied on the comments of the fans themselves to interlace our stories and contextually layer our understanding of what David Bowie means to his fans. The primary material gathered for this chapter now narrows the focus to specifically knit together the responses of Bowie fans that are also academics. We interviewed scholars in their home countries and in aca-fan focus groups that we convened at the international conferences on David Bowie for their response to personal fandom connected to their pursuit of research careers, creativity and scholarship. In the most intimate of ways, this has given us insight into the extent to which the emerging constituent of academia in Stardom and Fandom Studies offers ways to re-evaluate existent and deeply evocative star and fan interactions.

Recently arisen are the new spaces for discussion and commentary about star performers and the various affects of fandom itself (see also Chapter 8 on digital spaces of interaction). The importance of *affect* is elevated, equal with cognition, for shaping a wide variety of human behaviours by touching our feelings and sensorily moving us emotionally; the knowledge about which is fundamental for audience and reception studies researchers. Our approach then for this chapter was to create discussion spaces, either at conferences or at key sites, for the interactive flow of academic study and conversation both. Participants voluntarily attended these, engaged as aca-fans, for the critical study and contemplation of stars, celebrities and fandom—and David Bowie.

What we find worked throughout this chapter are the many familiar and broad issues that the aca-fans raised with us including their questioning (both privately and professionally) of: the nature of 'love'; the morality of sex and friendship; concepts of family; influence and cultural production to the more esoteric topics such as whether it is possible to grasp a definition of knowledge and understanding about the human condition. The aca-fans critically discussed such everyday issues called forth by the abstruse topic of 'David Bowie' and what this has meant for their own creative and/or scholarly practices. This chapter adds to our critical consideration of the distinctive ways that David Bowie has become an emotive subject within the media-rich world around us.

According to Professor of Media and Film, Matt Hills (2002) fan communities can be critically considered to be both within and outside practices of commodification at the same time. They are understood to be self-aware *and* self-absent, rendered simultaneously intellectual and performatively embodied. Of course, this begs the further question of whether researchers should be members of the population they are studying or should they not when engaged in fan ethnographic research. On this, Dwyer and Buckle (2009) have made a compelling case that it is in the space between that allows researchers to occupy the position of *both* insider and outsider rather than insider *or* outsider. Hills similarly fashions the provocation that researchers 'should treat self and other identically' (Hills 2002: 81).

As I have elsewhere argued (Cinque 2019), any attempt to define 'aca-fandom' (academic fandom and also scholar-fandom) is possibly a rhetorical manoeuver, and a point for discussion raised in *Punkademics* by Furness (2012) with recent fandom scholarship continuing to contemplate the relationship between fans and academics since Matt Hills' *Fan Cultures* (2002), including that of Henry Jenkins' ongoing blog *Confessions of an Aca-Fan* (http://henryjenkins.org/); Will Brooker's own studies of personal passion (fandom) vis-à-vis objective analysis of scholarship (professional academic writing) (2007, 2017), and studies of 'scholar-fandom' by Cochran (2009) and Phillips (2010). Later work by Hills (2012: 17) on scholar-fandom suggests that it need not be viewed as one thing to be celebrated or transcended, but as multiple and successive bids for identity wherein 'a coalition or conglomeration of academics whose hybridised "scholar" and "fan" identities can vary in a number of significant ways'.

Platt and Squire (2017: 48) support Jenkins' discussion of aca-fandom (2006, 2012) and emphasise how, within the broad church of fandom, the aca-fan researcher is entwined *with fans* and *as fan* both. As is the intension here, reciprocity and dialogue between researcher and subject are convincingly in the forefront of their work that examines the aca-fan position in relation to textual analysis of slash—a genre of (user-generated/created) fan-work, fuelled by an interpersonal attraction, that includes fan-fiction as well as fan-art and fan-videos among other subgenres (see also Chapter 8 on digital co-creation).

Epistemologically, what can be distilled from the experience of speaking with academics and creative practitioners engaged in research, in the context of fan ethnography, is that aca-fans produce work that encourages personal and often transformational understanding towards new ways of knowing. Self-reflexive questions fuelled communal and reciprocal dialogue on why aca-fans 'do what we do professionally?' and 'why aca-fans produce what we do', thus testing out-loud our 'truths'. Of course, like the liquescency of the un-fixed notional vessel discussed above, the aca-fan is also always already purposefully being formed and reformed because at the moment we receive the answers to our self-reflexive questions 'why am I ...' or 'why do I ...', our self-identity shifts and is immediately (re)fashioned only to be (re)shaped again and again when we quizzically (re)examine our everyday lived professional (and private) experiences.

From our developed mediations of contemporary aca-fandom, we take this journey that is specifically built in and around the star figure of David Bowie and the creativity he inspired. In other words, we begin to understand the importance of a creative work for the various nuanced emotional responses by aca-fans and their subsequent 'action' to explain some of the possible ways that David Bowie's works have 'tacked back and forth' between being specific (concrete and empirical) and abstract (allegorical or metaphorical) as they are (re)interpreted in multiple contexts by his aca-fans.

Variously woven throughout this book are the ways that David Bowie has acted upon his fans' assemblage and affirmative realisation of 'identity' variously conceived. As we have argued, Bowie's work also acts as a 'store' for aca-fans' special thoughts and feelings as they work on/through them towards (in ideal circumstances) active agency and positive emotional growth or individual 'becoming'. In the context we present here, this notion of 'becoming' translates as consequent academic activity and/or critical-creative work arising out of David Bowie fandom. When asked 'What does David Bowie mean to you?' during our Amsterdam focus group, participant BW1 enthusiastically relayed having found a purposeful career interest through their fandom:

> I became a Bowie collector but nobody else I grew up with was into David Bowie … it was in the 1990s and I also got involved in digital technology because I was in the fan-groups online.

Here is but one example in support of being able to make a claim to a certain 'intimacy' of emotive/affective significance existing between Bowie and his fans. This is seen in many aca-fans like BW1 who have used Bowie to spark deeper philosophical reflection and gradually intertwine experiences of him into their emerging self-awareness (see also Chapter 6). As we will see below with our other aca-fans, theirs is not unaffected, ephemeral identity construction; this is professional 'becoming' through critical exploration and is a serious and testing personal crossing towards expressive development as they push wilfully against all the socio-conventional and class confines to be and do more.

INTIMATE METHOD: MEMORIES, SHARING AND THE STORIES THAT FRAME US

As noted in our book's introduction, the academic focus groups comprised participants that had previously completed the online survey *Turn to Face the Strange: The Fandom of David Bowie* and who had indicated a willingness to participate during specially convened sessions. The initial survey comprised some 16 questions in both English and Japanese languages (see

Appendix A). The analysis of the impact of David Bowie's stardom for aca-fans was recorded using qualitative and quantitative data from respondents' online survey responses (see Appendix B). Two focus group sessions were then held at conferences dedicated to the theme of David Bowie or celebrity, precisely: (1) the *Celebrity Studies Conference* 2016 in Amsterdam (June) and the *David Bowie Intertext/Text/Media Conference* in Lisbon in 2016 (September). Further focus groups were convened with academic participants who were interviewed for their responses in London (June), Tokyo (June) and another in New York (July). Our aca-fan participants were recruited three months prior to the commencement of each of the focus groups. This was to ensure that individuals had appropriate interest in the research topic and were willing to participate.

The aca-fan focus groups comprised respectively: (1) 9 males and 21 females at the *Celebrity Studies Conference* 2016; (2) 11 males and 18 females at the *David Bowie Intertext/Text/Media Conference* in 2016 in Lisbon; (3) 2 males and 1 female in Tokyo; (4) 3 females in London; and (5) 2 females and 1 male in New York. The modal age across all groups was 40 years. The authors of this work also took active part in the focus groups. The global sample comprised participants living in New Zealand, Portugal, Ireland, Germany, France, Brazil, Australia, the UK, the United States and Japan. In line with the findings related to professions above, a number research and publish in the specific fields of celebrity, fandom, popular music, cultural studies and cinema studies while others work in media and the arts more broadly. Overarchingly, the findings drawn from the online questionnaire found that 25% of respondents were in the fields of arts, design, entertainment and media occupations, and 24% were employed in education, training and library occupations. Far fewer were from 'Business/ Financial Operations Occupations' (4%), Sales (4%) or 'Healthcare Practitioners and Technical Occupations' (4%) (see Table B.4: Occupation in Appendix B).

Each of these aca-fan focus group lasted for approximately one hour and was comprised only of the willing participants and undertaken in a designated space either as part of the conferences or set public location. As we did in all other focus groups, during these sessions Bowie's music was also played softly as a sonic companion and visual images of him from different points in his career were simultaneously screened. Colour photocopied images of David Bowie from various decades and periods were laid out on tables or the floor as additional visual stimuli. Participants were subsequently invited to look at and take their time in choosing one image that most 'spoke' to them and their sensibilities about David Bowie's music or filmic roles and the level of significance in their lives; that is, an image that they felt they most identified with to then talk through their choice and respond to open questions.

These particular focus groups were organised around questions designed to enable the participants to 'story' their fandom in relation to personal identity formation and development as academics. Our collective discussions then related to interactions with David Bowie's creative works (music, film, art) for how they positioned us as academics/scholars/aca-fans and what the impact might be. We started by asking the aca-fans about Bowie's processes of meaning making and significance for them in their lives. Each session began with asking each of these participants some framing questions: 'What does David Bowie mean to you'; 'what sort of role has he played in your social or private life'; 'what sort of significance, e.g., a major event'; 'how does David Bowie connect to your sense of yourself/your community/family/history/where you have come from and where you might be going?'; 'why are you here today?' and 'what is it about David Bowie you so identified with?' The conversation then continued with specific framing around how Bowie helped them each navigate their profession, with each participant drawing forth a memory, event, or series of events to story his impact upon their lives.

From the transcriptions and notes taken at each occasion, certain themes emerged and were drawn upon by respondents themselves either directly or in terms of supportive commentary and affirmative comments from others. There was a series of constellations of articulating or intersecting stories in relation to self as a fan and scholar both and are threaded through the eye of the needle hence for this chapter. Congruent to our findings in Chapter 4 for how new migrants to Australia came to critically develop a palpable self-invention by virtue of David Bowie, a number of the aca-fans in our study similarly understood or addressed identity and *becoming* through connections with family and/or community. Importantly here, the aca-fans made critical sense of their aca-fan writing and creativity which ultimately coalesced as a 'science of imagination' via thoughts on ontology and epistemology through and for their aca-fandom.

Of course, emotion and memory both underscore one's identity as an academic in the context of how Bowie's work has been interacted with, shared, translated and interpreted. Here we drew upon story-sharing, allowing the respondents to trace their fandom backward and forward to entwine their recollections in the context of their academic work, then speak to them publicly, thus bringing them to vivid life.

Aca-Fans' Thoughts on Forging Self and Subject

For the participants in the aca-fan focus groups, their memory traces allowed for instances of philosophical reflection in line with those of Antonio Gramsci (1971) and the similar contemplations in the same vein of 'thinking about self' by Woodward (2015: 62):

> In thinking about self, one of the key tensions and relationships that has to be negotiated is the relationship between personal responsibility and social, cultural, or other constraints. The concept of identity has been seen to take into account the extent to which individuals or groups participate actively in shaping selves who have responsibility for their own actions.

The aca-fan participants rendered important moments, negotiating key events in their lives that they mentally traced back and forward, entwined in remembrances of their growing up that were intimately shared. What we exposed is David Bowie fandom acting as an important medium through which they come to shape their thinking, actions and profession. One of the participants in the New York focus group was an African American novelist, academic writer and educator in an urban school district who has studied in Moscow and London and serves as a member of the National Council of Teachers of English in the United States. This scholar, RA4, recounted that:

> RA4: David Bowie was a touchstone for me in two ways. One, as a child he was the Goblin King. He was the apex of all things magical and fantastic. I mean, I came to *Labyrinth* as a fan of Jim Henson and *The Muppets* and you know, I was introduced to David Bowie because of my love of *The Muppets* growing up. We all grew up with the *Wizard of OZ*, but you also want something new, you want something different and, in a sense, you also want something sexy. For example, Linda the good witch is not sexy, Dorothy is not sexy - to me [laughs] - so I think that what David Bowie meant for me as a child was the difference in things, another facet, another darker facet of the things that I enjoy. I would say that same connection to difference expanded to his music, the ever-changing sound. I would joke that I was probably the only black kid in north-west DC that listened to David Bowie and was listening to 'old' David Bowie ... so what he meant for me was beyond the otherness of fantasy, beyond the otherness

of reality and always being different and being OK to be different ... and
this was before I knew I was gay ... and I don't draw a parallel between my
being gay and Bowie being gay, but being a fan did make my transition
and coming out when I was older easier - sort of.
I can't explain it. For me it wasn't a sexual thing and even though I am
gay I was never attracted to him. My thing with him was more paternal.
I was not raised with a father in my life and I thought if there was to be a
guy to show me the ropes then why not David Bowie. David Bowie is the
perfect storm for what I needed then as a child and what I need now as a
creative guide. I write and draw comfort from Bowie and am inspired by
the strength he gives me. For me Bowie isn't a touchstone for identity,
more for the important transitions and reminiscences, things like that,
the thinking about which I use in my writing.

In simpatico with respondent RA4's story, GG (in academic publishing)
verbally explored their own:

Why do I love him? Well the *Labyrinth* thing was funny because I saw it in
4th grade and I didn't know who David Bowie was and I was scared of the
movie in general, the goblins I think, so that was really my first introduction
to him ... maybe ...

... I am not sure what I listened to growing up. My brother worked for a
record company and I would meet various famous people, but I can't pinpoint
what I enjoyed then. But when I went to college and I met people that showed
me his records and I heard David Bowie, I was like "Oh, David Bowie", "O
My God!" His music was just this whole other world that collided with life
at college, experiencing new cultures and being exposed to new things ...
David Bowie was it for me.

Here GG was asked a further open-ended question for deeper insight: 'you
had exposure to so much music, why do you say Bowie was "it" for you?':

It was a feeling, it was intangible and I think because I was exposed to more
in his music my mind became more open to things, very appreciative of new
ideas which definitely guided me toward my career choice and the things that
I am interested in pursuing and developing. I like being known as someone
who likes David Bowie and in a certain part of my life, people I work with
get me. My dad calls me the rebel, well compared to my sister, but I feel it's
like part of this picture of me; "oh she lives in Brooklyn, she lives alone, she
likes David Bowie" ... I don't know how those things all go together, but

they kind of do … a kind of inner confidence in a way, you know. I guess I am strong you know. Yeah, intellectually, professionally, what I want out of life, all of that was really inspired by David Bowie.

We could understand both GG and RA4's self-reflections upon their fandom through the key moments in their lives that were usefully engaged with (and openly discussed above) towards their identity development. Drawing on Hills' (2002: 52) question of 'why do various fandoms become relevant and irrelevant to cultural identity at specific times?' provides a way to understand the implications of events in a 'life story' and here, for later aca-fan pursuits:

> These could be moments in a life-story (leaving home but using fandom to remain connected with a family-based identity); moments in the construction of age-based identities ('child'/'teenager'/'youth'/'adult'); moments when different cultural identities and contexts become dominant ('fan'/'academic'); or moments which emerge through the popular construction of cultural history ('the 1970s', 'the 1980s').

These positions raised by Hills (above) are indeed to be found. Both GG and RA4 intertextually came to David Bowie as 'the Goblin King' in *Labyrinth*. For RA4, it was as a child-fan of *The Muppets* and they shared with our focus group intimate instances of the 'moments' from their considered construction of self, using popular media (including *The Wizard of OZ*), in accord with Hill's 'age-based identities ('child'/'teenager'/'youth'/'adult')' and sexual awakening with Bowie as their physical and referential 'transitional object' (Winnicott 1971). Like the Wolf who would 'take' *Little Red Riding Hood* is what Bowie represents to girlhood and for GG, there is a sense of their crossing from childhood with fearful anxiety into an emerging womanhood. The words of GG 'Oh, *My God!*' were indeed inflected with breathless sensually in their confessed adolescence experience. Moreover, we see the cultural history and identity positioning in RA4's claim to being 'the only black kid in north-west DC that listened to David Bowie and was listening to "old" David Bowie' and in GG's reflection on how family 'see' her as the 'modern woman' pursuing a dynamic career in New York (a different cultural context from the one they left at home). We also find a 'family-based identity' in GG's reflection of themselves as a rebel in the eyes of their father and RA4's comments that Bowie represented for them an actual 'father' figure that modelled such positive patterns for creativity that would later become RA4's inspiration for writing literature and being an academic.

The nature of 'time' was important to a number of academics in our focus groups. When we asked participants to choose one picture of David Bowie from the colour photocopied images across various decades on display that most drew them, a participant picked up one from the video 'Lazarus' (*Black Star*, 2016). For this participant, BMR, in the process of writing an academic study of Bowie's work and having just made a documentary about the process, they spoke of the selected image and the way Bowie had fuelled their own creative process in reflection of past events:

> BMR: I chose a photograph of an older Bowie as it did speak to me in a way; in the way he is looking very serious and earnest. My feelings about Bowie now are a lot to do with age really, my age and my parents age and mortality and death, you know the whole idea – if Bowie can die, then anyone can die and we are all getting older. So, it speaks to me that when you look at the older person you see the younger person in it. In my film, there is a lot of personal history in the story or idea I wanted to connect with and tell in relation to Bowie.
>
> When I think on what it means to me personally it is the aspects of Bowie in the 1980s which I really enjoyed trying to connect with … I came to Bowie in the 1980s. I felt Bowie was a bit sexual, a bit 'rude' as we say, grown-up dirty and that he was a bit shocking … I liked that. Here was someone that looked straight, passes as straight, but was not really straight and he was importantly conveying the tension, but he was getting away with it … showing that he wasn't quite comfortable in it, which is what I felt, but everyone liked him.

In respondent, BMR's comments above are the affects of a personal historicity with its diffused and distributed modes of being. We perceive BMR's reflection upon the weight of their time in the 1980s. What they powerfully recall is that for them, David Bowie's work acted as a cultural bridge, from Bowie to the fans and with David Bowie they kindled the sparks that turned into their blazing fires of creative endeavour. BMR, like other participants in our study, shared with us that through Bowie they found that they had something in common, a shared sensibility. Bowie also allowed them a sense of recognition as being part of the world's stage at a time when they were trying to make sense of their place upon it. David Bowie validated their sensibility that he was an ingress for subsequent creative thinking and expression, confirming once again how his star image offered positive and progressive entry points for those feeling seemingly on the periphery to the rest of society or the world to find a place where they too 'fit in'.

We can see this personal mapping *over* time as well. Again, in the process of choosing an image, another participant felt impelled to share their story of their fandom from when they were an art student to becoming an academic and fine artist. They had chosen an image that had been a constant throughout their creative life and only in their later years did their way of working come to make personal sense nestled in, and comforted by, Bowie's own self-considered experiences. In London, when asked to choose an image that best represented for them Bowie's work, one fan, E8, told us that:

> [Holding up their chosen image of David Bowie] This is Bowie as 'The Cracked Actor' and this image I put up in my studio when I first came to art as a student and I have always had it hanging there. I did give up art for a while and went into Science and Politics. Now back in art though, I have all that knowledge and can put it all into my artwork. What assures me somewhat is that I read that Bowie described himself as a person with a very short attention span and would move from one thing to another rapidly, a little ADHD [Attention Deficit-Hyperactivity Disorder] and I have been recently diagnosed and I embrace all that fire-power and madness and energy like Bowie had—a kind of power straight from the stars that I channel into my own creative work.

This aca-fan uses the self-reflexive insights they unearth professionally in ways that allow for deeper engagement with their own creative and scholarly work. Our participants E8 and RA4's personal critical introspection in the aca-fan space, linking together personal interest in David Bowie and lived experience, produced revelations for them that subsequently led to thoughts long internally held being openly voiced. What was repeatedly accentuated by the aca-fan participants in our study was that there was a connection or shadowing of creative practice or ideas that David Bowie was pursuing that set a course in relation to their own professional lives. For our aca-fan participants RA4, BMR and E8, inspiration consequently seeped into their academic careers as creative artists and writers.

And, as we encountered in the previous Chapter 6, the similar experience of TS at a Bowie concert in Tokyo found them awake to the personal realisation that Bowie was for them '*the* rock star' affording the appreciation that 'for the first time I understood what a rock star is. His aura was so big.

From then I started to make my music. Bowie inspired me ... my life'. This inspiration was not only to become a rock musician, writing and performing their own original lyrics, but to share that journey with others as a music educator. Other participants relayed that they too used Bowie and his work as a template for their careers in music and academia. The story shared by TS was paralleled by a London-based composer/producer of eclectic instrumental music, born and educated in Australia, and also working as a university academic. In our study, participant GA recounted for us that for them, their long interest in David Bowie and consequent writing about his music was not about dissecting the Bowie music catalogue itself, but critically considering the systems, processes and practices that created it in the first instance for the meanings that are unearthed and exchanged by his fans. GA declared in the London focus group that:

> I love Bowie! I came from Australia originally, I came over to London for work, but part of my journey getting to England was pilgrimage-like. My life in Australia felt very isolated particularly being a Bowie fan. I became a Bowie fan in the late 1990s when I was at music college and it was just one of these "light-bulb moments" where as a music student I was very caught up in the idea of technique and creating clever intellectual music and we saw a lecture on David Bowie that included analysis of 'Life on Mars'. For me it was partly about the weird way he looked, he looked so unworldly and so really beautiful, but especially how he used his voice and the way he wrote songs, it was so clever, it was so soft but had this whole other "world" to it. He was using his voice like an actor, playing with references, there was lots of depth and suggestion there. It wasn't just good execution, it was all his other stuff as well and I just thought "Oh, my God" and just really got into it. Later I moved to England and I thought "great! [claps hands] now I am closer to Bowie".

This narrative of GA's professional journey serves as a good example of how participants have connected to something in David Bowie's music, often listened to in the present time, but created in different eras and sociocultural contexts. Despite everything seeming to be set to the contrary, Bowie's music and its messages still reflected the aca-fans' universe allowing for alternate transitioning in their academic cogitations and being in the world. For them, delight took over, but it was more than this. It was more than the notion of music that 'ought' to be listened to because it was created by an 'interesting figure'; David Bowie's aura pervaded mere appreciative delight leaving us with a sense of being awestruck.

Returning to Woodward's notion above of identity formation (2015: 62) and the fan responses we drew attention to in Chapters 2 and 3, these participants recalled the ways they actively fashioned their self-perceptions and subsequent interactions, sometimes negotiating complex terrains, with the effect that the normative borders around their identity were breached and consequently reconstructed as was the case for E8. Aca-fans have found in Bowie a mirror for their perceptibly different world-views and through him are made to feel comfortable in their own skin. This fashioning of their self-perceptions is frequently pleasurable and often stems from a conscious moment of personal understanding, like GA's 'light-bulb moment', through one or a series of poignant instances that lead thereby to personal, metaphysical introspection of the kind of reality they (want to) inhabit. A number of aca-fan participants told us that their own thinking and questioning were ignited for their professional work in possession of the strands of Bowie's creativity. As we have encountered so far in this chapter, the comments of our aca-fan participants closely trace the views of Schopenhauer (1962: 51) that our critical thinking of ourselves and the world around us frequently depends on things that concern us personally and deeply. Thus:

> Reading and learning are things that anyone can do of his [sic] own free will; but not so *thinking*. Thinking must be kindled, like a fire by a draught; it must be sustained by some interest in the matters in hand. The interest may be of a purely objective kind, or merely subjective. The latter comes into play only in things that concern us personally.

In GA's comments (above), we find an aca-fan locating something of themselves in what David Bowie creatively depicted which allowed them to feel attuned to a like-minded other and through what Bowie imparted for them, they were therefore set free. Another participant in our Lisbon focus group similarly found that David Bowie was the border of their soul and had used his creative ideas for inspiring their own:

> Y1: In Italy I was a revolutionary from a 'Left-wing' socio-critical approach. I discovered another culture through Bowie's music and another critical approach through Bowie's work as a result. I came to understand the 'Star system' as part of a wider cultural system, an important system – and for me it was important to be aware in my critical political-economy work.

Many aca-fan participants shared sheer joy amidst life experiences and environments imbued with key memories of Bowie—a study for this work in human flourishing, human strengths and virtues. We might claim then that professional identity is so much an important aspect of David Bowie's own work and those memorial struggles and celebrations within the identity politics of his *aca*-fans. For these reasons, we have spent some time critically unpicking the vectors of 'identity' and tracking memories in our other chapters. Consideration of identity formation by aca-fans through Bowie fandom does need special examination here too for the impact on the subsequent career trajectory. This suggestion finds light here, thoughtfully expressed by GA in the focus group in London:

> Through Bowie I emancipated myself. Bowie was my conduit to all the really juicy and great ideas in the world. He was the gateway really because he was just so intellectually entrancing and everything he did had layers with references like a treasure map to literature, history, art and philosophy. He was a way to all the best stuff and opened up my worldview. To the point which I relied on his considered work up until he died when I felt really lost. I had lost my gateway to all the good stuff. He was intellectually curious and I wanted to be intellectually curious and this led to my career, wanting to be an academic and wanting to be curious. Bowie brought that out in me.

We then turned the question of aca-fandom towards a fine focus on the aca-fan participants' views on whether it makes a difference that they are both an academic and a fan in terms of the correlations and (at times) collisions between the research that we do and the nature of fandom itself. Drilling down, they were asked to consider whether they think they can see themselves as aca-fans where their scholarship is never that far away from their fandom—or, just not in that realm at all (see questions 2[b] and 3 in Appendix C). From the focus group in Lisbon:

> *R*: Fandom has inflected my research. Things that I was obsessed with are still things I write about.

> *Z*: Fandom gives an entry point that we wouldn't normally have; a reference point, a richness for where to start in writing.

> *E*: Regarding Bowie and childhood and all the memories that go way back, this is the first time I have written about something that has made me cry.

G: I am not a fan of the term 'aca-fan', words aside however, the way I do feel about it [aca-fandom] is that what I do is write books and that is my art professionally, my way of celebrating Bowie. It is my creative expression – it is a tribute.

M: I would say that a lot of the things that interest me about Bowie's work are the same things I study in my work in academia. That is, different deconstructions of identity and the individual but beyond that I think Bowie just gave me a really great feel to just sort of play with and learn how to be critical – even with things that you like and that is what I like about Bowie. He gave me a way to be critical about things. He was definitely intellectual but not academic and that gives me hope that there are other ways that are not necessarily academic ways to work.

A respondent in the Amsterdam focus group shared that:

X: I have been wanting to write something about or on Bowie for a long time but I never have. For me it is as if Bowie embodies what I consider to be the collapse of the intellectual and the emotional in my work, that is, over-achingly I study what I love, I am an aca-fan in general.

For Toija, David Bowie's impact was similar to that in the examples from aca-fan participants cited above in that they too became 'free to play' and learn how to be critical, bound to his articles of belief sonically and visually made manifest. This fuelled their audacity to continue reaching beyond their potential:

For me he was a teacher as though he was saying: "have you listened to this …" or "go and read this …" and that was what Bowie did for me and what he was about. I found his music and oft-obtuse meanings would jar me into critical contemplation over what they might mean, why, what is a life (or death) and what options are there for the path in between the two. Thus, mine became and remains an academic endeavour, imbued by, and indebted to, Bowie's challenging ruminations about the world and its accepted associations between sensations, language, action and things.

For others:

F: Even though his music and his work has been studied and scrutinized, I think there is still this excitement that we can still find new things to analyse … I think that he has had this important part in my musical development and my academic journey.

> *J:* I feel a bit like an interloper because I would say that I love Bowie, but I wouldn't self-identify as a fan, which working in fan studies I find really interesting to try to unpick. I am kind of theorizing myself. In that aca-fan sense, I am more interested in the *academic* untangling than I am in the fan-ish untangling ...

The comments by J (above) here might be typical of the conundrum that aca-fans grapple with in their professional lives—that they put the *academic* first in the compound word to immediately ascertain their scholarly status because the other side of the hyphen is 'the fan'—which is tender ground. As noted by Cochran (2009: 7–8):

> I am not a fan who masquerades and parades about as a scholar. No, I am first a scholar and *then* a fan. That's what many scholar-fans like to tell ourselves, anyway.

The relationship between academia and fandom might be indistinctly drawn, but it is one in which a number have commented on having found the means to draw upon their fandom for academic expression in a variety of ways. In consideration of the creative, imaginative and academic displays recorded here, we confidently claim that at its core the story begins with the fandom. For the participants in this study, personal fandom created the conditions for these academic individuals to channel their passions towards their own empowered ontology in their fields of research. This argument raises at least two further important points relevant to our goals for this chapter. The first is an issue that the scholarly work by aca-fans, the 'neo-cognoscenti' (see Hills 2018: 480), who are deeply familiar with and knowledgeable about the affects of David Bowie's work in relation to their own, might act to culturally elevate David Bowie affording his work 'classic' status. Perhaps though, if aca-fans remain diligent researchers then 'they will be able to "slip in and out" of the experience being studied, slip in and out of intimacy' as Clandinin and Connely (2000: 82) gently suggest they can. Secondly, the aca-fans were working within a realm of inspired creativity infused by a particular experience of a particular materiality of David Bowie, a particular cultural phenomenon that matters to them. Their deep thinking together with critical self-evaluation, surprise and disclosure via discourse in the process of circumnavigating Bowie's work was apparent in the stories shared with us. David Bowie was a source of support and inspiration both, wherein the strongest connection was realising that he is, in some way across time and space, a part of you.

CONCLUSION

David Bowie created an artistic mosaic and its shards are scattered all over the world. The distinct parts form imaginative connections through our own lives because of what they mean personally to us. As aca-fans, there is a double engagement, one on the personal level or emotional level and one that is intellectual, and Bowie's work affords separate and peculiar sources of pleasure and darkness both because of our powers of reflection. Wondrously layered is the way the interaction of time, place and person can shape us so indelibly; then it is all gone, yet the traces remain. As academics and fans both, we unravelled our personal memories for their stories and what emerged was that though the multitude of ways that Bowie made us feel 'OK', we dared to try things and he was the reason why, as aca-fans, we were all there that day. Most participants were attuned to the need for examination or 'working through' of the everyday in their respective fields of research. This is in line with Schopenhauer's (1962: 51) argument on thinking for the self and that we frequently do so with regard to things that concern us personally. We had gathered in appreciation for the ways that David Bowie personally changed our lives and we found ourselves connected by intangible threads. Participants were honest about how they felt on the inside and out and their stories are testament that even the most difficult circumstances can be overcome with a different point of view and this template or attitude carried them into very successful academic careers. Indeed, a number of the participants have seen poetry, musical works, academic papers and books all emerging from the influence and 'support' of David Bowie as he afforded a sense of invincibility and ways to (re)interpret and understand the world. David Bowie was that 'alternate view' for them and that aspect of Bowie continued to be a template as they navigated their career trajectory to a high level in academia and productive creativity. In our respective ways, we have learned to reject the negative and embrace wondrous possibilities, pursue intrigue, and be our best creative selves without fear of alienation. Indeed, we revel in our 'strangeness' solely as ourselves.

REFERENCES

Brooker, W. The Best Batman Story: *The Dark Knight Returns*. In *Beautiful Things in Popular Culture*, ed. Alan McKee, 33–48. Oxford: Blackwell, 2007.

Brooker, W. *Forever Stardust: David Bowie Across the Universe*. London: I.B. Tauris, 2017.

Cinque, T. "Celebrity Conferences as Confessional Spaces: The Aca-Fan Memory Traces of David Bowie's Stardom." *Celebrity Studies* 10 (1) (2019): 44–59.

Clandinin, J. D., and M. F. Connely. *Narrative Inquiry: Experience and Story in Qualitative Research*. San Francisco, CA: Jossey-Bass Inc, 2000.

Cochran, T. R. "Toward a Rhetoric of Scholar-Fandom." Dissertation, Georgia State University, 2009. http://scholarworks.gsu.edu/english_diss/51. Accessed 5 June 2017.

Dwyer, S. C., and J. L. Buckle. "The Space Between: On Being an Insider-Outsider in Qualitative Research." *International Journal of Qualitative Methods* 8 (1) (2009): 54–63.

Furness, Z. M, ed. *Punkademics: The Basement Show in the Ivory Tower*, 5–24. Brooklyn, NY: Minor Compositions, 2012.

Gramsci, A. *Selections from the Prison Notebooks of Antonio Gramsci*. Edited and translated by Quintin Hoare and Geoffrey Nowell Smith. New York: International Publishers, 1971.

Hills, M. *Fan Cultures*. London: Routledge, 2002.

Hills, M. "'Proper Distance' in the Ethical Positioning of Scholar-Fandoms: Between Academics' and Fans' Moral Economies?" In *Fan Culture: Theory/Practice*, ed. K. Larson and L. Zubernis, 14–37. Newcastle upon Tyne: Cambridge Scholars Publishing, 2012.

Hills, M. "Implicit Fandom in the Fields of Theatre, Art, and Literature: Studying 'Fans' Beyond Fan Discourse." In *A Companion to Media Fandom and Fan Studies*, ed. P. Booth, 477–494. Boston: Wiley, 2018.

Jenkins, H. "'When Fandom Goes Mainstream …'." *Confessions of an Aca-Fan* [online], n.p., 2006. http://henryjenkins.org/blog/2006/11/when_fandom_goes_mainstream.html. Accessed 21 April 2015.

Jenkins, H. *Textual Poachers: Television Fans and Participatory Culture*. London: Routledge, 2012.

Marshall, P. D. "Productive Consumption: Agency, Appropriation and Value in the Creative Consuming of David Bowie." In Toija Cinque and Sean Redmond Special guest-edited edition, "Intersecting David Bowie." *Continuum: Journal of Media and Cultural Studies* 31 (4) (2017): 564–573.

Phillips, T. "Embracing the 'Overly Confessional': Scholar-Fandom and Approaches to Personal Research." *Flow* 13 (5) (2010): 1–15.

Platt, V., and M. Squire, eds. *The Frame in Classical Art: A Cultural History*. Cambridge: Cambridge University Press, 2017.

Schopenhauer, A. *The Essential Schopenhauer*. First published in *Parerga and Paralipomena*, 1851. London: Unwin Books, 1962.

Winnicott, D. W. *Playing and Reality*. London: Penguin, 1971.

Woodward, K. *Psychosocial Studies: An Introduction*. London: Routledge, 2015.

CHAPTER 8

Bowie Nets and Online Interactions

INTRODUCTION

In the context of online interactions, we seek to understand the extent to which fans experience a kind of 'digital shimmer' in contemporary life that deterritorialises David Bowie's star performances while simultaneously draws the willing into an intimate embrace. Indeed, the intricate dialectic of digital cultures conjoins and remerges texts and bodies as components in a code that suggests a wide range of messages. This chapter then acts to trace out an analysis of paratextual online media use organised through the experiences of Bowie fans. We argue that websites and social media such as Twitter and Facebook and the like together with imaging applications on mobile devices afford fans with intimate connections to like-minded others through increased opportunities for friendship or developing community bonds. Our approach here is to gauge the nature of public commentary, reaction and creative expression within the digital social spaces of Bowie fandom. Be it 'lurking' or actively posting comments and photographs, retweeting, creating personal websites, fan-fiction/art/vids among other subgenres or social media pages, we predict that there are subsequent valuable opportunities for shaping and engaging with public opinion. In addition to our other approaches, a non-intrusive methodology is also used for this chapter to specifically ask questions of: (1) how David Bowie has been engaged with by his fans using the Internet and social media; (2) how fans share their experiences online; and (3) the nature of the creative practices

© The Author(s) 2019
T. Cinque and S. Redmond, *The Fandom of David Bowie*,
https://doi.org/10.1007/978-3-030-15880-4_8

or shared stories that might emerge as a result. In a highly focused cultural analysis of fandom that brings to the surface identity politics and the wider social struggles in which a number might feel themselves to have a stake, this chapter explores the contested meanings and 'roles' for stars and celebrities online which are made salient.

The inclusion of Internet access as a basic capacity of many devices (fixed and portable) means that increasingly we use a connected range of media rather than single media in isolation. This affords a certain 'scalable sociality' to use Borgerson and Miller's (2006) term. Initially, many users would simply engage with existing 'real world' relationships online rather than forging new ones (see Ellison and Boyd 2013; Huijser 2008; Boyd and Ellison 2007; Ellison et al. 2007) such that respondents in research by Ellison et al. (2007: 1155) said that they viewed 'the primary audience for their profile to be people with whom they share an offline connection' and that: 'many use Facebook primarily to maintain existing offline relationships or to solidify what would otherwise be ephemeral, temporary acquaintanceships'. While this might be the experience of a number, other research of online communities by Tsaliki (2010, 2016), Shirky (2011) and Papacharissi (2010) confirms that individuals connect easily online to interest groups and society more broadly; findings supported by our fan feedback as we will see. Such online interactions allow for new connections to those with similar interests to be established, shaped and sustained. Indeed, the digital social encounters chronicled by respondents in our study attest to this model for online communication. Without doubt, access to news and information on the Internet about David Bowie, his videos, music, song lyrics and more via websites have changed significantly since the mainstream uptake of the World Wide Web (WWW) since the 1990s and this has grown with the additional uptake by users of social media including Twitter and Facebook.

A Pleasure Code

For many fans, much pleasure is to be found in the now globally accessible and interactive online commentary, creativity and digital content sharing with regard to stars and celebrities. This not least because for a number our digitally enforced lifeworld is an existential terrain. Questions concerning digital technologies are thus questions about human existence (Lagerkvist 2017). Digital technology has the capacity to heighten the cultural importance of both fandom and celebrity both through the augmented online interactions. In an observational ethnographic study of the capacity for more complex identification processes to be formed using the Internet, Soukup (2006: 319) established that fans can themselves influence substantially the meanings of media texts and use the iconography of celebrities to participate 'visibly' in public discourse via such digital means (also see Chapter 2). Specifically, fans have the capacity to enter into a dialogue with the 'artist' and the fan community both; to co-create the representation of the star or celebrity; and better establish personal identification with or through the star or celebrity. Decisively, G20 responded in our online survey to the question (Q6) 'Please recall and describe what your first memory of encountering David Bowie is?' that:

> I had seen Labyrinth as a small child, and watched it again in my early teens. From there, I think I found my way to Elizabeth A. Allans' essays on the character of the Goblin King on her fansite, *Jareth's Realm*. It was a hop, skip, and a jump from there to full-blown Bowie obsession.

Such co-creative opportunities are frequently found in ritualised forms of public online discussion and often characterised in recurring rhetorical devices, figures of speech or emotive words about a star/celebrity (love, real love, hate), that move back and forth on the stage of public culture. In their recent work on Web-based interaction, Siqueiros-García et al. (2018: 108) similarly find affective arrangements lure bodies to resonate thus causing the affective aspect of the engagement to become more prominent than encountered in other kinds of environments (see also Chapter 6):

> We use this notion to highlight the affective and embodied nature of Web-based interaction which is typically ignored. Digital affective arrangements can be described from two complementary perspectives: (1) In terms of what they afford: They offer action possibilities for both affective engagement and emotional expression that would be impossible in other settings. For instance, they afford public or intimate instant sharing of emotions, sending or receiving intrusive messages, abruptly finishing interaction by going offline, trolling or being trolled etc. (Lin et al., 2014). (2) In terms of the unfolding dynamics: They emerge from the spontaneous and meaningful actions that unravel when agents engage with others through the Web affordances. In posting, commenting, chatting, etc., agents bodily experience the affective dynamics they are contributing to. They feel the excitement of posting a picture that flatters them, the anger when confronted to negative content, and so on.

Commentary and user-generated stories via interactive fan sites such as BowieNet (community.davidbowie.com), BowieWonderWorld (www.bowiewonderworld.com/) and Teenage Wildlife (www.teenagewildlife.com/)—these sites are not dedicated to the commercial sale of merchandise such as CDs, T-shirts, photographs and the like—as well as social media, all act to offer representations of emulation and derision, connect people to each other, and operate within and across the streams of entertainment capital. Here, the circulation of public commentary produces a new melodramatic imagination (Beer and Penfold-Mounce 2009). Théberge (2005: 500) writes that:

> For both stars and fans, the Internet-based fan club offers a degree of access that is, without doubt, unprecedented in the history of fan culture. It offers the opportunity to perform their identities and relationships in an ongoing fashion, and what this performance may lack by way of intensity, it makes up for in the very quotidian regularity of its rhythms. In this way, a new set of relations may emerge that could help fans learn something about not only the stars that are the object of their desire, but also about themselves.

In this context, certain interpretations and understandings of 'real' space and place are less definitive, allowing for special encounters. The Internet and its social media forms have facilitated the coming together of formerly more separated youth taste cultures, such that literary, screen, music and graphic fandoms now more readily overlap across fan networks.

FANDOM ONLINE AND CREATIVE SHARING

Many years ago, Alvin Toffler (1970) used the term *prosumer* when he predicted that the role of producers and consumers would begin to blur and merge. The Internet era bears witness to this early premise yielding a new creative trajectory for many. Don Tapscott used the term *prosumption* (production + consumption) in his 1996 book *The Digital Economy: Promise and Peril in the Age of Networked Intelligence*. The 2000s witnessed the emergence of fan-created derivative works or the 'mashup' (music remixes, reboots, samplings, re-modelings) that involves rearranging isolated elements of a text, object, music, image or code. Australian researcher, Axel Bruns (2007: 6) consequently employed the term *produsers* to describe how participants in digital interactive spaces engage with content interchangeably in consumptive and productive modes at the same time. In this process of 'textual poaching' (to draw on Henry Jenkins' term), Bowie's star image has been used as a prominent subject for online memes via the digital mediasphere. Vernallis (2013: 131) has argued that online cultural production often instigates 'insistent reiteration' whereby successful memes and GIFs (a looping animation) become quickly and widely circulated encouraging the production of additional variations by other users. Here, David Bowie has been the subject of such creative works over many years, frequently encouraging fans ('old' and new) to delve into his past filmic works and music back catalogue. Fans use images that speak to them to then creatively share messages to others.

Their reintegration to form something completely new further develops for a number the creative impulse to adapt and appropriate visual and sonic aspects of Bowie's original work. Indeed, David Bowie remains one of the most highly 'mashed' artists due in large part to the observational and thought-provoking touchstones in his music and appeal that emotionally move his fans (Moore 2015). Bowie said himself that he was 'very comfortable with the idea and had been the subject of quite a few pretty good mashups … Mashups were a great appropriation idea just waiting to happen' (Bowie cited in Thompson 2006: 281–282). Such appropriations and new adaptations use David Bowie's cultural material in ways that are designed to appeal directly to participating fans'/prosumers' predilections. The creation and distribution of such memes, mashups and other re-edits occur typically within closed fan communities such as fan sites. This implies that the majority of content creators/users are intimately familiar with the original source material. Hence, they would immediately recognise the fan artist's version as encouraging of desirous virtual encounters and transformative readings.

Bowie himself predicted a future of newly emerging digital forms and Internet communications that witnessed his foundation in 1998 of the technology company Ultrastar (an Internet Service Provider [ISP] which launched BowieNet); his own bowieart.com aimed towards selling promising art students' work without the high commissions of terrestrial galleries; and his own fan club, BowieNet (viadavidbowie.com). As Morley describes Bowie's future thinking as a technological visionary (2016: 445):

> He could see one system coming to an end [industries being disrupted by digitalisation], and conceived another in a different sort of conceptual collaboration … Anticipating a communications revolution meant Bowie was the first major-level rock musician to release an online-only single in 1996,

and he was already experimenting with CD-ROMs and cybercasts of shows by 1997. He could already see how the internet offered a direct route to his fans, a way of communicating with them in an instant, and how it could become a vast interactive version of the late 1960s idea of the Arts Lab.

The Arts Lab at the Three Tuns pub in London's Beckenham High Street enfolded David's intention to: 'create an alternative environment to feature new and developing artists, providing a simple showcase for them' (Cann 1983: 52). More than the Arts Lab, however, BowieNet even preempted the later intentions of Facebook for its all-encompassing, daily *social-cum-commercial* interactions that connect our whole lives for news, entertainment, shopping, work and socialisation. But, David Bowie frequently treated his digitally struck stardom as a particular kind of game between himself and his fans as well. In the virtual realm and anonymously cloaked by an assumed identity, David Bowie would often engage with fans in his BowieNet forum using the pseudonym 'Sailor' and it is still possible as a BowieNet member to find Bowie's 'Sailor' profile and some of his posts from 2006/2007.

Fanpages online such as those on Tumblr and the like are themselves increasingly embedded in co-created media ecologies, and systematic analyses of how public communication takes place in the social mediasphere provide rich insights into a range of issues, emotions and behaviours called into being by fandom. Posted online to 'Archive of our Own', for example, is *Hamartia*, a dark story created by a fan which features an original plot with fictional characters of 'Jareth', also the name of the protagonist played by Bowie in *Labyrinth* (dir. Jim Henson, 1986), and 'David Bowie'. They are, however, written as different characters in this chronicle. The urban fantasy tells the tale of innocence lost, angst and shared intimacy. On this story's page, others can leave comments or 'kudos' (a button selected by users akin to Facebook's 'Like' function). Here where identification with a star performer/celebrity is expedited in increasingly individualistic and digital media-saturated cultures, it is reasonable to offer conjecture that, among others motivations, overcoming one's sense of invisibility or perceived anonymity is underscored as being a fundamental driving force for a number of fans (Soukup 2006: 334).

Fans are creating content and garnering feedback and comments forming as they do so friendship communities that are welcomed, or accepted, and which are successively managed through multiple layers of personal access. With reference to the concept of community formation, the remarks

of Anderson (1983) and later Boyd (2006) are lucid without being unten-
able in that the footprint of our new media engagement and habits enables
others to locate us in our friendship/fan communities and interconnect
with our 'imagined egocentric communities'. Such that, James (2013: 388)
contends with a focus on individual empowerment: 'At the core of our
"MEdiaverse" is the constant representation and reinvention of our personal past and present biographies ... We choose to connect, or not'. An
Australian now living in England and participating in our London-based
focus group described their conscious connection to a digital social circle
when recounting the nature of their own international community:

> I joined BowieNet in the 1990s ... so, I became friends with lots of people
> here in England and who are my friends to this day. We party and they are my
> social circle. Very much my fandom feels like it doesn't belong in Australia
> because I didn't have people that I could talk to there [about Bowie]. My
> fandom was definitely a world-wide network of people online. So, I do have
> these really strong friendships that last to this day and we are all over the
> place.

A follow-on question to this participant (GA) was: 'In terms of these friendships, how would you define them?', to which the participant stated:

> Before the internet had gotten so social, there was a time for me that the
> internet felt that it was a conduit to this immediate intimacy with other people
> that you didn't know like in chat-rooms you would really bear your soul and
> trust these people and only based on a really flimsy premise that we like
> similar music. But with these people I spent a good 25-30 years watching
> these people grow up, get married to each other and divorce each other. I'd
> go on holiday to see them and when they'd come to Australia they'd stay
> with me. We'd be talking on the phone and racking up bills ... you know,
> these people are real friends.

At first blush, study of online interactions yields insights into the lives,
opinions and feelings of fans. What is then set to work are the deeper
contemplations about the proliferating layers of their affective experiences.
With seemingly wistful remembering, one of our online survey participants
G1 responded in a similar vein to GA above. To the question (8): 'what
does David Bowie mean to you?', G1 stated that going online connected
them with like-minded others in collective, but virtual conversations with
significant consequences:

He has changed my life. I loved him when I was younger but to be honest he lost me in the 90s somewhat. So I can't say he formed my worldview or taught me about culture, like everyone seems to say. He came to mean everything to me from 2002 onwards when I joined BowieNet and found myself at the heart of a loving, warm, intelligent, funny community of creative people. I wouldn't be getting through what's happened without them.

And, similarly for BG:

David Bowie's music has had a profound impact on how I see myself and others. I started listening to him at an age where I was really discovering who I was and forging my own identity. I believe that I was always a nonconformist, but listening to his music and engaging with other Bowie fans on sites like Teenage Wildlife helped me feel like I belonged somewhere. I often got ridiculed at school for my clothing, my interests, my intelligence, my religion, etc. But Bowie helped set an example for me that it was alright to exist outside of contemporary norms and social expectations.

Two provocations are being intertwined here, the first being that the star is fundamental to the fan for the purposes of, in ideal circumstances, positive and purposeful identity formation through social interactions in the digital realm. The second summons the first, whereby the changed nature of contemporary communication bears witness to a digital shimmer that draws the relationships ever closer, intimately and perceptibly reducing their non-physical distance from each other. For G2:

He has been my idol and role model for 30 years of my life … I've seen him live well over 20 times, and met some great friends through BowieNet.

Bowie fan participants readily share their real-world experiences with others in the 'Bowie Net'. Yet again we found real-life intersecting with the virtual; their online interactions being drawn into everyday encounters in the real world and vice versa:

G3: [He] pretty much became an anchor-point for my socialisation: Bowie's music helped me to define myself, pretty much set the bar for what I ask of art/entertainment, and of course I met other Bowie fans online and in real life, which also became a portal to find more music, literature, art … Some of Bowie's abilities became ideals I strive for.

G4: 2003 was my first concert after moving to Berlin … I met other fans I knew online after the concert.

G5: [In] 2003, I won tickets through the fan section of his website and the whole experience was just so special. From meeting fellow fans who I'd only ever spoken to online (who are still friends almost 13 years on) to seeing him performing in such intimate surroundings, the whole thing was magical.

The axis upon which this digital shimmer is turning is a certain *phaino-ken*, a term established to capture the essence of one's knowledge or experience of a particular medium, its distinct materiality, and the particular cultural phenomenon of consequence that results (Cinque 2016: 444). Such is the vital spark of the star/fan relationships we are unpacking above as to what is rendered large in terms of how fans form groups around/through their Bowie fandom—and the means by which a star is 'seen' to metaphorically glow with the 'reflected light' of the immediate culture that has been forged and the broader social context in which they exist. The bond linking fans via a star performer, and their art has deep significance for those interlaced together online and acts to reinforce fundamental connections. We can see in the instances above, the shared feelings of personal friendships, together-ness and social ties that are fostered. On the heels of this comes a wonderful response by one of our participants who had a brush with Bowie:

G6: I did have him reply to a comment I made on his website's message board once, though, and that meant the world to me …

What is registered by G6 (above) points to online play as spectacle, the forging of links between star and fan, intimacy and revelation, in the process of reading and response. In any number of ways, the digital BowieSphere presents opportunities to make connections with/for his fans and increases affective investment. The added capacity for a star and their polysemous meanings to transubstantiate across time, place and cultural contexts also denotes that the star is no longer tethered to a particular time or setting and is absorbed as significant into the weft of society (see Boorstin 1964). Our star in the digital BowieSphere can now remain *forever* present for his fans.

Digital Interactions via Facebook: Bowie Conference Friends

For lovers of Bowie, who all had the pleasure of getting acquainted during the Lisbon Bowie Conference 2016, and in the evenings that followed ...

Where the preceding section has drawn on examples of online Bowie fandom more broadly, this section considers the more recent phenomenon of Facebook (since 2004) through a close analysis of a closed group that arose out of a Bowie aca-fan conference held in Lisbon in 2016. That David Bowie is the topic and avocation spurring discussion and commentary in online spaces among others is not unexpected.

The authors participated at the Lisbon conference and are friends in this Bowie Conference Friends Group. To elaborate, immediately after the conference the Facebook page was created and has been actively used on a regular basis by the participants. The group comprises members living in Portugal, America, Australia, England, Germany, New Zealand and Italy. The group ritually share pictures of Bowie, Bowie facts and invitations to tribute parties and showcase events such as film screenings, exhibitions, Bowie festivals and conference events that stretch across the globe.

We Are Social Planners

The Bowie Conference Friends page remains a site for conversation and connection between its followers. While members are internationally dispersed, we hope that our respective travels will bring us together again at some point for the enjoyment of our shared fandom. On a documentary film screening event related to David Bowie, BCF1 shared an invitation with an accompanying flyer (May 2017):

If you're around London on the 9th or 10th of May.

In a post, featuring another Bowie event flyer:

(from Lisbon) If you have nowhere else to go on May 6 ...

In this post about a Bowie event in the United States, in Philadelphia, BCF3 shares an invitation to friends (15 December 2017)

This is becoming a yearly event. If you happen to be near Philadelphia ...

And, when a group member planned a Bowie-themed conference, they posted:

> *BCFX* (6 September, 2017): I know you can't all be there, but I wish you could.

What we find here in these posts is the amity between these like-minded friends and colleagues, sharing and connecting online through their Bowie fandom regardless of the distances (and time zones) that physically separates them.

Bonds of Fandom

Another time, one of the participants BCFX in the group experiences 'six degrees of separation' sharing in April 2017, that:

> I'm hanging out with some American cousins right now. Turns out that the husband of one of my cousins used to work as a security guard or something like that for the Rolling Stones, amongst others. The Stones had to cancel their concert in an MTV show back in the late '90s and David Bowie replaced them. My cousin's husband says Bowie was the most amazing artist he had ever met and he didn't even like his music much before meeting and talking to him. I'll try to get the most I can out of him!

To which another respondent shares a video taken from that very concert. Upon confirming this as the very one being referred to, BCFX further comments:

> Yes, that one! We know, of course, Bowie is great, but it's exciting talking to someone who actually met him and thinks the same. I can say I had a Bowie night ...

Noting this significance of online sharing and connecting, when one group member posts an image of a fan love letter from a teenage 'Sabrina' hand-written to David Bowie many years ago, stating: 'Dear David Bowie, I love you very much. I would love it if you would send a picture of you to me'; another group member reflectively comments that to receive a single picture by post is set in opposition to how online access changed the nature of fandom in the digital age with a plethora of images readily available on demand:

> BCF4: Ah, bless: just 'a picture of you' ... if only Sabrina had had the 'interweb'
> :)

Bonds of Friendship

A number in the group regularly share weekend well-wishes, Christmas greetings and photos. The friendship of the group can be fluid yet remains close as can be seen when BCF1 checks in with the group (12 June 2018):

> I haven't been here in a while. Hope you're all doing well!

When a number of the aca-fan friends caught up in London, their *amicus curiae*, BCF2, posted to their Facebook page (6 April 2018):

> I had the great honor to host BCFs [name deleted] and [name deleted] at the Drexel University Audio Archives today. Listening to Bowie tapes!

The group has also offered each other council and support when in June 2017 came a very upsetting post. The trimmed conversation follows:

> Does anyone know how our dear friend [name deleted] is doing?

> If you are in contact, please give them my best.

A number respond that they had not had contact.

> Thanks [name deleted] and [name deleted] for letting me know.

> I hope they comes back to us soon.

Transcribed here are stories of optimism wherein exuberance makes itself felt in both subtle and overt ways. As we see above, there are also personal and existential vulnerabilities set out. We are flawed creatures that exist in a fugacious state. Underpinning the posts is a sense of searching to connect; yearnings and the joining of circumstances across time, place and space that makes themselves felt. We might have started out at the conference as individuals gathered in rapport, but formed a connected community where shared friendship now preponderates.

For a number, there is much delight within the digital matrix of textual forms across time, place and space. As can be understood from the examples above, an important narrative is around the affective role that celebrities and stars play in the digital sphere; the argument being that there is a mutual relationship between stars, together with their associated textual objects including 'gossip', and the receptive individual ('fan'). Here too we can see the camaraderie of like-minded friends connecting, revealing and disclosing through their shared Bowie fandom. Important aspects of stardom and celebrity studies in contemporary societies now span 'new' and social spaces for commentary, discussion and thinking about star performers and the various affects of fandom itself. Such is the nature of the 'Twitterverse'.

TWITTER: DIGITAL METHOD VIA POETIC LANGUAGE

When *The Next Day* was released in 2013, it was David Bowie's first album in ten years and for a fan used to bi-annual if not annual releases, this was a long time coming and an anticipated joy. Not long after came reports of another album for planned release in 2016. Fans waited with bated breath. Underscored by anticipation came *Blackstar* on 8 January 2016, just two days after David Bowie's birthday; the work a dark, moody, contemplative offering—then two further days later, David Bowie passed away. This section seeks now to narrow the focus to concentrate upon the complex relationship between David Bowie's star performativity as projected and perceived through the filter of online interactions and the emotive/affective responses that were produced at a significant time for David Bowie fans—at the released of his final album and then when he was brought out of his physical existence. We might intimate in line with Derrida (2001) that examination of the networks of mourning also evokes a typology of ritualised and networked mourning practices. The further need then becomes one to explore the affective ways in which sites, genres and platforms for mourning practices are mediated.

I'm a #Blackstar

The album's title is believed to symbolise death; it is the name given to a cancerous lesion, as well as the term for the transitional state between a collapsed star and a singularity. It is also reminiscent of the name of a little-known song 'Black Star' (Wayne and Sherman 1960) by one of Bowie's own musical idols, Elvis Presley. The song was recorded for the movie *Flaming Star*, but not used after its own title was changed to 'Flaming Star' for the film (dir. Don Siegel, 1960). Elvis' own 'Black Star' is about death and features the lyrics: 'Every man has a black star; a black star, over his shoulder. And when a man sees his black star, he knows his time … has come'. A reasonable question in this instance then arises from speculating upon whether Bowie felt an obligation to write the parting *Blackstar* album for his fans so that we would feel less alone. Perhaps, even so that he felt less alone in his last few months—a 'celebrity' self-fashioning of a posthumous identity.

Fan conversations were examined about David Bowie on social media at the time of the *Blackstar* album's 2016 release and the day Bowie died which happened just days later. This focus because an increasingly important aspect of stardom and celebrity in contemporary societies has found 'new' central spaces for discussion and commentary about popular music, its star performers and the various affects of fandom itself via the digital mediasphere. Of 'star' deaths and the reaction to them in the online spaces, Burgess et al. (2018: 1) convincingly argue that:

> deaths not only heralded intense affective and discursive activity on social media of the kind associated with public mourning, but they also enfolded ordinary users' biographies into public expressions of memory, or provoked adjunctive conversations about other topics.

This means that as new platforms emerge they encourage the filling of niches and gaps. As a result, we can now have greater choice over the degree of privacy or size of group we might wish to communicate to, what we share or interact with. Presently, we can see changes to Facebook and Twitter both in terms of how groups might be formed and used for the various interactions therein. Twitter hashtag research specifically involves searching Twitter for tagged tweets, collecting these tweets and using a range of analytic methods to interpret and display the data. Such research assesses how people are using the platform to communicate and interact with its content. There is a growing body of important literature associated with the collection and analysis of Twitter data and networks (see, for example, Hemsley et al. 2018).

This Twitter hashtag study involved harvesting relevant tweets (including original tweets and retweets) from Twitter for a mixed methods analysis

blackstar vs time

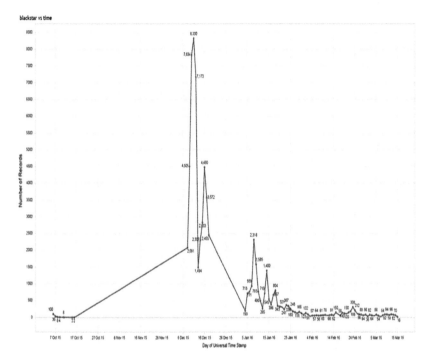

Fig. 8.1   The use of Hashtag #Blackstar from October 2015 to March 2016 (*Source* Created by Toija Cinque)

using established computational and hand-coding methods. A systematic Twitter search process used the most commonly occurring David Bowie related hashtags, previously determined through repeated scans of Twitter, as follows: '#Bowie', '#David Bowie', '#Blackstar'. Because data can be difficult to collect retrospectively from Twitter, a six-month period between 2015 and 2016 was initially chosen to begin gathering data for the 2016 release of the *Blackstar* album as part of the preparatory research for this book (see Fig. 8.1). As it turned out, it was also the time that David Bowie died.

Tweets captured through a search in Twitter are typically limited in quantity and time frame. Therefore, to capture the most tweets possible using the Twitter search bar, tweets were collected on a daily basis from October 2015 to March 2016. Tweets were captured before being exported to Microsoft Excel and Tableau for further analysis. Tweets outside the date range of data collection and duplicate tweets were removed so that only original tweets and retweets sent during the set time frame were included. Tweets were then examined to exclude: irrelevant tweets and those not related to David Bowie; tweets written in a language other than English; tweets that contained no text; spam (e.g. bulk advertising or marketing); and advertisements (e.g. for competitions). This was done to increase the relevance of the tweet content to meet the aims of the research.

Tweets in the dataset were analysed both qualitatively and quantitatively using a variety of methods. The quantitative analysis determined the overall number of tweets and the number of unique contributors (@users) over the pre-determined time period. The fan statements of unique @user profiles were classified as @users who: (a) tweeted using the hashtag '#Blackstar'; (b) tweeted using the hashtag '#Bowie' or '#DavidBowie'. This information provided context for the subsequent qualitative analysis of the data. Following the quantitative analysis, tweets identified as being written by fans about Bowie were further analysed by their linguistic content which formed a narrative coding.

Specifically, from fans that posted tweets using the hashtag '#Blackstar', the peak (8330 tweets) came on 6th of December 2015 and a smaller peak on 16th of December 2015 (4480 tweets) when fans avidly posted about the forthcoming release of the *Blackstar* album (see Fig. 8.1). The third peak was on 10 January 2016 when David Bowie died (2318 tweets). The assemblage of #Blackstar tweets at this time featured words including: 'genius', 'the goodbye album', 'requiem' and 'religious symbolism' (Fig. 8.2).

When looking at the retweet data in Fig. 8.2 above for the comments circulated to other users from an originating source (the initial tweet) using hashtag '#DavidBowie' or '#Bowie', there is an expected peak on 8 January 2016 at the time of David Bowie's birthday and the simultaneous release of *Blackstar*, but they climbed to 18,155 retweets on 13 January after Bowie's passing.

From fans that posted tweets using the hashtag '#DavidBowie' or '#Bowie', their tweets could be usefully divided into five distinct narrative domains: (1) words of expectancy regarding the impending release of the *Blackstar* (2016) album such as: 'Not long to wait now' and 'looking forward ...'; (2) words regarding the 2016 album's release and the contextual weight of his death e.g. 'devastated', 'sad', 'poignant', 'epitaph', 'grief' and 'obsession'; (3) comments reflecting personally upon the magnitude of David Bowie's passing for these fans such as: 'David Bowie RIP' and

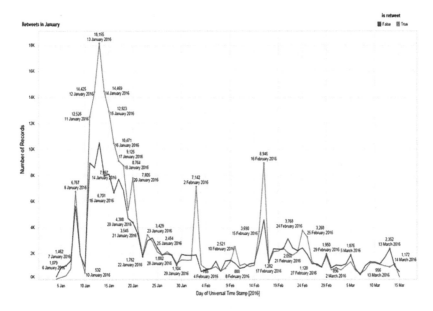

Fig. 8.2 Retweets using hashtag #DavidBowie in January 2016 to March 2016 (*Source* Created by Toija Cinque)

'Our hearts are aching'; (4) comments of representation such as 'Icon' as a term to indicate the significance or impact of David Bowie's creative work on them personally; and (5) negative comments (trolling) in the public domain. In detail:

1. *Anticipating the 'Blackstar'*

In the lead up to the release of *Blackstar*, a gathering of tweets using the hashtag '#Blackstar' was collected (scrapped) from Twitter to assess the public's reaction to the forthcoming release of the album. We estimated that there would be much anticipation within the fan communities at least as this was Bowie's first album in three long years. From thousands of statements, we found that there were much expectation and excitement. Indicative comments included: 'Happy David Bowie release week! It's gonna be really weird, so right up Bowie's alley. And it's called Blackstar' (2016-01-04 T08:05:14); 'Not long to wait now Bowie fans' (2016-01-04 T15:10:08);

and 'Looking forward to @DavidBowieReal new album on the 8th January' (2016-01-04 T17:11:18). We can see from these statements (and the many other similar assertions online) that fans were building up the suspense with like-minded others. They were sharing their hopes for yet another inspired musical creation from their hero.

What happened during the monitoring of the tweets was, however, quite unexpected. The authors initially thought that they would simply find the affirmation and a little consternation that naturally surrounds an impending new creative work and its release by an artist. What happened instead was in every respect intense and shocking and not just for fans as popular media reports from around the world at the time attest to.

2. *#Blackstar Is a Masterpiece*

Upon David Bowie's passing on 10 January, just days after the release of the album *Blackstar*, his shocked fans came to virtually gather, not just to ponder the surface weight of the work, but to lament his passing and grieve together. His new songs took on a vastly different set of possible meanings for many as a number came to study the lyrics from within the drastically changed frame that now surrounded the album. Typical comments on Twitter from 2016 include: 'Rock Star #DavidBowie left us devastated, with the devastating last album #Blackstar' (2016-01-11 T12:05:19); 'Interesting to read the lyrics of the seven songs on #Blackstar after today's sad news' (2016-01-11 T19:49:11); and '"Songs About Death": Thursday's now-poignant review of @DavidBowieReal's new album Blackstar' (2016-01-11 T19:45:47). Other fans were wistful in thinking through this new work: 'Blackstar sounds like his requiem #BowieForever' (2016-01-11 T10:46:51), and 'Blackstar is a masterpiece. Will stand as sonic lesson in making death/horror/trauma poetic, dreamy, hopeful, wondrous, beautiful & sensual' (2016-01-11 T19:49:36).

3. *David Bowie RIP*

Fascinating is that while the following statements are accompanied by the use of the hashtag #DavidBowie and circulated virtually to/for others in the very public spaces of social media, they are also heartfelt tribute statements, much the same as might be fervidly, but privately, spoken and heard at a friend's or family member's funeral. For example, in their own words:

'RIP David Bowie. Our hearts are aching. You left us a beautiful parting gift, and we thank you. #BlackStar' (2016-01-11 T19:48:51); 'R.I.P. David Bowie. A very special creative force. You will be missed. #Major-Tom #Blackstar #DavidBowie' (2016-01-11 T15:22:20); 'The Stars Look Very Different Today #BlackStar' (2016-01-11 T20:21:57); 'Hard to believe @DavidBowieReal could create something as hauntingly beautiful as #Blackstar in final days … RIP you beautiful human being' (2016-01-11 T11:33:38); 'Bowie, synonymous with innovation and intrepidness, we all mourn #Blackstar' (2016-01-11 T18:17:58); and ' Bowie all day, Bowie all week. Fuck it, Bowie forever. RIP #Blackstar' (2016-01-11 T14:23:39).

4. *David Bowie Is*

A number of fans emotionally contextualised their past pleasure, desire and identity politics through perceptions of David Bowie as an icon. Representative examples from the many comments posted online are: 'Reflecting on the impact @DavidBowieReal had on my life… A true #Icon. Listening to #Blackstar. Thank you for all the music' (2016-01-11T11:51:28); '"I can't give everything away". Oh David, genius to the last. Heartaching, poignant, beautiful. Love it so much. #Blackstar #DavidBowie' (2016-01-11T19:47:48); 'Today we lost a great musician, visual artist and creative genius. It is appropriate to cry… #Bowie #Blackstar' (2016-01-11T19:19:23); 'Thank you #DavidBowie for being one of my biggest inspirations. Forever in debt to you. #RIPDavidBowie #Blackstar' (2016-01-11T23:48:51); 'So sad to hear about the loss of #DavidBowie. He was a legend and a major influence on me. #Blackstar is a brilliant album' (2016-01-11T20:10:32); 'A genuine icon and music innovator has been lost to us today. A Star has gone out #Blackstar #RIP' (2016-01-11T11:00:41); and 'DavidBowie has gone to the stars. Whether he'll be a #Blackstar or #stardusttostardust he was a bright star for many of us' (2016-01-11T18:46:57).

As can be observed, for many of David Bowie's fans, their sensitive nucleus was ruptured the day he died and their lamentations resounded in this public, social mediasphere. Undeniably, 'a star has gone out'. Here we find posts by fans trying to comprehend the impact and the significance of the moment. The ruminative posts could be read as an even deeper proclamation that something seems to have shifted within these fans and nothing would be quite the same again—for any of us.

5. *The Trolls*

The analysis here did find some negative commentary in the popular press spurring consequent remarks online. For example, the popular press *The Sun* (UK) and *Daily Mail* (Australian edition) both ran with headlines purporting: 'EXCLUSIVE: David Bowie's sex addiction drove him to sleep with 13-year-old groupies, engage in wild orgies and declare he was bi-sexual with a "permanent erection"—but he turned down an offer to "f*** a warm dead body"' (http://www.dailymail.co.uk/news/article-4800164/David-Bowie-slept-13-year-olds-engaged-orgies.html). Social media was also used communally by fans to refute the notions presented by the reported allegations pointing out that no conviction eventuated: 'Lol, these trolls make me laugh. It's sensationalism, it's a story geared to sell papers … The police have never been involved' (20 August 2017), and 'he is dead now, he cannot defend himself over these stories' (20 August 2017) (see https://www.thesun.co.uk/news/4276028/david-bowie-13-groupies-age-dead-body-new-book-gay-sex/). Some Twitter comments were levelled against David Bowie's wife, Iman. Typical of a number of responses, however, was this one that countered: 'The man just died, leave his wife alone #blackstar' (2016-01-11T18:56:19). This troll's account is now suspended.

While the focus thus far has been on the text (coded pink in Fig. 8.3 below), it was also accompanied in many cases by emotive imagery that fans felt connected to: photographic (coded purple), audio (coded orange) and video material (coded grey in Fig. 8.3). The larger the circle below the more content shared on that day/date:

What emerged as interesting is that while David Bowie is frequently associated with music rather than his other art forms, the day after he died (11 January 2016) the majority of content being circulated was photographic (1262) as opposed to links to audio (in blue and orange respectively in Fig. 8.3). In line with the focus groups that we ran in Berlin, Lisbon, New York, London, Tokyo, Melbourne and Amsterdam—within which we asked participants during the study to choose a particular image of David Bowie and speak to why they chose it or what it meant to them personally—here again, fans chose visual images that spoke to them and shared this 'moment' with others.

There were two limitations associated with the dataset here to note. First, of the thousands of tweets checked and analysed manually only a

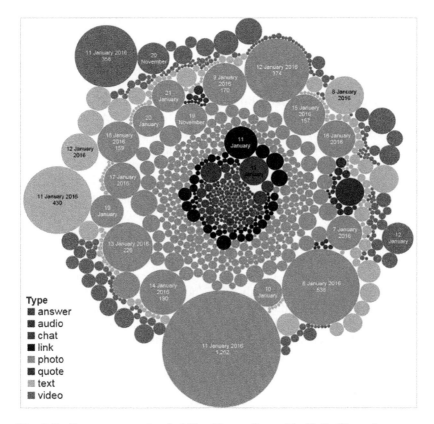

Fig. 8.3 Dataset versus time bubbles (*Source* Created by Toija Cinque)

select number of tweets were used (approximately 10,000 of a possible 50,000 available) because a number were in languages other than English and were removed from the set along with advertisements and multiples of a single post. This study does, however, still represent a significant sample size from which to draw critical conclusions. Second, because only English-language tweets were included for analytical review, a potentially rich store of information was left untapped and unrepresented because of the incapacity to reliably translate all non-English-language tweets. This is a cultural bias that might be addressed in future studies with consideration given to the 'cleaning' of the data and how many and the types of responses that are removed so there is greater representation from international fan communities.

Coded into the DNA of Our Souls

An expected portrait of David Bowie and the 'digital sphere' emerges then; one arranged from the increased ubiquity of the distribution platforms, essentially blog sites, social media forms of Twitter and Facebook and imaging devices on mobile screens that afford amplified fan interactions connected to him. The qualitative analysis and quantitative analysis here using online data demonstrate that the social mediasphere played an important role for a number of David Bowie fans over time and when he passed away, for mourning and remembering his virtues collectively without resorting to hagiography. While plausibly fortifying David Bowie's now iconic image (his myth), his death might have prompted instead a reputational re-evaluation through the (re)emergence of scandalous or unsavoury posthumous revelations resulting in the desecration, rather than the enhancement, of his star identity. But, no substantial negative effect was found in this content analysis. Using the fans' own narratives demonstrated a range of thoughts and feelings in which their value and significance were invested in relatively stable digital ensembles of experience that conveyed the meaning of a life to self and others and found embodied resonance.

For many fans, there is much delight in the direct actions and capacity for community building afforded by connection to David Bowie that is linked online. This radical ubiquitisation of digital paratexts, the visual forms and virtual conversations together, alongside communications technologies certainly interrupt the present and fertilise the immediate contemporary experience of popular media use and practices for fans. What became apparent through this research of the digital discussions around the topic of David Bowie is that while we have all seen the same 'officially produced' footage and images and heard the same music—arising from those that Bowie generated, featured in or has been associated with—we each read Bowie's work in slightly different ways. By way of creative extension, the digital mediasphere has conferred the means for many to recreate the 'conversation'. But like the torments of Tantalus, the circulation and recirculation of video footage, images, sound and user-generated content online means that he is eternally present, rendered large yet now, always out of our worldly reach. It is undoubtable that the Starman has left his imprint on the DNA of our souls. In the dark spaces, fans are the secrets between the stars.

References

Anderson, Benedict. *Imagined Communities: Reflections on the Origin and Spread of Nationalism*. London: Verso, 1983.

Beer, David, and Ruth Penfold-Mounce. "Celebrity Gossip and the New Melodramatic Imagination." *Sociological Research Online* 14 (2) (2009): 1–15. http://socresonline.org.uk/14/2/2.html. Accessed 24 August 2017.

Boorstin, Daniel J. *The Image: A Guide to Pseudo-Events in America*. New York: Harper & Row, 1964.

Borgerson, Janet, and Daniel Miller. "Scalable Sociality and 'How the World Changed Social Media': Conversation with Daniel Miller." *Consumption Markets & Culture* 19 (6) (2006): 520–533.

Boyd, dana. "Friends, Friendsters and MySpace Top 8: Writing Community into Being on Social Network Sites." *First Monday* (2006). http://firstmonday.org/htbin/cgiwrap/bin/ojs/index.php/fm/article/view/1418/1336. Accessed 10 August 2018.

Boyd, Dana M., and Nicole B. Ellison. "Social Network Sites: Definition, History, and Scholarship." *Journal of Computer-Mediated Communication* 13 (1) (2007): 210–230.

Bruns, Axel. "From Production to Produsage". In *Uses of Blogs*, ed. A. Bruns and J. Jacobs, 6–7. New York: Peter Lang, 2007.

Burgess, Jean, Peta Mitchell, and Felix Münch. "Social Media Rituals: The Uses of Celebrity Death in Digital Culture." In *A Networked Self: Birth, Life, Death*, ed. Zizi Papacharissi. New York: Taylor & Francis Group, 2018 (forthcoming).

Cann, Kevin. *David Bowie: A Chronology*. London: Vermilion, 1983.

Cinque, Toija. "Digital Shimmer: Popular Music and the Intimate Nexus Between Fan and Star." In *Companion to Celebrity (Studies)*, ed. P. David Marshall and Sean Redmond, 440–456. Boston: Wiley Blackwell, 2016.

Derrida, Jacques. *The Work of Mourning*. Edited by Pascale-Anne Brault and Michael Naas. Chicago: University of Chicago Press, 2001.

Ellison, Nicole B., and Danah M. Boyd. "Sociality Through Social Network Sites." In *The Oxford Handbook of Internet Studies*, ed. W. H. Dutton, 151–172. Oxford: Oxford University Press, 2013.

Ellison, Nicole B., Charles Steinfield, and Cliff Lampe. "The Benefits of Facebook 'Friends': Social Capital and College Students' Use of Online Social Network Sites." *Journal of Computer-Mediated Communication* 12(4) (2007): 1143–1168.

Hamartia. Posted to 'Archive of Our Own'. https://archiveofourown.org/works/5990221.

Hemsley, Bronwyn, Stuart Palmer, Stephen Dann, and Susan Balandin. "Using Twitter to Access the Human Right of Communication for People Who Use Augmentative and Alternative Communication (AAC)." *International Journal of Speech-Language Pathology* 20 (1) (2018): 50–58.

Huijser, Hendrik. "Exploring the Educational Potential of Social Networking Sites: The New Line Between Exploiting Opportunities and Unwelcome Imposition." *Studies in Learning, Evaluation, Innovation and Development* 5 (3) (2008): 45–54.

James, Martin. "A Silent Voice Across the MEdiaverse: The Next Day as Identities Prosumed." *Celebrity Studies* 4 (3) (2013): 387–389.

Lagerkvist, Amanda. "Existential Media: Toward a Theorization of Digital Thrownness." *New Media & Society* 19 (1) (2017): 96–110.

Lin, Han, William Tov, and Lin Qiu. "Emotional Disclosure on Social Networking Sites: The Role of Network Structure and Psychological Needs." *Computers in Human Behavior* 41 (2014): 342–350.

Moore, Christopher. "2004 (Bowie vs Mashup)." In *Enchanting David Bowie: Space/Time/Body/Memory*, ed. Toija Cinque, Christopher Moore, and Sean Redmond, 153–168. Bloomsbury: New York, 2015.

Morley, Paul. *The Age of Bowie: How David Bowie Made a World of Difference.* London: Simon & Schuster, 2016.

Papacharissi, Zizi. *A Private Sphere: Democracy in a Digital Age.* Cambridge: Polity Press, 2010.

Shirky, Clay. "Political Power of Social Media-Technology, the Public Sphere, and Political Change." *Foreign Affairs* 90 (1) (February 2011): 28–41. http://heinonline.org/HOL/Page?handle=hein.journals/fora90&div=8. Retrieved 17 December 2017.

Siqueiros-García, Jesús M., Laura Mojica, and Susana Ramírez-Vizcaya. "The Affective Affordances of the Web: A 4E Approach." In Artificial Life Conference Proceedings, No. 30, 107–108. Cambridge, MA: MIT Press, 2018.

Soukup, Charles. "Hitching a Ride on a Star: Celebrity, Fandom, and Identification on the World Wide Web." *Southern Communication Journal* 71 (4) (2006): 319–337.

Tapscott, Don. *The Digital Economy: Promise and Peril in the Age of Networked Intelligence.* New York: McGraw-Hill, 1996.

Théberge, Paul. "Everyday Fandom: Fan Clubs, Blogging, and the Quotidian Rhythms of the Internet." *Canadian Journal of Communication* 30 (4) (2005): 485–502.

Thompson, David. *Hallo Spaceboy: The Rebirth of David Bowie.* Toronto: ECW Press, 2006.

Toffler, Alvin. *Future Shock.* New York: Random House, 1970.

Tsaliki, Lisa. "Technologies of Political Mobilization and Civil Society in Greece: The Wildfires of Summer 2007." *Convergence: The International Journal of Research into New Media Technologies* 16 (2) (2010): 151–161.

Tsaliki, Lisa. "Tweeting the Good Causes: Social Networking and Celebrity Activism." In *Companion to Celebrity (Studies)*, ed. P. David Marshall and Sean Redmond, 235–257. Boston: Wiley Blackwell, 2016.

Vernallis, Carol. *Unruly Media: Youtube, Music Video, and the New Digital Cinema.* New York: Oxford University Press, 2013.

Wayne, Sid, and Sherman Edwards. "Black Star" Later Changed to "Flaming Star." EP Recorded on 8 August 1960 at Radio Recorders, Hollywood, California.

CHAPTER 9

Ghostly Pilgrimages

Introduction

There are many ways to move through place and space—one can haunt a city, trace a journey or encounter the aliveness of memories. Albeit that they are derived therein, our memories are not confined to the past, but reach forward to be felt in the present time. *Time* then takes not a realist's view of temporality but exists in a circularity of continually folding back upon itself. Here, we find spaces to reinterpret our memories, feelings and experiences and all the intervals in between. Time is what we have, what we lose, a point we might look forward to or backward upon. It is simultaneously all and nothing, neither an event nor a thing. Within time, it is the assembly of memory that catches our breath through re-imagining key moments or people that needles the body to respond. Over the last century, advances in transportation and the instant and global circulation of multiple and networked digital media forms have allowed for a non-Euclidean perception of place to arise that subsequently emphasises 'time axis manipulation over the fixity of location' (Graves-Brown 2009: 220). In this chapter, we explore how David Bowie is an artist who always is/always was, futuristic and nostalgic, always present in memorial motifs and haunted places through time and the temporal.

With reference to Jacques Derrida's neologism, 'hauntology', we focus in this chapter on the tracing of times and places for the conversational rhythms, for the physical journeys through memorial spaces and of cities associated with David Bowie. Specifically, in 2016 we travelled to Tokyo (June), London (June), New York (July), Berlin (September) and we undertook research during conferences dedicated to celebrity and David Bowie in Melbourne (February), Amsterdam (June) and Lisbon (September) for the ghosts that every naturally constituted fan feels an irresistible urge to encounter. In these contexts, we come to understand the events, locations, circumstances and desires as recalled by the fans, both historically and philosophically. We find the spectre of David Bowie emerging by anamnesis in cities and important locations, bringing forth ghosts as flaring but ephemeral nostalgic images in the process. In this chapter, we encounter fans recalling their travels in pilgrimage to live events and locations, often driven by 'a myth' or nostalgia, which have afforded them purposeful exploration of their motivating circumstances and desires.

Spectres of Bowie: Myths and the Rhizomatic Entwining of Memories

'David Bowie' was always beginning so the conjunctional use of the theory of hauntology keeps the future open, since the spectre ends, only by coming back and is always to come (Derrida 1994: 2). Time is punctuated by returns such that '[t]he specter is thus both past and future; it is from the past, but waiting to come back. The metaphor of a specter haunting the present establishes the idea/image of the existence of something ghostly which stands over and outside the present, something which does not belong to time, and is waiting to come' (Hughes 2012: 15). The prosopopoeial 'specters of Bowie' (see also D'Cruz 2015) act here to position memorial moments in/across time revealing aspects of the arras of a fan's significant lived experiences.

But, the tale does have to start somewhere. Familiar to fans is that David Robert Jones was from London. As it is told, at the start of 1947 in London, climatic conditions were freezing and the exceptionally cold weather caused the Lambeth Town Hall clock to strike thirteen times at midnight, while just half a mile away Margaret Mary Burns gave birth to a baby boy, a son to Haywood Stenton Jones, born at 40 Stansfield Road, Brixton on the 8th of January (Pegg 2011: 5). Biographer, David Buckley, atmospherically recounts that the attending 'midwife-cum clairvoyant … allegedly remarked, "[t]his child has been on earth before," as the babe snuggled into one of the coldest, snowiest winters of the century' (2005: 11); a seemingly providential introduction to his world marked by the war-damaged infrastructure of Brixton outside his home windows that would tinge later visual imagery and lyrics. This damage of the recent past in sites of destruction and abandonment representationally addressed 'not only the unsaid but the unsayable', the 'unconstituted' and that which 'remains outside discourse' (Buchli and Lucas 2002: 12). In Leigh's (2014: 15–16) biography of Bowie she further underscores the impact of the war:

> As history tells us, during the Second World War German bombs didn't drop on London's historical landmarks, like Westminster Abby, the House of Parliament, the Tower of London, St Paul's Cathedral ... but rather on the East End and South London which bore the brunt of the bombing ... [The devastations] were in evidence within a few miles' radius of David's home and would remain there well into the early fifties, when most of the houses were replaced with prefabricated reinforced bungalows, known as "prefabs." Hurriedly thrown together eyesores with seemingly paper-thin walls, prefabs rose up from bombsites that resembled the desolate craters on the surface of the moon: forbidding, barren, like some bleak mysterious planet - all gist for David's creativity.

While a full account of Bowie's life is beyond the scope of this chapter (for detail see among others: Morley 2016; Trinka 2011; Spitz 2009; Stevenson 2006; Buckley 2005), many fans in London have haunted Brixton and the Jones' first address and 4 Plaistow Grove in Bromley, Kent. This was the later home in which David Jones lived with his family for fifteen years from 1955. A number have peregrinated through London, to the former Trident Studios where *Space Oddity* (1969), *Hunky Dory* (1971), *The Rise and Fall of Ziggy Stardust and the Spiders from Mars* (1972) were recorded; Heddon St, Mayfair where Bowie was photographed as Ziggy Stardust for the 1973 album; the then Marquee Club (where he performed as Ziggy Stardust in 1973), and; the former Hammersmith Odeon where Bowie announced his last show with the Spiders from Mars.

Brooker (2017: 171) writing of fans experiencing pilgrimage and the motivations that lie therein conjectures that many fans: 'depart from their own habitus and the frameworks of everyday life, but those who travel to the homes and final resting places ... [can similarly] experience their destinations as familiar, safe, places of communion and reassurance'.

On the topic of pilgrimage to certain 'sacred' places, we asked the participants in our survey (Q13): 'Have you ever visited a site or place that is given significance within David Bowie's career?' and so many had:

H1B: I picked where I live. To be closer to the spot. I'm very addicted to everything Bowie. It feels cool, knowing he walked the same streets.

H1A: I have been to Heddon Street where the iconic Ziggy album cover was shot. I had been collecting something from a shop in Oxford street and was really just wandering around the area, I found myself in Regents street and I just happened to look up and see the sign for "Heddon Street", so I ducked in and got some poor photos on my phone. I felt kind of sad I suppose, because of how much it had (of course) changed, and I'd have liked to have jumped in a time machine and gone back to when David and Marc Bolan were bright young things kicking about in the general area!

H22: I visited the studio in London where he recorded Major Tom. I visited the Bowie exhibition twice at The Victoria and Albert Museum in London.

These comments above of wandering and dreaming in the streets while thinking of David and Marc Bolan 'kicking about' draw on what participant H1A was themself doing in the very area. For H1B, that they chose to live near a sacred site meant that they could readily trace Bowie's spectral footsteps in the familiar locales and be actively confronted with feelings of wonder while roaming the liminal spaces. Dyer (1979) contends that when we examine our stars, our intellectual and emotional anchor-points, we are also examining ourselves. This march of thinking is borne out by our quantitative online survey results (see Table B.7, Appendix B) that finds that respondents summarise David Bowie's place for them as being 'Life' (170 respondents used this term by way of description) and 'Imagination' (116 respondents used this term by way of description).

Others also recalled details of their personally significant, azimuthal travelling to hallowed locations and the special atmosphere that they experienced:

H1: I went to the Hammersmith gig in 2002 because it is a historic venue (Ziggy's farewell). It was a great concert and when he wore the boa that I had thrown on stage that made it extra special.

H2D: Yes, a few through the years. Most notably Berlin, and Heddon Street and The Phone Box from the Ziggy Stardust cover. I went up to Heddon

Street the night of the day I heard he'd died (Jan 11th). It was one of the most heartbreaking moments of my life.

H2D: The Heddon Street phone box. I think every lifelong Bowie fan makes that pilgrimage. I was living in London, and on a night out with a pack of other Bowie fans, we happened to be walking down Regent Street when somebody said: "let's go to the phone box in Heddon Street!" We took pictures, including one of all of us squeezing in.

One finds in the responses above from participants that the Heddon Street phone box is now a fane for fan-pilgrimage and 'Ziggy Stardust' a name to conjure with. Since his death, we find David Bowie's cultural currency posthumously circulating as Walking Tours that offer guided tours of Bowie's 'hometown' of Brixton (see https://bowietourlondon.co.uk/ and https://freetoursbyfoot.com/david-bowie-sites-london/) and most recently the Bowie Mural, painted in 2013 on the side of a Brixton department store by street-artist, Jimmy Cochran, that became a public shrine and central location for fans in the UK to go to and mourn his 2016 passing by way of leaving tributes such as flowers, letters, photographs and other mementos. Many participants noted for us the important touchstones grounded in memories and shared, communal experiences of their fandom:

H3C: Heddon Street in London, with friends on several occasions. Brixton at the mural last week for obvious reasons. I think I went with a group to Stansfield Rd once years ago on a tour that also took in Beckenham.

H3E: I went on a Bowie tour of London once. I have also made pilgrimages to the location of Haddon Hall, Heddon Street and the Bowie Mural in Brixton.

That fans themselves have fashioned these makeshift memorials honours the personal significance of David Bowie for affording them ways to feel and acknowledge their own unique thoughts, emotions and experiences. In their individual and collective mourning, candles were lit, handwritten notes, flowers and cards lined the department store wall. Friends and strangers gathered in support and found reassurance; together they talked, sang and remembered.

When we asked participants in our online survey (Q11): 'Have you ever seen David Bowie live in concert or on stage?' other fans revealed that they had undertaken the 'road trip' across time to place. Outlined in detail below:

H3A: 16 times in a dozen cities in half a dozen countries from 1990-2004. Not as many as I'd have liked, nor as many as friends have under their belts, but I can't complain. *Sound and Vision* 1990, then the Freddie Mercury concert. Twice in 2002, including Hammersmith. 10 times in 2003 including a New York Bowie net show and Riverside in London, the final time in 2004 in Holland. Also had a ticket for the last (?) show in Monaco which was cancelled.

H4: I've seen him twice. The first time was at Area 2 in Tinley Park, Il. I was a junior in high school and I made the 4-hour drive with two of my friends. It was at an outdoor venue and the sound was awful. The stadium was also huge and probably less than half full. I think I was a little disappointed at the lack of intimacy but I did enjoy the performance. The second time was better. I saw him at Madison Square Garden on the *Reality Tour* with friends from a David Bowie fan site. We were maybe halfway back in the arena, so significantly far away, but I remember thinking how amazing it was that he could hold such a huge audience in the palm of his hand. The show was fantastic and I think it might have been my first visit to NYC as an adult.

H5: Yes, about 50 times since 1973. Each tour was so different from the previous one meaning every show was a slightly different experience.

H6: I've seen David around 192 times live, all over the world (UK, Europe, Japan, New Zealand/Oz and the USA) including concerts and TV shows between 1987 - 2004

H7: Yes! 13 December 2003, Bell Centre, Montreal QC, Canada. I went with my dad … It was a divine experience to me, and no concert will ever top it … Bowie started singing Ziggy Stardust (I think? It was from that album though), my dad asked me, "Is that from his fucked-up phase?" I didn't really answer that, and honestly I wanted to respond with "Which one? The one where he idolized Hitler? Nope." but I didn't want to ruin this incredible experience.

H8: I did get to see him 3 times, on the *Serious Moonlight Tour* in Perth of November, 1983. I camped out for two weeks outside the Perth Entertainment centre for good tickets, during my school holidays. I managed lounge tickets a few rows from the front in the centre. Managed to jump all seats to get to the front for both Saturday and Sunday concerts. On the first concert, on the Friday night, I went and hung out with my older sister at the backstage exits, and a bouncer have us all a free ticket each to the concert that had already begun. In a mass of excitement, we ran inside and took our seats and remained dancing for the entire concert.

H9: Yes, six times (Vancouver 1997, NYC 2000 & BowieNet show, NYC 2002, Calgary 2004, Edmonton 2004). Imagine a dose of adrenaline and serotonin, and you can possibly imagine only part of how in awe and fascinated I was at my first Bowie show. It was one of the smaller *Earthling Tour* shows, and felt very intimate. Bowie was only a few rows away, and I'd been dying to see him for ages already then. (and I missed the *Outside Tour* because it only went to Toronto and I couldn't afford it, and was only 15.)

H10: Berlin, December 2009. I purchased *Low*, *Heroes* and *Lodger* before my trip and I transited the frozen city for a week with Bowie as my soundtrack. Ethereal.

The comments above reveal that emotion will always be in motion as fans recall overlapping events related to their experiences from different eras as memorial moments from *then* are pulled into the *now* of their pilgrimage. As we see from H10's statement, they used Bowie's music from the 1970s as an *aide-mémoire* that sound-tracked their movements through 'modern' urban Berlin by way of memorially (re)constructing their perception of the city as sacred place. For H9, experiencing Bowie was felt akin to 'a dose of adrenaline and serotonin'; or for H7 the 'divine'. Others were also moved physically as H8 was, first sleeping on the street for many nights to get tickets in the first instance, then jumping over venue seats towards Bowie's presence with a 'mass of excitement', to dance all night.

Some fans regularly travelled extensively in the hope of more personal encounters. In our study, KJ revealed to us that they had met David Bowie some twelve to thirteen times in international pilgrimage for this express purpose. While some of these 'meetings' were just a quick 'hello' as Bowie walked past, others were more meaningful making KJ's travel worthwhile. Their first especial meeting was recounted in detail as being on 2 July 1989 and the second some seven years later on 8 June 1996, but for this participant, the strong emotion for the object of their inspiration remained fresh:

> We followed the tour bus during the Tin Machine tour from Usk, in Wales up to Bradford, but lost it *en route*. We decided to travel via Stratford Upon Avon - we don't really know why but, luckily, our route took us past a pub called the March Hare in Broughton Hackett, Worcs, where David and the band were having Sunday lunch. We patiently waited until they were leaving and asked David for his autograph, which he very kindly gave. This was my first time meeting him.

> The second time, I was following the tour around Japan with 2 friends. We waited outside the back entrance to the venue in Hiroshima to see David arrive, around 3pm. When his car pulled up, he pointed at us and said something to his bodyguard, Erik, then went inside. Erik came over to us and said, "can you 3 come through, David wants to say hello". When we walked in, David was waiting and said, "what on earth are you guys doing here?" Probably recognising us from the front row at about 30 of the shows around UK/Europe on the tour so far. He had a brief chat with us and asked Erik to arrange tickets for us for the show that night. A truly memorable experience!

The thread being drawn throughout each of the recollections above is that, albeit differently anticipated by fans, Bowie 'myths' of performance and the man himself have, over many decades, contributed to certain expectations preceding the fans' travel to notable sites and attendance at concerts. KJ above repeatedly found in David Bowie someone warm, accommodating and perhaps familiar; they sensed that Bowie had remembered them. Respondent H5 noted that 'every show was a slightly different experience' and of the many they attended, each one was special.

Catherine Soussloff (1997) explains compellingly that the figure of the artist in historical contexts has been produced by way of biographies and anecdotes that work up and reinforce the myths of the artist. *Myths* in this sense relate to Roland Barthes' (2000: 142) epistemology of them being structures that are greater and more enduring than 'reality', replicas of sorts, as opposed to notions of complete falsehoods:

> What the world supplies to myth is an historical reality, defined, even if this goes back quite a while, by the way in which [people] have produced or used it; and what myth gives in return is a *natural* image of this reality ... The

world enters language as a dialectical relation between activities, between human actions; it comes out of myth as a harmonious display of essences.

To varying degrees, fans put their faith in the 'myth' to the extent that David Bowie becomes someone 'known' to them in different ways and is one they expect to find; a special presence they seek in their travels. Noted in this chapter is that many fans have travelled to experience Bowie, to be 'there' with and/or imaginatively 'like' him. Sometimes, their 'sacred' pilgrimage or tourism can also act to take fans away a little from their everyday modes of life that are difficult. Support for this is found in the work of Porter (2004) and drawing attention to research by anthropologist E. Alan Morinis (1992). Here, we find that travel can be appreciated as pilgrimage if the: 'journey [is] undertaken by a person in quest of a place or a state that he or she believes to embody a valued ideal' especially where these destinations might be: '… an intensified version of some ideal that the pilgrim values but cannot achieve at home' (Porter 2004: 161). The travel in such instances plays the role of pure feelings such that fans are able to (re)build themselves through Bowie—from the inside out—as S recounts:

> Over the years a couple of things have happened to me, and Bowie has dom-inated my mind and everything I did really centres around him so it really did become a bit of an obsession where from 1976 to 1983 I was travelling around to see him all throughout Europe and in 1987 I started going to America and I have been very fortunate over the years to do two things – I have seen some really special shows and to meet him twice. The first time I met him I said to him "It took me 27 years to meet you" and he looked up at me and he said "Yeah?" and then the second time, and I had thought a bit about this, I said "I just want to thank you for all the pleasure you have given through your work over the years" and this time he seemed genuinely sincere and he looked at me like I was the only person in the world. Looking back, I am so pleased with myself that I managed to do that.

Myths and also memories cannot then be understood as formed from a continuous series that might progress in neat order from a beginning to end. Rather, they must be taken as *gestalt* in that the whole is made up of the sum of the individual parts—as are we, overlapping and rhizomatic entities. Lévi-Strauss (1978: 45) tells us that myths are 'bundles of events' that might arise at different points in time in the story and explains that to understand a myth we might liken it to all the necessary individual elements that make up a complete musical score:

Therefore, we have to read the myth more or less as we would read an orchestral score, not stave after stave, but understanding that we should apprehend the whole page and understand that something which was written on the first stave at the top of the page acquires meaning only if one considers that it is part and parcel of what is written below on the second stave, the third stave, and so on. That is, we have to read not only from left to right, but at the same time vertically, from top to bottom. We have to understand that each page is a totality. And it is only by treating the myth as if it were an orchestral score, written stave after stave, that we can understand it as a totality, that we can extract the meaning out of the myth.

The extraction of a myth is not an endpoint in itself for myths are not static but open to polysemic interpretation and reinterpretations over time and in different places, changing with the telling and retelling and the experience. The motifs arising around David Bowie's stories have simply not been produced through a unidirectional process, prepared by a PR agent for the fans, for example. Instead, the multiple contradictions 'are all absorbed into a glorious fluidity, both clear and indecipherable, crystallised, perhaps in the notion of Bowie as simultaneously *sui generis* and an amalgam of multiple influences' (Readman 2016: 2). The stories of Bowie, his myths if you will, have evolved (like our own) in iterative processes and encounters, affording mutually constitutive opportunities for construal and interpretation. Karan Barad (2007: ix) adroitly writes that:

> Individuals do not pre-exist their interactions; rather, individuals emerge through and as part of their entangled intra-relating. Which is not to say that emergence happens once and for all, as an event or as a process that takes place according to some external measure of space and of time, but rather that time and space, like matter and meaning, come into existence, are iteratively reconfigured through each intra-action, thereby making it impossible to differentiate in any absolute sense between creation and renewal, beginning and returning, continuity and discontinuity, here and there, past and future.

Beautifully recounted by another fan were memories of imaginatively seeking Bowie's ghost in many cities around the world, weaving in new stories that were overlaid with associated emotions cultivated across (re)disturbed time; statements from their own reminiscential experiences:

H3D: Ziggy Stardust facade in West London. A road used in the Let's Dance video filmed in Sydney. Berlin, I kissed my girlfriend by the wall. She put her head through and I took a picture from the other side. We arrived at the Banhf Zoo from east Berlin, after a long ride from Prague the day the two 'marks' came together in a single currency in 1990. I looked for Christiane F. but she had gone. Helden echoed in the arrival hall. Years later I went to the V&A touring exhibition at Martin Gropius Bau, just up the road from Hansa Studios. Primrose Hill, London - I always imagined it as high on Poachers Hill, gazing down on Hunger City. Kyoto - listening to Japanese koto music and thinking of Moss Garden. Amalapura in Bali. Before the second Tin Machine album, so it was retrospective memories of lava-filled destruction and historical overlays.

To accept timelessness (for all possible beginnings) is epistemologically rooted in the history of modernism. At the macro-level spanning some two centuries, Jameson (1999) classified no fewer than thirteen beginnings of the 'modern' and signalled that many more can be anticipated to creep from the edges. Modernity and postmodernity both embrace the flows of variability. Making the in-depth observation for the micro-level of the individual, Marshall Berman writes in *All That Is Solid Melts into Air: The Experience of Modernity* (1982: 345–346) that:

> To be modern is to experience personal and social life as a maelstrom, to find one's world and oneself in perpetual disintegration and renewal … To be a modernist is to make oneself somehow at home in the maelstrom, to make its rhythms one's own.

In Derrida's view, meaning is never self-present because objects and places signify through the traces within them of other details. The overlapping stories then are important for appreciating David Bowie's apparitional 'absent-presence' as fans travel in pilgrimage (literally or by imagination) and engage with his creative works (Derrida 1997). With this deconstructive logic, Bowie's interesting and obscure work is frequently (re)manifest allotropically, subtly familiar forms of his re-occurring 'presence' for the fans. By way of example, the spectre of Bowie as Major Tom (*Space Oddity*, 1969) resurged in his video clip for 'Ashes to Ashes' (*Scary Monsters … and Super Creeps*, 1980); Aladdin Sane (1973) was made manifest in *Little Wonder* (1997); an impression of The Thin White Duke (*Station to Station*, 1976; *Low*, 1977) is made obvious in 'The Stars (Are Out Tonight)' (*The Next Day*, 2013). And, years after Pierrot in Turquoise (1967) and the clown of 'Ashes to Ashes', Bowie's Halloween video of 'Love is Lost' (*The Next Day*, 2013) depicts life-size wooden puppet-bodies, one dressed as The Thin White Duke cradling Scary's 'blue clown' in its arms as Bowie croons 'say hello to the lunatic men' over the self-referential melody from 'Ashes to Ashes' but in this recent song. In the film, Bowie's shade is felt keenly in *Velvet Goldmine* (1998, dir. Todd Haynes), a movie in which Bowie is both entirely absent from, and fully present in, the fictional account of Brian Slade and his space alien alter ego Maxwell Demon. Bowie and Ziggy are conspicuous in their (non)presence in the paradoxical fairy tale that demythologises glam rock's emancipatory appeal and rediscovers a sometimes ambiguous and electrically seductive period (see D'Cruz 2015; Bennett [2010] for a reading of shame's difficult part in the pleasure of queer reception). David Bowie's perceptual embodiment (re)draws/repels in the screen world of children as echoes of Jareth the Goblin King (the antagonist in *Labyrinth*, 1986, dir. Jim Henson) are felt through Bowie's voiced and animated evil Emperor Maltazard, a charming antagonist ever cursed, in the children's adventure film *Arthur and the Invisibles* (2006, dir. Luc Besson).

Bowie's work has thematically featured the sociopolitical stories of 'alienation and technology through folk music (*Space Oddity*), sexualized mysticism through heavy metal (*The Man Who Sold the World*), messianism and apocalypticism through blues-based rock-and-roll (*Ziggy Stardust, Diamond Dogs*), the American Dream and totalitarianism through soul and disco (*Young Americans, Station to Station*), solipsism in tension with global consciousness through avant-garde expressionism (*Low, "Heroes", Lodger*)—and [from the 1980s] … signalled a return to rock-and-roll and R & B in order to confront modernity (*Scary Monsters, Let's Dance*)' (Finn 1983: 467). Rock-and-roll gave way to an undercurrent of (post)industrial music in the 1990s that emphasised social change for music in an era of networked digitalisation, disruption and global flows of capital. Bowie with many artists wanted to highlight issues of access and control of information and did so via musical themes to tear apart the preconceptions used about the 'necessary rules' of musical form by way of representation (in collaboration with Trent Reznor and Nine Inch Nails). In a stable marriage with a young daughter the 2000s, Bowie's intellectual energy turned to the study of the positive and necessarily contemplative facets of human experience in a number of important ways (*Reality, The Next Day*). Conceptual hierarchies then abound, to be easily re-engaged with, over and over, as the phantom of David Bowie continues to haunt the spaces/places that he is popularly associated with across time.

The spectre of Bowie raises questions then about the special and temporal sedimentation of his past/our past and the impact upon the possibilities for the intricacies of (re)tracing memories, personally, individually and collectively. Moreover, emerging social screen technologies with Application Programming Interface (APIs) linked across Facebook, Instagram, Twitter and the like today contribute to practices of fan sacralisation by allowing user-driven, conversational and networked content to define and grow the communities that it serves (see Chapter 8). The technological affordances act to: 'augment existing narratives about sacred places and people's experience of them' (Otter Bickerdike and Sparrowhawk 2015: 53). Moreover, virtual travel via Google Earth that allows one to 'walk' the city streets and visit memorial places mean that; 'even before the tourist visits the site, he or she will have an imagined set of imprinted expectations of the place before they arrive' (Otter Bickerdike and Sparrowhawk 2015: 53).

Access to his 'ghost' is also exacerbated by the workings and trajectories of digital tentacular technologies and media forms such as photography shared on social-screens. Moreover, while one might be physically present in one location, we are frequently absorbed by a technologically vicarious world of elsewhere through video, film and photographic images, increasingly circulated online that shatter 'real' time and place. We can instantly feel and 'see' Bowie in difference eras as if it were always 'now'. Evermore, ours is increasingly a world of social online connection that is dynamic and mediated both, wherein the domains of meaning are being created, circulated, recreated or sustained.

Haunted Tourism and Pilgrimages in Time

David Bowie was himself a pilgrim seeking places that were strange, fascinating and that might stretch his imagination, the ones of special significance for his own intellectual inspirations and new aesthetic developments. In this section, we consider 'the journey' itself as sacred for the traveller. We get the sense that David Bowie was always questioning how ordinary places are themselves transformed as culturally important whereby he goes as a pilgrim to Berlin in an attempt to try to reclaim that which he interprets is lost through the search for what is/was authentic. Of Bowie's Berlin, McCombe (2017: 956) critically observed that:

> Berlin offered its own extremes: a site where drag queens shared cafe tables with Marxists and the rubble of World War II coexisted with unparalleled eco-

nomic growth of the Bundes-republik. Having earlier conversed in Los Ange-les with a one-time German emigre, writer Christopher Isherwood, Bowie learned that Berlin "was by no means as exciting a place as [Isherwood's] writings from the 1930s suggested," and that Bowie could make use of the city's extremes to fuel his song writing. (Seabrook 64)

At the turn in time when Bowie left Los Angeles after having lived in the United States for a year and a half to go to Berlin, it was to detoxify his damaged body and live an 'authentic' life: 'I had a more-than-platonic relationship with drugs. Actually, I was zonked out of my mind most of the time. You can do good things with drugs, but then comes the long decline. I was skeletal. I was destroying my body' (Bowie cited in Young 1978). There was also a strong sense that he needed a new creative outlet and different collaborators: 'In L.A., I fell into the trap of referring back to rock all the time … I had blinkered myself to all the other musical possibilities' (Bowie cited in Young 1978). In Bowie's words on Berlin then:

'Low' is my reaction to certain places. 'Warszawa' is about Warsaw and the very bleak atmosphere I got from that city. 'Art Decade' is West Berlin - a city cut off from its world, art, and culture, dying with no hope of retribution. 'Weeping Wall" is about the Berlin Wall - the misery of it. And 'Subterraneans' is about the people that got caught in East Berlin after the separation - hence the faint jazz saxophone representing the memory of what it was. (Bowie 1977 cited in Miles 1980: 97)

In their lucid observation of Bowie's travels, Otter Bickerdike and Spar-rowhawk (2015: 50) reflect that Bowie became a pilgrim himself as he searched for something that might be identified as meaningful to him; "something more 'real'". Bowie in this sense was:

searching for the authentic – thus, he is not so much the tourist as he is a pilgrim. We suggest this works, as rigid distinctions between pilgrimage and tourism have become much harder to define; indeed, some would argue that as such these distinctions do not exist at all. It is not impossible to suggest there must inevitably exist a close interaction between people and places that ultimately work together to socially construct the landscape as sacred. It is often the actions of fans themselves who create, maintain and evolve the meaning of specific spaces, underscoring and often validating the same behavior in others.

Many of his fans made their own pilgrimage to Bowie's Berlin, searching with energetic nostalgia to remobilise forgotten histories from their specific contexts (also see Chapter 3):

> *H2A*: Yes. I travelled to Berlin in 2013 and shot photos of places he lived, visited, worked and mentioned in his work. The images were used as part of a stage set when a Dutch cover band went on a theatre tour in 2014. I later compiled some of the photos into a short film that was screened at the interfilm festival in Berlin in 2014.

> *H22*: I lived and still live close to the place where he lived in Berlin in the 1970s. I went there mourning when he died … I was several times at the place where in former times the Hansa studio in Berlin was located where he recorded the Berlin trilogy. I visited … the Martin Gropius Bau in Berlin.

> *H1K*: After moving to Berlin I immediately went to Bowie's former apartment in the Hauptstraße and I passed several times the Hansa Studios.

> *H3*: Yes … I did a Berlin Bowie walking tour just a few weeks ago. The description of David singing Heroes at the wall in the *Glass Spider Tour*, the crowd building up behind the wall as he sang to those in the west - that covered me in goose bumps and still does …

With emphasis, many participants in our focus groups were in attendance having travelled great distances because of their prime interest in David Bowie—many arriving from international destinations. In Amsterdam during the *3rd International Celebrity Studies Conference: Authenticating Celebrity* (28–30 June 2016), the authors scheduled a focus group with interested participants (see Chapter 7). During the session, AG responded that the reason they attended that day was because:

> … from the earliest time that I can remember there has been this entity who had done things that I didn't expect and I always marveled at that and everything else that came along with it, the music.

And, in Lisbon was run the *David Bowie Interart|text|media Conference* (22–24 September 2016) and another focus group was convened by the authors structured around a number of key questions. In particular, we asked participants about why they were there that day and 'M1' indicated that while travel brings people together, it has the duel capacity for unfastening:

> *M1*: I first got into Bowie when I was 11 or 12 years old … we, my friends
> – these two guys I am still really good friends with, were all obsessed by
> Bowie and he was a big part of our growing up in a boring suburb/town
> and what we liked about Bowie was that you could play Bowie against
> Bowie, how many different Bowies there were, we didn't articulate that
> in terms of the ways that we have been talking about it at this conference
> in the past couple of days but I think that is what it was – our elaborate
> inside Bowie Jokes, favourite 'Bowie' and we had preferences for different
> Bowies, the stupid things Bowie would do, we were just being sarcastic
> teens and trying to rebel a bit and we did that within Bowie fandom …
> [when David Bowie died] I skyped with them, they are in Vancouver …
> I was flying back to Belgium from visiting them and news broke while I
> was on the flight and it was like the worst because I was *so alone*, ah, and
> had just left everyone I would want to be with.

For M1 their fandom was about finding the space to intellectually stretch and even 'rebel'. As a young child, it must have seemed as though this wondrous creature had beamed down to land in their midst and was calling for them and their friends to join in some grand adventure. M1 genuinely recounts how Bowie afforded playful experiences bounded by a 'boring suburb/town' and of friendships that were made possible therein. M1 and their friends created their own world, entering through the door that David Bowie had fashioned, one that appealed to them. At the time of David Bowie's death, these friends were separated and the physical distance seemed then to have stymied the resonation of their inter-corporeal forms.

As we note in our Introduction to the book, the authors employed an auto-ethnographic methodology to 'story themselves' as lifelong David Bowie fans into the study's approach. During our fieldwork, we also participated in the focus group sessions. In the course of conducting the fieldwork, each was on their own pilgrimage to visit a number of the locations that Bowie had worked from such as London, Berlin and New York. Of specific interest to Toija was Tokyo, Japan where they started their journey with the Japan focus group being held in the lobby of the Imperial Hotel where Bowie had given his own press conference in 1973.

ACROSS TIME IN TOKYO

I went on a walking tour through the heart and soul of Tokyo's aesthetic cultural tapestry as a way to touch on David Bowie's mythical history as past/present which vivified my memories. I remember reading as a young fan that among other flamboyant happenings at the time that he had taken his wife and son with him on the 1973 *Ziggy Stardust Tour*. I had my own family with me and together we were tracing imagined events from Bowie's time in Japan drawn from my reading and an article that originally appeared in *Mirabelle* magazine (1973) recounting their time there (albeit that it now understood to have been 'ghost written' by his then publicist, Cherry Vanilla). The story gave an account of the Bowies' visit to Japan which included the family's travel itinerary of visits to the Imperial Gardens at the Emperor's Palace, and Angie and baby Zowie enthusiastically seeing David perform in concert in Tokyo's Shibuya district (see http://www.davidbowieworld.nl/mijn-bootlegs-2-2/tour-recordings/1972-1973-the-ziggystardust-tour/attachment/folder-47/). I imagined David Bowie in Tokyo, perhaps walking around the same markets and taking trains as the 'every-day' pilgrim/tourist (but ironically photographed by Masayoshi Sukita). What was writ large for me was that I was now (re)storying my own fan-history with those closest to me in the process of reflexive travelling.

My personal travel to locate the hall in Shibuya where David Bowie performed as Ziggy Stardust in the 1973 concert, however, proved not a little heart rendering. Incredibly, after so many decades the hall was literally torn down before my eyes on the day that I arrived there to photograph it, the unsayable moment of its collapse central to my memorial making and unmaking. Was this the metaphorical collapse of my world; one so recently without him in it? Felt still thrillingly, however, was the 'ghost' of Ziggy Stardust and the Spiders from Mars appearing to so many Japanese fans in 1973 as alien creatures.

In these locations, a technological embrasure of sorts was created for collecting photographic images gathered in my pilgrimage of the sights seen in this most personal of 'grand tour'. The images and memories recalled were always imbued with a certain *invisibility*, that *which is* veiled by that *which was* across time. The invisibility of ellipsis and interruptions across time were felt most keenly. As del Pilar Blanco and Peeren (2013: 201) write:

Photography, as well as other technologies that have become integral parts of our everyday existence, such as the cinema, the sound recorder, and the television, aims to commemorate persons, places, and events. But the very moment of commemoration (that "simple click" to which Barthes refers) reminds the collector of memories of the passing of time, and the entry of death into the world of the living. The Ghost, to borrow Gilbert Ryle's [1984] famous phrase ... has always occupied an important place within the Machine.

Of cinema particularly, but by extension other images that we record, the *trace* is the; "'that-took-place-there" of the[image]...', and haunting of people, places and events now past but frequently recalled (Derrida 2015: 31). Wistfully then of past events and people: 'By its own spectral miracle, it [the image] points out to us what ought not to leave any trace' with the passing of time. That is: 'the ... image allows the thing itself ... to be not reproduced but produced with immediacy once again "itself there"' (Derrida 2015: 32); indeed, 'of the image' we find 'the ghost in the machine'.

As observed and recorded in this study, many fans reported that while privately experiencing David Bowie's spectral nearness in the locations for which he was known to have lived or worked that they had always wanted to actually run into him in their travels. Bowie moved to the United States in 1974 before travelling again in Europe and Australia (living for a time in Sydney during the 1980s), then finally settling in New York and 'the best city for a restless traveler to end up if they have to end up anywhere, with enough in walking distance of a Manhattan home to feel constantly in touch with a wider, shifting world' (Morley 2016: 452). Drawing now not on the spectral but focusing upon the literal, we asked fans in the online survey for their thoughts on travelling with the precise hope of encountering David Bowie in the street in (Q12) 'Did you fantasize about meeting David Bowie—or meet him for real?':

> *H3B*: Yes, New York, although I never saw him I felt empowered that I may be walking on the same pavement on which he walks to the music studio, shopping etc.

> *H3C*: I have walked past his NYC apartment a few times, a couple of times on purpose but mostly not. I admit I've walked the streets of NYC thinking what I'd do if I ever saw him, off duty, dressed like a dad. I'd have frozen in terror, most likely!

The fantasy of randomly finding David Bowie in a public space and encountering the 'everyday man' was earnestly shared by fans in our study with one (HL) summarising their recent personal musing thus:

> *HL:* I will say that a year or two ago, Iman was on social media, posting pictures of photos of scenes in London such as the London Eye, London Bridge et cetera, and it was clear that the Jones' were happily strolling about fairly anonymously in my home town, after that I did think, imagine just strolling around the British Museum or somewhere like that, and looking up from an exhibit to find David Bowie standing next to me! ... and ever since it's kind of always been in the back of my mind that one day something like that could actually happen, it was an actual possibility! ... I will miss that 'possibility' now that he is gone ....

For these fans just being on the very same streets allowed an intimate connection to Bowie to be sensed during the process of retracing his footsteps and aspects of his private daily routine.

Toija picked up on David Bowie's resounding echo in one of the world's busiest and most vibrant cities in the world—New York: 'I had always wanted to go to New York and maybe there I would encounter David Bowie in my travels'. Alas, it was too late:

> *Toija:* I can remember my husband and I, with our little-ones in hand, standing across the road from the Bowies' 285 Lafayette Street apartment. We were gazing up at the top of the building across the street where David Bowie and his family had lived together. An amiable couple approached us and asked if we were looking for something. I answered that we had come to see where David Bowie lived. 'Oh!" they blurted out in shock and pity for us: "He's not there anymore!" Pointing upward, they told us "That is his home, he lived at the top of the building". We thanked them for their kindness and crossed the busy road.
>
> We then walked the cobbled stretch of Mulberry Street and I was transported back across the years. I could hear the murmur of David Bowie's artistic New York. We traced his footsteps to The Basilica of St. Patrick's Old Cathedral and I wondered if he ever went in; just because? We found McNally Jackson Books where he shopped and then had dinner in Little Italy. We wandered to Washington Square Park (did he take his little daughter there I wondered), visited MOMA and smaller art galleries (did these places inspire his young son toward a career as a film director I considered). On the Fourth of July we stood in light warm rain and watched the fireworks ignite over the Statue of Liberty from Battery Park. As we

walked, I told my children about 1970s New York and the art scene I loved and David Bowie's place in it; we talked, laughed and learned a little more about each other and the world in the process. Bowie was for me 'a beginning' of my entangled intra/inter-relating with my important others and he afforded me the capacity to take it from there.

Another fan (BC) whom self-identified as African-American shared during the focus group conducted in Amsterdam what they thought David Bowie brought out powerfully in the culture and music scene in New York:

> BC: I wanted to talk a little bit about how Bowie reconfigured our sense of national identity when he arrived in New York and the way he positioned himself and rejected certain forms of glamour and certain chic circles that he certainly had access to and preferred instead to work in Harlem with African-American musicians and was deeply invested and interested in Soul and R&B and those musical histories and he made people famous – He was incredibly generous artist and always pushing himself, very prolific and flexible and willing to go out of his area of comfort. Of course, then inevitably you are going to make a bad choice when you go out of your area of comfort, most people live very safe lives and tend to reproduce the thing they did before that was successful because the alternative is scary. I think he shared his fame with people that wasn't just about advancing his own name but wanted to learn. He changed the music scene. He shaped himself in a Trans-Atlantic way, he became a New-Yorker and it reshaped us and the way we felt in New York at that time. Interesting was his horror at what 'Americanness' meant in those days at that time was a good way for us to channel our own disappointments and aspirations.

Towards the end of the London focus groups session, our participants were called upon to crystalise one cherished moment or one overriding memory and what that might be. GA participating in our London-based focus group recalled a very special pilgrimage

> The trip to New York that happened in December [2015] with a lot of the BowieNet friends because he hadn't played for over ten years, so we hadn't all been together since then. So, we all decided 'let's go to Lazarus', so people flew from all over. I had a best friend from Uni in Brisbane in Australia and he flew from New York to come and we were all there and we were so happy. We saw the play three times and we'd stay up all night at a gay bar singing Bowie songs off the Jukebox … and it was just the best thing ever; we were all so happy, all of us. We saw him at the opening and were chuffed. And it

was this moment of just pure and absolute happiness and it was so close to the end. I think that is why I sort of elevated that memory now; it's just that it was the last time we were all together and he was there too and it feels like that was the last 'Hoorah'; yeah, it feels really special to me that I could do that and I am so glad I went.

CONCLUSION

Our collective stories form a metaphorical cartography of haunting; one that topographically maps the geography of thinking and being through pilgrimages—those physical and memorial journeys. The spectres that we have considered in this chapter speak neither for each other, nor do they speak over each other, but form an indelible chorus of memory that supports tales of travel and pilgrimage. David Bowie was also a pilgrim, but his visual and sonic navigation has itself been a journey by which he long questioned the obstacles of the inherited established metaphors that bind many to a version of reality, to ask his fans to undertake a more sincerely lived experience because of their contemplation. Stories about David Bowie, his 'myth', have been collected and shared. In the process, Bowie is seen as vital to the way his fans story their own lives and agentially configure their becoming despite (and often because of) imperfections in the face of impermanence; a process then never finished, but always evolving. With David Bowie's passing, his spectre might (like Cathy in *Wuthering Heights* or the mysterious Bob in David Lynch's *Twin Peaks*) over time similarly come to epitomise the tangible (and anthropomorphic) manifestation of the ambivalences of being human, the strange complexities of love, fear of and desire for eternal life, technological agency and the unknown lands of the unconscious (Van Elferen 2011).

The commemorative remembering and telling of fan pilgrimages have illuminated the entanglements of memory and imagination for how they are quintessential to the back-and-forth of one's simultaneous past/present/future and (re)configure the path of chronology. The moments drawn from the distillation of fan experiences and outlined here cast light on the process of remembering. Music and photography both are rudimentary to congealing memorial encounters that form identifiable 'texts' that capably unfold a story of a life. The distillation of lived experience reveals that a place, a *sanctum sanctorum* accorded with significance requires the ephemeral, kinetic nature of myth and memory. Accordingly, revered ensembles of experience afford the meaning of a life to self and others. Pilgrimages to memorial places trace the memories that are thickened over time in the remembering. Shared collective stories of pilgrimage are akin to establishing new growths; like rhizomes that put out vigorous shoots, our memories are buds that are metaphorically connected subterraneanly/inter-corporeally, sensed in our hearts and echoed in time.

References

Barad, Karen. *Meeting the Universe Halfway: Quantum Physics and the Entanglement of Matter and Meaning.* Durham, NC: Duke University Press, 2007.

Barthes, Roland. *Mythologies.* Selected and Translated from the French by Annette Lavers. London: Vintage Books, 2000.

Bennett, Chad. "Flaming the Fans: Shame and the Aesthetics of Queer Fandom in Todd Haynes's 'Velvet Goldmine'." *Cinema Journal* 49 (2) (2010): 17–39.

Berman, Marshall. *All That Is Solid Melts into Air: The Experience of Modernity.* London: Verso, 1982.

Bowie, David. "The Albums: Bowie and Eno." In *Bowie in His Own Words*, compiled by Barry Miles. New York: Omnibus Press, 1980 (1977).

Brooker, Will. "A Sort of Homecoming: Fan Viewing and Symbolic Pilgrimage". In *Fandom: Identities and Communities in a Mediated World*, ed. Jonathan Gray, Cornel Sandvoss, and C. Lee Harrington, 157–173. New York: New York University Press, 2017.

Buchli, Victor, and Gavin Lucas. *Archaeologies of the Contemporary Past.* London: Routledge, 2002.

Buckley, David. *Strange Fascination David Bowie: The Definitive Story.* London: Virgin Books, 2005.

D'Cruz, Glenn. "He's Not There: Velvet Goldmine and the Spectres of David Bowie". In *Enchanting David Bowie: Space/Time/Body/Memory*, ed. Toija Cinque, Christopher Moore, and Sean Redmond, 259–273. New York: Bloomsbury, 2015.

del Pilar Blanco, María, and Esther Peeren. "The Ghost in the Machine: Spectral Media/Introduction." In *The Spectralities Reader: Ghosts and Haunting in Contemporary Cultural Theory*, ed. María del Pilar Blanco and Esther Peeren, 199–206. New York: Bloomsbury, 2013.

Derrida, Jacque. *Specters of Marx.* London: Routledge Classics, 1994.

Derrida, Jacques. *Of Grammatology.* Translated by Gayatri Spivak. Baltimore, MD: Johns Hopkins University Press, 1997.

Derrida, Jacques. "Cinema and Its Ghosts: An Interview with Jacques Derrida." *Discourse* 37 (1–2) (2015): 22–39. Interview with Antoine de Baecque and Thierry Jousse; translated by Peggy Kamuf.

Dyer, Richard. *Stars* (1979). London: BFI Publishing, 1998.

Finn, Deborah Elizabeth. "Moon and Goom: David Bowie's Frustrated Messianism." *Commonweal* 110 (9) (1983): 467–468.

Graves-Brown, Paul. "Nowhere Man: Urban Life and the Virtualization of Popular Music." *Popular Music History* 4 (2) (2009): 220–241.

Hughes, Chris. "Dialogue Between Fukuyama's Account of the End of History and Derrida's Hauntology." *Journal of Philosophy: A Cross-Disciplinary Inquiry* 7 (18) (2012): 13–26.

Jameson, Fredric. "Time and the Concept of Modernity." In *Anytime*, ed. Cynthia C. Davidson, 208–217. Cambridge, MA: MIT Press, 1999.

Lévi-Strauss, Claude. "Myth and Music." In *Myth and Meaning*, 44–54. Toronto and Buffalo: University of Toronto Press, 1978.

Leigh, Wendy. *Bowie: The Biography*. New York: Gallery Books, 2014.

McCombe, John. "David Bowie and the Myth of the Berlin Trilogy: Tearing Down Musical Walls in the 1970s." *The Journal of Popular Culture* 50 (5) (2017): 949–967.

Morinis, Alan, ed. *Sacred Journeys: The Anthropology of Pilgrimage*. New York: Greenwood Press, 1992.

Morley, Paul. *The Age of Bowie: How David Bowie Made a World of Difference*. London: Simon & Schuster, 2016.

Otter Bickerdike, Jennifer, and John Charles Sparrowhawk. "Desperately Seeking Bowie: How Berlin Tourism Transcends the Sacred." In *Enchanting David Bowie: Space/Time/Body/Memory*, ed. Toija Cinque, Chris Moore, and Sean Redmond, 49–60. New York: Bloomsbury, 2015.

Pegg, Nicholas. *The Complete David Bowie*. 6th ed. London: Titan Books, 2011.

Porter, Jennifer E. "Pilgrimage and the IDIC Ethic: Exploring Star Trek Convention Attendance as Pilgrimage." In *Intersecting Journeys: The Anthropology of Pilgrimage and Tourism*, ed. Ellen Badone and Sharon R. Roseman, 160–179. Urbana and Chicago: University of Illinois Press, 2004.

Readman, Mark. "Editorial—David Bowie". *Journal of Media Practice* 17 (1) (2016): 1–3.

Ryle, Gilbert. *The Concept of Mind*. Chicago: University of Chicago Press, 1984.

Soussloff, Catherine M. *The Absolute Artist: The Historiography of a Concept*. Minneapolis: University of Minnesota Press, 1997.

Spitz, Marc. *Bowie: A Biography*. New York: Crown Publishing Group, 2009.

Stevenson, Nick. *David Bowie: Fame, Sound and Vision*. Cambridge: Polity, 2006.

Trinka, Paul. *Starman*. New York: Little Brown Company, 2011.

Van Elferen, Isabella. "East German Goth and the Spectres of Marx. *Popular Music* 30 (1) (2011): 89–103.

Young, Charles, M. "Bowie Plays Himself: Ziggy Stardust Returns to Earth." *Rolling Stone*, January 1978. https://www.rollingstone.com/music/music-news/bowie-plays-himself-240811/. Accessed 16 September 2018.

CHAPTER 10

Conclusion: Everyone Says 'Goodbye'

Everyone Says 'Goodbye'

Everything! He's been in my life for 30 years. I've listened to him almost daily since then. He's always been there when I've felt low, or worried, or scared. I can play his music and it consoles me. He entertains. He inspires. He's the reason I've been to various places around the world and the reason I've met many great friends. I can't my imagine my life without him in it.

(Q 8 What does David Bowie mean to you?)

Here in F4's response to the question of what David Bowie means to them, we find many of the layers of productive fandom that the book has addressed. For F4, Bowie is a constant aural and symbolic presence, his importance and influence shaping their life decisions and effecting their mood and well-being. Their fandom has led to new friendship circles, soothes and heals them in times of crises, and both narrate a journey of selfhood and one of accumulations. That F4 cannot imagine their life without Bowie in it recalls the power and importance of the fandom of David Bowie.

During the course of this book, we have explored the way that David Bowie fans from across the world draw upon his music, live performances, films and media output generally, to make sense of their lives, and for the pleasures it brings them. In many respects, the structure of the book was led, determined, by the fans: their responses to the questionnaire, through

© The Author(s) 2019
T. Cinque and S. Redmond, *The Fandom of David Bowie*,
https://doi.org/10.1007/978-3-030-15880-4_10

the social media, and in the focus groups, produced the memorial material out of which the threads and patterns of the chapters emerged. From the start of the research, we wanted to ensure that it was the voices, feelings, memories and emotions of the fans that built the rooms we 'visited'. We also wanted to draw in our own voices, to engage in conversations with fellow fans about what Bowie meant to us.

In the Introduction, we defined this approach as a form of triangulation or multiple operationalism where we would lattice together four ways of working with our fans, the data, and each other. The questionnaire gave us both qualitative and quantitative data to draw upon, as did the social media we analyzed. The focus groups were all story driven but were differently constituted: the ones in Melbourne, London, Tokyo and New York were populated by people who had completed the questionnaire; the ones in Amsterdam and Lisbon by 'aca-fans'; and the one in Berlin by Sean's life-long friends. This 'spread' offered us diversity and the ability to work with articulations that were both distinctive and personal. The two authors bring different methodological and theoretical trajectories to this wealth of data, and each uses different analytical and conceptual tools to hear the voices being aired. Brought together in the same book, then, they create new interpretative layers, if not also moments of productive tension. The book draws upon the approaches of cultural studies, phenomenology, feminism, new materialism, embodiment theory, critical race theory, discourse analysis, narratology and auto-ethnography to make sense of the voices being shared. When these approaches are combined, Bowie fandom emerges as participatory and shared, and interiorised and personal; and as ideological and sensorial, and social and psychological. We feel the full sensorial and cultural individual emerges from such a fashioning of the self.

Nonetheless, three criticisms of the book's approach might be aired. First, what can a case study of one star really reveal about the matters of the world? Textual analysis of one star within the field of stardom and celebrity has often come into criticism (see Turner 2014) because it, so it is suggested, fails to look at commercial or industrial elements, and is seen to be difficult to 'extract' from. Our approach of course would argue the exact opposite: it is in the everyday where material life is played out and it is only in hearing what people productively 'do' with stars that we can get close to understanding about such things as power, ideology and pleasure. The data that we have been able to share with you in this book point to the ways that David Bowie was utilised to negotiate a range of identity positions often running counter to dominant ideology and the forces of patriarchy and heterosexuality. Of course, as the book detailed, Bowie was also a totemic figure for the migrants we spoke to. The bow of his stardom crossed many lands.

The second criticism of the book might be that it eulogises David Bowie. The book seems to ignore or only briefly touch on the way that Bowie was arguably connected to fascism, embodied a hyperwhite masculinity, and was involved in lurid tabloid tales of sexual perversion and abuse. In some respects, this is a fair criticism, but perhaps more one of method than deliberate structured absence: the questionnaire we designed and the focus groups we ran were intended to find out what bowie *meant to fans* and they duly, rightly obliged, filling the pages of this book with hopeful, uplifting storied memories.

One aspect of the research we would change, in hindsight, is to have these 'questions' raised and aired. Of course, the 'gap' is more than a method problem: fans rarely if ever see the bad side of the star they so admire and will do everything they can to protect their name. The perversity of this type of fandom has, of course, serious consequences for addressing important political questions, as can be seen by President Donald Trump's die-hard Republican Party supporters in the United States.

The third criticism of the book might be that David Bowie as 'David Bowie' is nowhere to be seen: in the main, we have not drawn upon interviews with him, and only very marginally drawn into the book his own fandoms. The question of authenticity is an important one in this respect, as is the myth that somehow by mining this public, mediated material we will get closer to knowing the *real* David Bowie. Our preference in getting to know David Bowie since this cannot be found in the media is through the talk of fans. David Bowie only becomes meaningful, pleasurable and desirable at the point of consumption, in the homes of the fans who have adored him so.

The research for the book began before David Bowie's death, but the bulk of it was conducted after. For the fans who took part, and for the authors themselves, this was a haunting experience, as we have shown through various threads in this book. This haunting continues today in culture more broadly.

Now We're at Sea: Thoughts on Death and Dying

Almost all of the fan participants can recall where they were the moment they learnt that David Bowie had died. Toija's personal recollection is of driving a white rental car late in the afternoon—such superfluous details to recall—when they got a call from a local broadcaster about an interview. A strained voice at the end of their phone carried the news: "Hello, Dr Cinque … I am not sure if you have heard, but David Bowie has just passed away …."

Sean was at home with his kids, who were visiting from New Zealand where they normally reside. The TV was on in the house, and it was a breaking news story, reminiscent, for Sean of Bowie's song, Five Years. Sean recalls that the fact didn't really register, or rather, because his children were with him, he was surrounded by love.

We asked those taking part in our focus groups: 'When did you hear of his death and how did you respond?'. Emotionally they recalled for us that:

> *F001*: I heard about it on TV, I stayed glued to the set; it was like losing my Dad, it was devastating.

> *F002*: I thought "we are screwed; the guardian angel for all freaks is gone and we are doomed".

> *F003*: I found out on Twitter … I thought not that his illness was kept 'secret' but that it was kept '*private*', a really cool thing to do.

> *F004*: My husband told me, but he waited for me to wake up. I was in complete shock – in disbelief, and he held my hand and said that David Bowie had passed away. I had to go to social media, even though I knew my friends would know how I felt about this, and to report my feelings on it.

In such moving responses, one can see that Bowie's death was not just met with grief and surprise but engaged reflection and shared empathetic communication. To draw the arc of the book back, picking up the threads we outlined in the Introduction, when David Bowie died in 2016, there was a type of public remembering that bordered on hysteria, in part fuelled by the media coverage of the time. The media were full of stories of collectivised gatherings, pilgrimages, temporary shines and outpourings. There was also a weightier response, laced with the various types of profound life story memories that we have shared here, as Bowie fans searched for temporal moorings, aide-memoirs and recuperating measures to enable to make sense of their loss. Of course, the contemporary therapeutic and confessional discourses that position grief as to-be-shared and yet also privatised and internalised, provided the dichotomised space for this to take place.

This in the face of contemporary Western constructs of bereavement that frame grief and mourning as psychological processes where modern grieving practices are now individual, internal and private (see Freud 1917). What is fascinating with regard to the reporting of David Bowie's death (and the same happened with Princess Diana, George Best, and to a large degree, Prince) is how ancient rituals of mourning that once helped to channel the experiences of death and loss, such as collective wailing and worship, were found in the media coverage, and with many of our respondents. The social and communal grieving of David Bowie might be understood then as a form of positive cathartic release, where it is not born silently. In our study, fans told us their stories of remembrance and reflection in tribute:

> FTS: I was born in the 1990s so when I started to like rock music David Bowie was not that famous. The first idea that I got about David Bowie was in a rock magazine that I must have read over and over before I actually got to listen to him because in Spain he was not played on the radio. A friend of my father used to burn some CDs for me and burned me *Ziggy Stardust* and it was one of the first CDs and I used to listen to it a lot. I didn't understand a lot of his work, for example, I was thinking that if *Blackstar* had come out when I first listened to him I would not have understood anything.
> I bought this album *Blackstar* just last week and I think it is the album that I would like to hear the most from all his work. When he died it was quite striking to see the media attention and the general grief around him which is quite strange and sorrowful to think about it. All the newspapers with 20 pages about David Bowie and it made me get more deeply into him in that last month.

FTS here takes up a meta-position, aware of the grief countenanced in/by the media reporting, while assessing Bowie's meaning to their own biography. *Blackstar* becomes a mausoleum piece, a place to go to hear and see Bowie pre- and post-death, caught between living and expiration. For academic fan, FD, who was at the conference in Lisbon, their thinking about the harrowing song 'Lazarus' in relation to Bowie's passing confirmed its resonance linking the theme of resurrection to Bowie as the Messiah figure:

> FD: This is really where [sigh] this has just dominated my life and our lives probably since it came out. I heard about Bowie's death in a very traditional way via word-of-mouth not social media. It is one of those instances in which I will remember where I was always. I think because I have almost been able to validate myself, my identity, as a researcher through

the popular culture research I do, and this is the pinnacle now. Taking me on intellectual journeys that I never thought I would go on. It has given me a new appreciation of my own identity and its relationship with popular music so it is quite a strong statement. He is that sort of 'Messiah' figure.

The events immediately surrounding Bowie's passing were evoked by others in our study as being somewhat surreal:

> F5: I'm sure I dreamed about it, although I can't recall any details just now. I'm sure I thought that it would just be nice to meet him … When I became a big fan, he had been on hiatus for years; even after *The Next Day* came out, he seemed a fundamentally otherworldly figure. I had a lot of difficulty processing his death for that reason.

> F6: I went to the Bowie mural at Brixton following his death. It was very moving and I felt some peace from being there amongst other fans.

> F7: I visited his mural, it was a really sad but lovely vibe.

> F8: After he died, his fans gathered at his Hollywood star. It felt surreal and heartbreaking. It gave me some closure knowing so many others loved him.

As these statements show, a number of fans found a sense of meaning in being physically with others to mourn, creating candlelight ceremonies and sharing their grief together. The realisation that grief was indeed being shared, and that one could pilgrimage, one could offer up one's love for Bowie, proved essential to the healing process. Centrally, Bowie's last album, *Blackstar*, was referred to frequently by fans as a touchstone for thinking about and getting to make sense of his death. That he made the album and produced the stage musical *Lazarus* in the face of his closely impending death indicated Bowie's own 'stake' in the fan gift economy, in which the gift is ultimately himself:

> F9: It is very curious that after his death, I've been listening *Blackstar* endlessly. I think "Blackstar" is the farewell gift from Bowie.

> F10: I think I may be keeping the receipt from my purchase of *Blackstar* (on the day of release) as a reminder of the emotions and thoughts that prevailed

for the two days when that album was unburdened by the knowledge of his death.

F11: Although incredibly expressive with his work Bowie was always incredibly cryptic. The Video for 'Blackstar' was such a patchwork quilt of references and symbolism that only he himself really knew the meaning of. There is a sense of foreboding and mysticism to it that really draws in the viewer. The same can be said for Lazarus however upon hearing it I knew that something was not right. Bowie (or the tracks I favor) always had a sense of melancholy or that he was searching for something, however 'Lazarus' seemed like he had reached an end, as if he was letting go (I originally thought it was just him referring to his age and physical state with regards to performing) then of course we found out he had been battling cancer. This is why 'Lazarus' (or 'Blackstar') is my favorite, I feel it is his most raw, true and brilliantly executed of all his personas. He is not playing a character, more creating a striking visual that communicates his inner struggle.

Blackstar can be understood as the unmasking of David Bowie, each star image being referenced and reflected, and then withdrawn, leaving fans with 'David Jones' contemplating his stardom; his aging, dying body; his mortality and pending death. During the Lisbon focus groups, we asked fans the questions: 'Why did he matter so much?' and 'Why did his death have such an impact/or matter culturally?' F0013 and F0014 suggest that,

F0013: The impacts when he died were huge – there was a realisation that he wasn't immortal and all of a sudden, he was dead. For me he was always there and everything I did centred around him; makes you think …

F0014: In terms of his death, the ability and vulnerability in making his art at the time he was dying; to make art out of that – of something so private (no pictures of him in hospital, no funeral) but the last album and Lazarus – we never knew it was coming … he didn't give everything away.

To many fans, David Bowie exists now beyond his physical presence through the memories and meanings that he is connected to, that are drawn upon and housed in studies like this, and in the keepsakes and mementoes that are kept in homes all over the world. These meanings are personal and social, individual and collective, ensuring that as long as he is part of us he will continue to live in us.

LIVING ON

Since his death in January 2016, David Bowie has appeared on screen and in the fabric of peoples' everyday lives in a different and particularly moving way, as a type of fan wish-fulfillment and cultural haunting, filling the mediated world with his presence. He has re-entered the spaces of popular culture, and newly adorned the walls and rooms of our streets and homes, through song, quotation, allusion, product, homage, enigma and mystery. He has been given new life in the margins of public spaces and peripheries of art. These are ghostly performances of subversion and resistance—he often appears as an alien modernist punctuating the humdrum of the 9-5. And in living on so strongly, if in part as apparition, he perhaps points to the material thinness of how our cultural world is held together:

> Spectrality does not involve the conviction that ghosts exist or that the past (and maybe even the future they offer to prophesy) is still very much alive and at work, within the living present: all it says, if it can be thought to speak, is that the living present is scarcely as self-sufficient as it claims to be, that we would do well not to count on its density and solidity, which might under exceptional circumstances betray us. (Jameson 1999: 29)

There has been the street art revisioning of Bowie and apartment blocks build with his visage on its side, in Melbourne, Australia, for example. For the *David Bowie Is* (2018) exhibition at the Brooklyn Museum, David Bowie's 'Subway Takeover' in the city's interconnected Broadway-Lafayette and Bleecker Street stations, becomes a deeply researched museum piece in itself, a mausoleum to the black star, celebrating the artist's relationship with New York throughout his career.

Tributes have emerged, some, small and local like the Thin White Yukes, and some global such as Lady Gaga's performance at the 2016 Grammys, and Lorde's cover of *Life on Mars* at the 2016 Brits Awards—each of them embodying Bowie, unstitching gender and sexual binaries as they do so. In the ballet tribute dance glam-opera 'Stardust' by Rhoden (2018), a representation of Bowie's gender-bending style and music is captured in poses and arcs that conjoin and confuse high and low art together.

In the *Doctor Who* episode, 'Smile' (BBC 2017), the Doctor faces an army of robots who are programmed to incinerate people if they detect that they are not happy. Retreating while smiling, the Doctor calls out, 'I'm happy, hope you're happy too', linking the scene to the lyrics of the song *Ashes to Ashes* (1980). Peter Capaldi's Doctor was also initially modelled on the Bowie star image, The Thin White Duke (Renshaw 2014), and so Bowie is constantly re-materialised in the body of this alien time-traveler, who has the ability to resurrect or rejuvenate.

In *Stranger Things* (Season 2, 2018) a haunting Peter Gabriel cover of *Heroes* provides the non-diegetic score to what seems to be a death scene—to a series whose feet and hands and heart is set in the 1980s, where David Bowie was at the height of his commercial success. In *Guardians of the Galaxy*, *Moonage Daydream* blasts out over the cassette player as they land on a sublime station/planet, bringing the man who fell to earth, to earth. Bowie of course has been ghosted into this franchise with the director, James Gunn, suggesting he was earmarked to play the part of one of the ravagers: enabling us to sketch him into the lining of the film each time we see it.

Of course, one of the most powerful examples of David Bowie entering a text comes with the latest series of *Twin Peaks* (Lynch, Showtime, 2017). Numerous interviews with key players involved with the series suggested that if not for his illness at the time of production, Bowie would again have taken on the role of Agent Jeffries as originally scheduled (Ekstein-Kon 2017). The reporting of such facts stems from a longing to see him return, a nostalgia for what was once brilliantly there, and an allusive way to *presence* him into the series. We see him in *Twin Peaks* even before he appears.

David Bowie's Agent Jeffries does appear in a dream sequence, in the episode, 'The Return, Part 14', using footage of him that was shot for *Twin Peaks: Fire Walk With Me* (1992). This is an uncanny cameo: it is about the strangeness of a dead David Bowie giving animated life to the estrangement of the show; it is wanting to see an iconic, ghostly narrative foreshadow come to full apparition; and it is a loving, painful, wishing to see and hear the Black Star rise again, if only because our lives are painfully bare without him. Bowie now exists as a form of spatial dread for many of us... These 'haunted spaces... bear the traces of repressed personal or national traumas' (Thompson 2012: 129). Where Bowie should be there is only his ghost, living on. As Z20 notes:

> I didn't adore him, he wasn't my idol. It wasn't like that at all. He was like the dearest of my friends and even though we had never met, he would sing songs about me as if he wore my heart on his sleeve.

I grew up with him. I could always recognise his powerful voice from afar. He had been my companion, my confident. I had no idea he was sick, that I'd lose him today. My friend is gone. He is forever gone.

I have loved him since I can remember. He will never know me. But somehow, somewhere down the road, he was more than a genius, a legend, a rock star. He was the sound of my cold, hardened, broken soul and he sang a sounding hope to a girl who once had nothing but a leg tattoo and a dead smile.

It's the end of an era. I'm no longer lost. I'm no longer dwelling in the chaotic mess I used to. But even when it was all OK, we still sang together. He was always there.

He makes me thankful.

We would like to conclude this conclusion with one final story about Sean's trip to Bowie's Château du Signal, situated next to the Sauvabelin forest in Lausanne, Switzerland, where for him the very fabric of loss and longing takes final flight.

On Not Finding David Bowie

My partner and I had left Melbourne together for a European adventure that would also take in the *Celebrity Studies* conference in Amsterdam (2016), and a pilgrimage to Lausanne, to visit the Château that Bowie had once lived in and to retrace the steps of where he had married Iman in a private, civil ceremony in 1992. When the trip was planned I had wanted us to do this together to both share the pilgrimage experience with someone I cared about, and because I had hoped or intended for the experience to be a romantic one. At perhaps some subconscious level I was imagining that the love we shared at the time would further blossom in the picturesque town of Lausanne. We would be David and Iman, just for one day.

Up until Lausanne, the trip had been a wonderful success: we had grown closer and closer and we were looking forward to travelling from Lake Como by train, crossing international borders as we did so. However, as we set off and as the day of our arrival went by, the mood between us changed. We fell silent and the wet weather matched the melancholy that had arose, seemingly out of nowhere. I became cold and surly: they became distant. When we set off on foot to find the Château we were barely speaking to one another, and the phone map we were using was not really showing us the exact location. The walk, uphill, took 40 minutes and ended with us at the forest edge, looking back to Lausanne and the breathtaking views of the lake. We spent some time trying to locate the Château but couldn't and, at my suggestion, we gave up. I realised I didn't want to find the Château in that state: that I was glad that we hadn't found David Bowie and Iman there. My partner told me later that day that they felt overwhelmed by the expectations I had brought with us to Lausanne and I felt deeply sorry about that. Fandom had got in the way, but it had also shown us the way: without each of us saying, I know we knew then that our relationship wouldn't stand the test of time.

Zygmunt Bauman writes:

> In other words, it is not in craving after ready-made, complete and finished things that love finds its meaning — but in the urge to participate in the becoming of such things. Love is akin to transcendence; it is but another name for creative drive and as such is fraught with risks, as all creation is never sure where it is going to end.

I had gone to Lausanne hoping to participate in the becoming of love: and all the risks it entails. I had hoped to share my love of David Bowie and for Lausanne to provide a romantic backdrop. While my partner and I didn't find David Bowie, or the love we were looking for, as we have seen in this book a large number of fans have described their fandom as a type of love for David Bowie and the freeing transcendence it offered them. Their love for David enabled them to grow, to become, to resist, to be happy, to find new love. This is what I take home from the memorial stories shared in this book. It makes me thankful.

CONCLUDING REMARKS

In our Introduction, we outlined the notion that fandom is emotionally experienced and 'a process of being' whereby the star performer acts not as a particular possession or even an activity but as 'a continuing presence to which they [the fan] may turn again and again' (Daniel Cavicchi 1998: 59). Presence, for us, is not just a cultural or psychic condition, but an affective one, so that when one returns, and returns again, to a favourite star, it is through the body, the senses, the emotions, and the joyous affects they unleash. As F0011 reflects, 'Bowie has been part of my life for many years through his music. I listen through all the emotions that life brings and always end up with a smile on my face'.

Such serious moonlight.

REFERENCES

BBC. Doctor Who. 'Smile', Television Series, Episode 2, Series 10, BBC One, Lawrence Gough (dir.), Written by Frank Cottrell-Boyce, Broadcast on 22 April 2017 on-demand via. https://www.bbc.co.uk/programmes/b08nz0vk.
Cavicchi, Daniel. *Tramps Like Us: Music & Meaning Among Springsteen Fans.* New York: Oxford University Press, 1998.
Ekstein-Kon, Alexandra. "David Bowie's Agent Jeffries Was Going to Be in Season 3 of *Twin Peaks.*" *Movie Pilot,* 5 April 2017. https://moviepilot.com/posts/3912307.
Freud, Sigmund. *Mourning and Melancholia.* Standard edition XIV. London: Hogarth Press, 1917 (1915).
Jameson, Fredric. "Marx's Purloined Letter." In *Ghostly Demarcations: A Symposium on Jacques Derrida's "Specters of Marx",* ed. Michael Sprinker, 26–67. London and New York: Verso, 1999.
Renshaw, David. "Peter Capaldi 'Bases Doctor Who Look on David Bowie.'" *NME,* 30 June 2014. http://www.nme.com/news/tv/peter-capaldi-bases-doctor-who-look-on-david-bowie-874668.
Rhoden, Dwight. *StarDust.* Dance Performance in Melbourne Choreographed by Dwight Rhoden, the New York Company Complexions Contemporary Ballet, April 2018.
Thompson, Kirsten Moana. *Apocalyptic Dread: American Film at the Turn of the Millennium.* SUNY Press, 2012.
Turner, Graeme. *Understanding Celebrity.* London: Sage, 2014.

Appendix A

Turn to Face the Strange: The Fandom of David Bowie

Are you a Bowie fan? Did you grow up listening to David Bowie?

Did you dress or 'perform' like David Bowie?
Has his music, films, shows, artwork or fashion had an impact on your identity?
Is there something about the star image of David Bowie that maintains its hold on your imagination and sense of being in the world?

    1. What is your Age?
    2. What is your Gender?
       ◯ Female
       ◯ Male
       ◯ Not-specified

© The Editor(s) (if applicable) and The Author(s), under exclusive license to Springer Nature Switzerland AG 2019
T. Cinque and S. Redmond, *The Fandom of David Bowie*,
https://doi.org/10.1007/978-3-030-15880-4

3. What is your Sexuality?

◯ Straight

◯ Bi

◯ Lesbian

◯ Gay

◯ Trans

◯ Other:

4. Please describe your Race/Ethnicity
   This information will be kept anonymous.

5. Which of the following best describes your Current Occupation?

◯ Management Occupations

◯ Business/ Financial Operations Occupations

◯ Computer and Mathematical Occupations

◯ Architecture and Engineering Occupations

◯ Life, Physical, and Social Science Occupations

◯ Community and Social Service Occupations

◯ Legal Occupations

◯ Education, Training, and Library Occupations

◯ Arts, Design, Entertainment, Sports, and Media Occupations

◯ Healthcare Practitioners and Technical Occupations

◯ Healthcare Support Occupations

○ Food Preparation and Serving Related Occupations

○ Building and Grounds Cleaning and Maintenance Occupations

○ Personal Care and Service Occupations

○ Sales and Related Occupations

○ Office and Administrative Support Occupations

○ Farming, Fishing, and Forestry Occupations

○ Construction and Extraction Occupations

○ Installation, Maintenance, and Repair Occupations

○ Production Occupations

○ Transportation and Materials Moving Occupations

○ Protective Service Occupations

○ Other:

6. Please recall and describe what your first memory of encountering David Bowie is?

7. What is your Favourite Album (s)?
   Why is this your choice?

8. What does David Bowie mean to you?
   Please summarise his place in your life.

9. What has been your favourite David Bowie 'character' or 'performance'?

○ Major Tom

○ Ziggy Stardust

○ Aladdin Sane

○ Halloween Jack

○ The Thin White Duke

○ Jareth

○ Nathan Adler

○ 'Lazarus'

○ Other:

10. Considering your favourite David Bowie 'character' or 'performance', please give a reason for your choice.

11. Have you ever seen David Bowie live in concert or on stage?
    If yes, please describe the experience.

12. Did you fantasise about meeting David Bowie—or meet him for real?
    Please explain how this (might have) played out.

13. Have you ever visited a site or place that is given significance within David Bowie's career?
    If yes, please describe why you went there and how it felt?

14. What description best sums up David Bowie for you?

15. Do you have a cherished piece of David Bowie memorabilia?
    Please state what is it and what it means to you.

16. Would you be willing to take part in a 1 hour Focus Group with 6–8 other David Bowie fans?

APPENDIX B

See Tables B.1, B.2, B.3, B.4, B.5, B.5a, B.5b, B.5c, B.6, B.7, B.8, and B.9

Table B.1 Gender

Gender	Frequency	%
Female	165	58.3
Male	114	40.3
Not-specified	4	1.4

According to the survey results, 58% were female and 40% were male respondents

Table B.2 Sexuality

Sexuality	Frequency	%
Straight	199	70.3
Bi	41	14.5
Gay	32	11.3
Other	11	3.9

According to the survey results, 70% were straight sexuality and 14% were bi sexuality. Gay sexuality represented 11% of the survey respondents

© The Editor(s) (if applicable) and The Author(s), under exclusive license to Springer Nature Switzerland AG 2019
T. Cinque and S. Redmond, *The Fandom of David Bowie*, https://doi.org/10.1007/978-3-030-15880-4

Table B.3
Race/ethnicity

Race/ethnicity	Frequency	%
White	61	21.0
Caucasian	59	20.3
White British	25	8.6
Unassigned	11	3.8
British	4	1.4
Chinese	4	1.4
White Caucasian	3	1.0
European	3	1.0
Other	121	41.6

According to the survey results, 21% were of white ethnicity and 20% were of Caucasian ethnicity. White British ethnicity represented 8.6% of the survey respondents

Table B.4   Occupation

Occupation	Frequency	%
Arts, Design, Entertainment, Sports and Media Occupations	67	24.5
Education, Training and Library Occupations	64	23.5
Management Occupations	18	6.6
Office and Administrative Support Occupations	16	5.9
Healthcare Practitioners and Technical Occupations	12	4.4
Sales and Related Occupations	11	4.0
Business/Financial Operations Occupations	10	3.7

According to the survey results, the majority of survey respondents reported occupations were in Arts, Design, Entertainment, Sports and Media Occupations (24.5%). Second highest reported occupation was in Education, Training and Library Occupations (23.5%)

Table B.5   Favourite character or performance

Character or performance	Frequency	%
The Thin White Duke	79	28.3
Ziggy Stardust	74	26.5
Aladdin Sane	21	7.5
Jareth	20	7.2
Major Tom	13	4.7
'Lazarus'	8	2.9
Halloween Jack	7	2.5
Nathan Adler	5	1.8

According to the survey results, 28% of respondents mentioned 'The Thin White Duke' as their favourite David Bowie character or performance. 26.5% of respondents mentioned 'Ziggy Stardust' as their favourite David Bowie character or performance

Table B.5a Gender vs favourite David Bowie 'character' or 'performance'

Character or performance

		Major Tom	Ziggy Stardust	Aladdin Sane	Halloween Jack	The Thin White Duke	Jareth	Nathan Adler	'Lazarus'	Other	Total
Gender	Female	6	44	13	2	39	16	1	4	39	164
	Male	7	28	7	5	40	4	3	4	12	110
	Not-specified	0	2	0	0	0	0	1	0	1	4
Total		13	74	20	7	79	20	5	8	52	278

This table shows respondents' favourite David Bowie character or performance based on their reported gender. For females' the highest reported favourite character or performance was Ziggy Stardust (44 females). Males' highest favourite character or performance was The Thin White Duke (40 males)

Table B.5b Sexuality vs favourite David Bowie 'character' or 'performance'

		Character or performance									Total
		Major Tom	Ziggy Stardust	Aladdin Sane	Halloween Jack	The Thin White Duke	Jareth	Nathan Adler	'Lazarus'	Other	
Sexuality	Straight	9	51	14	3	60	14	2	4	39	196
	Bi	2	10	2	2	11	3	2	2	7	41
	Gay	2	9	2	2	8	2	1	1	4	31
	Other	0	4	2	0	0	1	0	1	2	10
Total		13	74	20	7	79	20	5	8	52	278

This table shows respondents' favourite David Bowie character or performance and their stated sexuality.

Table B.5c Fan Occupation vs favourite David Bowie 'character' or 'performance'

Occupation	Character or performance									Total
	Major Tom	Ziggy Stardust	Aladdin Sane	Halloween Jack	The Thin White Duke	Jareth	Nathan Adler	'Lazarus'	Other	
Arts, Design, Entertainment, Sports and Media Occupations	1	14	5	1	24	4	1	5	12	67
Education, Training and Library Occupations	2	16	8	1	15	5	2	1	13	63
Other	2	8	1	0	9	2	0	0	9	31
Management Occupations	1	7	1	1	4	1	0	0	3	18
Office and Administrative Support Occupations	0	5	1	0	6	2	0	1	1	16

(continued)

Table B.5c (continued)

	Character or performance									Total
	Major Tom	Ziggy Stardust	Aladdin Sane	Halloween Jack	The Thin White Duke	Jareth	Nathan Adler	'Lazarus'	Other	
Healthcare Practitioners and Technical Occupations	1	3	0	0	4	2	0	0	2	12
Business/Finantial Operations Occupations	2	2	0	1	1	1	0	0	4	10
Sales and Related Occupations	0	1	0	1	4	2	0	0	2	10
Community and Social Service Occupations	1	4	1	1	0	0	0	0	0	7

This table shows how respondens' favourite David Bowie character or performance change based on their occupation

Table B.6   Favourite David Bowie Album

Album	Frequency
The Rise and Fall of Ziggy Stardust and the Spiders from Mars	161
Hunky Dory	153
Station to Station	104
Scary Monsters	62
Diamond Dogs	56
Blackstar	31
Heroes	29
Reality	24
Young Americans	22

This table shows respondents' reported favourite David Bowie album. 'The Rise and Fall of Ziggy Stardust and the Spiders from Mars' was the highest favourite album reported by respondents

Table B.7   Fan Responses to the Question: 'What does David Bowie mean to you?'

Fan Descriptors	Frequency
Music	171
Life	170
Imagination	116
Father	114
Fashion	95
Spirit	93
Love	91
Influence	81
Knowledge	72
Universe	67
Artist	62
Human	54
Inspiration	52
God	46
Origin	45
Friends	43
Sexual	31
Everything	29

This table shows how respondents summarise David Bowie's place in their life

Table B.8 Fan Reported Description that Best Sums Up David Bowie for Them

Description	Frequency
Character	78
Love	72
Bowie	65
Ziggy	52
Performance	43
Music	33
Fashion	30
Songs	29
Human	28
Album	24
Station	18
Dark	18
Artistic	16
Movie	16
Alien	15
Rock'n'roll	15
Something	13

This table shows how respondents describe David Bowie for them using key descriptors

Table B.9 Fans' Cherished Piece of David Bowie Memorabilia

Cherished piece	Frequency
Albums	49
Photographs	49
Book	47
Records	47
Drawing	34
Vinyl	32
Ticket	23
Concert	20
Framed pictures	18
Biography	18
Bowie collected Item	17
Music	16
Autograph	15
Ziggy picture	15
Poster	13
Collection	12
Shirt	12
Stardust image	11

This table shows the recorded range of cherished pieces of David Bowie Fan memorabilia

Appendix C

Focus Group Questions

1. Overview

The focus group will be organised around what Bowie means to you and why you think he was such a significant figure. We will also relate our discussion to how your position as an academic/scholar/fan impacts, if at all, on the way you interact with David Bowie. We will have some visual material to share and discuss. The session will be audio recorded. Memorabilia *only* will be photographed with permission.

1. If we could start with a simple question: What does David Bowie mean to you?

    a. What sort of role has he played in your social/private life?

2. Would you consider yourself a 'fan' or aca-fan of David Bowie?

    a. If a 'fan', what does or has this fandom involved?
    b. If an aca-fan', what role does the 'aca' play in the way you address your fandom?
    c. If you consider yourself neither, how would you define your attachment?

© The Editor(s) (if applicable) and The Author(s), under exclusive license to Springer Nature Switzerland AG 2019
T. Cinque and S. Redmond, *The Fandom of David Bowie*,
https://doi.org/10.1007/978-3-030-15880-4

3. Does your role as a scholar of popular culture/music/stardom impact upon the way you identify with Bowie, make sense of that identification?

4. Please choose an image from the collection here, one that speaks to your memories or interest or fascination with David Bowie, and talk through what it means to you and why?

5. Discussion of personal respective memorabilia. How is this item tied with your sense of how Bowie connected with/to a key period of your life?

6. Why you think he was such a significant cultural figure?

7. Why do you think his death generated such levels of mourning or was at least represented as such?

8. Do you remember where you were or what you were doing when you first heard that he had died?

Index

© The Editor(s) (if applicable) and The Author(s), under exclusive license to Springer Nature Switzerland AG 2019
T. Cinque and S. Redmond, *The Fandom of David Bowie*,
https://doi.org/10.1007/978-3-030-15880-4

Printed by Printforce, the Netherlands